US ARMY VEHICLES OF WORLD WAR TWO

JM. BONIFACE
JG. JEUDY

A FOULIS Military Book
First Published 1991

© J. M. Boniface and J. G. Jeudy

First Published in French in France as
Les Vehicles de L'US Army 1939-45 by
Editions Press Audiovisuel, Paris 1987

All rights reserved. No part of this book may be reproduced or transmitted in any form or by any means, electronic or mechanical, including photocopying, recording or by any information storage or retrieval system, without permission of the publisher.

Published by:
Haynes Publishing Group
Sparkford, Nr. Yeovil,
Somerset, BA22 7JJ, England

Haynes Publications Inc
861 Lawrence Drive, Newbury Park,
California 91320 USA

British Library Cataloguing in Publication Data
Boniface, Jean-Michel
The vehicles of the United States Army 1939-1945
1. United States. Army. Military land vehicles, history
I. Title   II. Jeufy, Jean-Gabriel
623.747973

ISBN 0-85429-811-8

Library of Congress Catalog Card No.
90-84481

Editor: Michael G. Burns

Typeset in 10/11 pt Times roman medium 19 picas
Printed in England by J. H. Haynes & Co. Ltd

DEDICATION
To Bart,
who showed us the way

SERIES
This title follows the titles previously published by Collection Bibliotheque E.P.A./G.T. Foulis:

The GMC, A Universal Truck:
Haynes W048
[Le GMC, un camion universal O/P]
(J-M Boniface & J-G Jeudy)
The Dodge, Five Generations of All-Terrain Vehicles
(Le Dodge, cinq generations de tous-terrains) [O/P]
The Jeep, Haynes F584
[La Jeep, un defi au temps]
(J-G Jeudy & M. Tararine)

CONTENTS

Introduction	5
Origins and Development of the Motorization of the US Army	7
Example of Equipment: 'TO&E US Army April 1943'	18
Identification of Vehicles	25
Tactical Markings and Paint Schemes	29
Motorcycles	33
Liaison and Command Vehicles	40
Tactical Vehicles	42
Jeep	42
Dodge ½ Ton, ¾ Ton	44
Trucks, 1½ Ton	48
GMC, 6 x 6 Ton, and other 2½ Ton trucks	55
FWD, 4 x 4, 4 Ton	62
Trucks, 6 x 6, 4 Ton	63
Tractors, 4 x 4, 4/5 Ton	65
Heavy Trucks	68
Trucks, 6 x 6, 6 Ton	69
Mack, NO, 6 x 6, 7½ Ton	74
Workshop and Repair Vehicles	76
Recovery Vehicles	78
8 x 8 Heavy Trucks	85
'Low Silhouette' Truck Series	87
Trailers	89
Amphibious Vehicles	92
Crabs and Alligators in Indochina	99
Landing Vehicle Tracked, LVT	92
Amphibious Jeep	103
GMC Amphibious DUKW 353 'Duck'	104
M29 Weasel	106
Weasel and Expeditions Polaires Française	109
Tank Transporters	112
M20 Diamond-T 980 and 981	113
M25 'Dragon Wagon'	116
Artillery Tractors, Tracked	119
Scout Cars	123
Half-Tracks	125
Armoured Cars	144
Road Vehicles	151
Mack EH, 4 x 2, 5 Ton	157
International K	159
M 425/426	164
6 x 4 Vehicles	166
Coaches	168
Engineering Vehicles	170
Fire Fighting Vehicles	188
Signal Corps Vehicles	197
Medical Service Vehicles	206
Chemical Warfare Service Vehicles	210
US Army Air Forces Vehicles	213
US Navy, Marine Corps and Coast Guard Vehicles	226
Vehicles Supplied to Allied Nations	236
The Post-War Period	252
Bibliography	263
Acknowledgements and Photographic Credits	264

M26 towing a Panther knocked out in November 1944 to the north of Aachen. The streets of Geilenkirchen are littered with the equipment of the US Ninth Army.1

INTRODUCTION

Traditionally, American military vehicles are presented and categorised by weight classification. However, American and European weight classifications differ. The American weight classification uses the load that a vehicle, in running order, complete with all fuel, spare wheel and regulation spares aboard, is capable of carrying, whereas the 'European' useful load is the weight that the vehicle is permitted to carry on its chassis longerons, which therefore includes both the weight of the body and the transported load. This difference of interpretation leads to American vehicles appearing to carry loads considerably smaller than is allowed in Europe. Moreover, the US ton, whether long or short, does not have the same value as the metric tonne.

This impression is again reinforced by the fact that, for all-terrain vehicles, the weight class is calculated according to very different and restricting requirements which result in halving the relationship to its potential on the road. For articulated tractors, the weight information given corresponds to the load transferred through the 'fifth wheel'—the tow attachment point—and not to the total weight of the combination, or to the useful load of the semi-trailer.

This presentation has the benefit of grouping around one chassis all the types of bodywork with which it has been equipped, and of allowing comparison between competing vehicles from several manufacturers. However, this method does not clarify the reasons which have influenced an Arm, the Ordnance Services or the Quartermaster in adopting a particular marque, model or item of equipment. Likewise, the particulars of military use are passed over in silence.

This is why we have attempted in this book to reclassify the equipment by the Arms or Services using them, as is done also in *Technical Manual 9-2800,* (US Army, 1943), in order to find the logical imperatives of the period to explain what actually happened when the United States confronted the problems of going from peace to war in a matter of months.

Thus, in this book, the reader will find series-produced equipment (excluding prototypes and tracked fighting vehicle) presented according to their employment or to the Arm or Service using them. The authors hope that they have thus explained several things which the usual system of classification does not permit, without having disconcerted the reader.

Origins and Development of the Motorization of the US Army

Following repeated incursions into American territory, and especially those into the little town of Columbus in New Mexico on March 8th and 9th, 1916, by Mexican rebel bands led by the famous Pancho Villa, whose real name was Doroteo Arango, the United States, at the decision of President Thomas Woodrow Wilson, decided to send what was called a punitive force placed under the orders of General John J. Pershing (1860-1948). On this occasion, and for the first time in its history, the American army used motor vehicles for transport and logistic support of its troops. At that time, the US Army's vehicle fleet numbered only a little less than a thousand vehicles dispersed through the whole territory of the United States and overseas, in the Philippines and Hawaii.

This expedition, a prelude to the United States' joining World War One, was completed on February 15th, 1917. It provided an opportunity for intensive training for motor transport personnel, drivers and support. It was also rich in lessons on the tactical and technical planes, unfortunately not always exploited as they should have been, especially in the matter of the need to standardise equipment. Indeed, of the approximately two thousand lorries in operation within seventy transport companies at the height of the conflict, as many as 128 different models could be counted. This posed problems which were, to say the least, difficult in the matter of maintenance. The multiplicity of makes employed during this expedition—FWD, Jeffery, Locomobile, Packard, Pierce-Arrow, Republic, Lippard-Stewart, Dart, White—although providing evidence of the richness of the American automobile industry of the time, also constituted, on the other hand, a cause of the heterogeneous nature of the vehicle fleet.

When the United States entered the war on April 2nd, 1917, at the side of the Allies, the US Army was capable of lining up about two thousand five hundred lorries. The automobile industry, which had already been working since the beginning of the war for Great Britain and France to supply White, Packard, Pierce-Arrow, Jeffery and FWD lorries, Knox tractors and Ford Ts, made a big production effort to meet the needs of the Allied armies. Thus, in 1918 alone transatlantic manufacturers supplied 227,250 vehicles.

The problems of maintenance which had already appeared in Mexico reared their heads again in an aggravated form. For reasons of maintenance and repair, it was estimated that one vehicle in two was

The famous Ford T was widely used as an ambulance during the First World War. This example is seen in the Reims area in the spring of 1918.2

FWD truck Type B of the California National Guard at the end of the 1920s.

Hudson Super Six ambulance capable of transporting four stretchers. The Type B appeared in 1917.

out either directly by the army as for the 3 Ton Molitor, or were conducted on behalf of the automobile industry by the Society of Automotive Engineers for the famous Standard B Liberty. The Liberty, with the letters 'U.S.A.' stamped on the radiator as the only maker's mark, will remain, like the GMC for World War Two, a legend. A total of 43,005 was ordered from twenty-nine manufacturers, of which 9,452 were produced by November 1918 in fifteen factories (Garford, Pierce-Arrow, Republic, Selden, etc.) Of this total, 7,655 were used in Europe. At November 11th 1918, the American Expeditionary Corps in Europe had at its disposal 62,818 motor vehicles, including 13,784 motorcycles.

The Inter-War Period. Attempts at Standardisation

The experiences gained in the course of World War Two had clearly shown the need for the army to have at its disposal robust vehicles, capable of travelling along bad roads, fording water courses or shallow flooded zones, and simple to maintain in the field. In addition, the necessity of all the wheels being driven, a four-speed gearbox, a good ground clearance, strong bumpers and a radiator protection grille had also been shown.

Undoubtedly, one of the features which had appeared most fundamental was the imperative of a standardisation of military vehicles, together with a proven system of maintenance and supply of spare parts. As a result, the history of American military motor vehicles was largely dominated in the period between the two world wars by the pursuit of a policy of standardisation, a pursuit that was unfortunately fruitless. From the setback to the efforts made, big problems of maintenance were to arise which the services of the US Army had to face during World War Two.

Those in charge of the Quartermaster Corps (QMC), which was to be succeeded by the Ordnance Department in 1942, were constantly pleading in favour of standardisation, but they had their hands tied by regulations and legislation controlling the supply of army *matériel*. These laws and regulations implied on the one hand that any contract was obligatorily given to the firm which presented the lowest offer and on the other hand prohibited the QMC from imposing detailed specifications for its

permanently immobilised. With 294 different models of vehicles in service in the US Army, in particularly difficult conditions of use, such problems were inevitable.

An effort to standardise was made and the Quartermaster Corps, which was responsible for motor vehicles, developed and classified (Class Standard A. B, etc.) the motor vehicle chassis which it needed by weight class. Furthermore, it launched design studies for standardised lorries, studies which were carried

More than 4,000 Mack 'Bulldogs' were ordered by the US Army during the First World War. This 'Bulldog', built in 1921, transporting a lighting unit, is fitted with two radiators. One serves for the cooling of the engine and the other for that of the generator mounted in front of the engine and providing the power for the searchlight. Eighty-four were still in service in the 1930s.

The Quartermaster studies the modernisation of his fleet either by building experimental models in his workshops, or by modernising (tyres, mounting of engine-gearbox units, four-wheel drive etc) those that he had put in hand during the First World War. W. Herrington, in his capacity as engineer-consultant, played a considerable part in these studies. Here is seen, based on a standard Liberty at the right, the evolution of this research into a 6 x 4 with balloon tyres (High Flotation), then into a 4 x 4.

lorries. Thus there could be no special vehicles for the army, but only civil vehicles of commercial types with, at the most, a few specific modifications. Another constraint, albeit ultimately fairly limited in its consequences, was that the army could not adopt any vehicle under its maker's name. The only specifications authorised were limited to very general details, such as useful load, speed and weight. Specifications which could have created uniformity in general

Harley-Davidson sidecar Model 74 used as a fire engine by the US Navy on its air bases (extinction by CO_2, 1927).

6 x 6 artillery tractor designed for Persia by Marmon-Herrington (Type DSD 400-6).

appearance, shape, materials, or dimensions were not tolerated.

One can understand that such administrative and regulation burdens prevented a harmonious and efficient development of the motorisation of the US Army until the dawn of the 1940s. Each time that the Army manifested its intention of ordering a new vehicle, a multitude of companies tendered and, practically each time, a different firm offered the lowest prices and thus received the contract. Such a regime only increased the heterogeneity of a motor vehicle fleet which was already rich in *matériel* of very varied design and makes. The intrinsic quality of this different *matériel* was not necessarily bad: on the contrary; but in terms of maintenance and management of spare parts the difficulties were bound to increase.

The principle of requests for tenders and submissions certainly sprang from very praiseworthy motives, such as that of avoiding any fraud or any favouritism in the placing of orders, since only the objective criterion of price came into it. The notion that this procedure was well founded was rooted in the idea that in the event of war mass production would be possible more quickly if the civil production lines did not have to be modified. Some people summarised the situation by declaring that the Army bought vehicles which it could have found in the street. However, the partisans of standardisation for their part advanced the idea that maintenance in the field was at least as important as ease of construction and that, after all, standardisation and mass production were not in opposition to each other, quite the contrary.

The Quartermaster Corps Standard Fleet

At the end of the 1920s, the QMC tried, relying on its own experience, to develop a standard fleet with what were called lorries class B. In 1928, it bought civil assemblies—engines, transmissions, axles—so as to build two complete lorries in its Holabird depot. This constituted a first attempt at standardisation. Colonel Herrington, civilian consultant of the Quartermaster Corps in the matter of mobility and future partner in Marmon-Herrington, played a very important part at this time, particularly in the field of tyres. Subsequently, between 1928 and 1932, eighteen other lorries were made using various standardised commercial components, so as to cover the spectrum of needs. These eighteen vehicles were arranged in five groups in function of their sizes. The primary mechanical components were interchangeable. In addition, which was important, the fact is that this *matériel* could as well be produced by private industry as by the workshops of the QMC.

In spite of its evident advantages, this plan failed. It must be admitted in this context that the majority of American car manufacturers were rather opposed to this system, and their views triumphed. Besides, in 1933, the War Department prohibited the QMC from proceeding to acquire sub-assemblies and parts for the manufacture of lorries. The Army had to remain outside the automobile industry and was not permitted to undertake any research or development in this domain.

The credits for studies with a view to standardisation were cut off. Obviously, the problem of maintenance was not given due weight. The officer commanding the Holabird depot noted in this respect that in 1935 the approximately 360 models of vehicles then in service in the US Army required the management of about a million spare parts. This situation was absurd and sharply criticised, especially as at the same time the Germans pronounced themselves in favour of a standardised fleet on the basis of studies carried out in the USA (Schell Programme)!

In September 1939, after the declaration of war in Europe, new regulations decreed that the vehicles of the US Army were to be limited to commercial models produced by one or more constructors. Thus, the Army was only allowed to use commercial lorries, with a few modifications such as protective grilles for the radiator, optics and towpoints! All components of vehicles intended for the US Army had to be standard articles of the civil automobile industry. The great idea underlying this step was to be able to ensure rapid production as soon as war broke out, without worrying about the problems of maintenance and management of spare parts. However, in order to minimise in a small way the inconveniences of this principle, the authorities limited the needs to five classes of chassis types: $\frac{1}{2}$ Ton; $1\frac{1}{2}$ Ton; $2\frac{1}{2}$ Ton; 4 Ton; and $7\frac{1}{2}$ Ton. As can be seen, the only element of standardisation that was retained merely concerned the useful load. Therefore, the door remained wide open as far as the number of manufacturers and models was concerned.

In 1935, Congress declared surplus and too old to be kept or repaired vehicles dating from World War

The War Department ordered sixty-four of these 4 x 4, $\frac{1}{2}$ Ton, Ford Marmon-Herrington pick-ups, Model LD3-4.

Built in 1940, this prototype 5 Ton tractor, Oshkosh Model TR, had four-wheel drive to pull 8-inch (203 mm) artillery guns hitched on by means of a goose neck like a semi-trailer.

Little by little, America got used to the idea of entering the war. After the proclamation of the state of 'imminent danger' in 1940 by the President, the country suddenly saw its Army on manoeuvres everywhere. Here, a convoy of Dodge 1½ tonners of the 18th Engineer Regiment, led by a ½ Ton VC 3, goes past a line of Plymouths of the US Army.

One. This brought into sharp focus the problem of remotorisation of the US Army. In July 1935, experts estimated an efficient and coherent programme of remotorisation for a peacetime army would cost 60 million dollars annually. This emphasises the state of denudation arrived at by the US Army, which possessed practically no recent *matériel* and had to buy everything. In 1937, it possessed 11,600 vehicles.

Although the vehicles had not been able to be standardised for all the reasons which we have outlined, the Quartermaster Corps nevertheless succeeded in taking two measures which tended to rationalise the choices. On the one hand, while remaining within the sacrosanct framework of requests for tender-submission, the QMC succeeded in only being confronted with a relatively limited number of constructors. Thus, in 1941, the QMC only had to buy sixteen different models. Furthermore, another important element, it succeeded in persuading the constructors to adopt an increasing number of common components such as batteries, spark plugs, alternators, petrol tanks and speedometers. But the great leap forward—abandoning the system of requests for offer in favour

An unparalleled instruction programme was undertaken by the US Navy and Army, and also by the manufacturers, who opened numerous classrooms to teach the maintenance to be given to their vehicles. They also sent to the front, technical missions to see the problems at first hand. Here is an instructional course at Mack's factory working on a NO.

of directly negotiated contracts—could not be effected. In June 1940, the QMC tried out and adopted three products derived from commercial vehicles: the Dodge 4 x 4, ½ Ton, the GMC 6 x 6, 2½ Ton and the Mack 6 x 6, 6 Ton.

To face up to the enormous needs of the US Army, certain responsible persons had wanted to rid themselves of the procedures of requests for offer-submissions, but the hierarchy and especially the Senate did not always agree. In July 1940, Congress tried to authorise the US Army to order its vehicles by negotiated contracts. The inertia of the authorities, however, put a brake on the effective application of this decision. It was only in summer 1941 that the procedure of negotiated contracts was finally admitted.

Starting up the War Economy

From about thirty thousand in summer 1940, the total number of military vehicles in service reached a little more than seventy thousand at the beginning of 1941 and two hundred and fifty thousand units at the end of the same year. That was the tangible proof of the effort agreed by industry. However, the rhythm of production remained insufficient to meet the needs of rearmament. To accelerate deliveries, the US authorities decided in August 1941, while the country was still at peace, to reduce by half for a period of six months, the production of vehicles intended for the civil market. Thus freed, the automobile industry could better devote itself to the needs of Defence.

The construction of vehicles none the less encountered a few difficulties arising from an underestimate of the real needs, both in quantity and in types of models to be produced, and with 'bottlenecks' in the production of certain mechanical components: homokinetic joints, drive axles, gearboxes. At that time for example, only two companies produced

homokinetic joints, Bendix and Gear Grinding Machine Cy. The situation would only improve when other companies, notably Ford and Chrysler, were able to manufacture these parts. Mack refused a design contract for high capacity rear axles which would have been very useful a few months later because the company would only be producing for the Army tipper trucks and fire engines. In the event of hostilities, thousands of motor car sub-contract workshops had in principle to cease their normal manufacturing work and devote themselves to munitions. After the attack on Pearl Harbor on December 7th, 1941, things evolved more rapidly, but still with quite a few gropings.

The Stopping of Civil Production

From January 1942, the USA took drastic measures in order to adapt their industrial potential to war production. The turning taken by the automobile industry at that time may be considered as particularly symbolic of this change.

The War Production Board, which had just been created to organise and harmonise production of *matériel* necessary for armed forces, asked the automobile manufacturing industrialists to devote themselves henceforth exclusively to the war industry, stopping commercial sales on January 1st, 1942 and stopping the manufacture of civil lorries in March 1942. Thus it is that on February 2nd 1942, General Motors ceased all automobile activity intended for the civil market. This event caused the weekly magazine *Newsweek* to comment in its issue of February 9th,

Lease-Lend did not only go in one direction, even if it was predominantly the United States who supplied the aid. France contributed tropical produce (oil, spices) and Britain especially aeroplanes and vehicles. A less known fact, the USSR also participated in Reverse Lease-Lend, quite timidly and very symbolically, notably by supplying timber to the Aleutians which did not have any. The photograph was taken on Adak Island in May 1945.

To try to make people understand the importance of maintenance, the US Army published in its manuals humorous drawings, often by the great comic strip artists like Will Eisner, the creator of Spirit. This one is taken from the manual of the Mack 6 Tonner and reminds one that the radiators have to be kept filled. The vehicle sketched by Will Eisner is a Diamond-T with its Rogers trailer.

1942 that 'this week the first American industry has died at Detroit'! The expression, lapidary but somewhat pessimistic, was not going to be long in being invalidated by the facts. Hundreds of thousands of Jeeps, lorries, tractors and trailers were indeed to come off the production lines of Detroit, Dearborn, Toledo and South Bend to equip the Allied forces. The authorisation to devote themselves again solely to the production of civil vehicles was only given again on August 20th, 1945, while the rationing of petrol ceased on August 15th, 1945.

The Office of Defense Transportation assumed responsibility for the allocation of industrial vehicles. The War Production Board only authorised, for example, the production of 7,500 lorries of more than 3 tons for the second half of 1943 for priority enterprises and 139 cars in 1943 and 610 in 1944, and others using spare parts in stock. However, the firms were authorised from 1944 to resume partially the building of lorries for civil transport and distribution, Chrysler reopening its production lines at Mound Road from the middle of the year and International producing ten to twelve model Ks per day at the Fort Wayne Plant alongside the sixty-five lorries manufactured for military needs. Thus, the production of lorries of more than 3 tons increased six-fold and that of pick-ups was able to resume that same year in the USA.

For all that, the problems of production did not disappear. Notably, there were deplorable shortages of certain supplies—steel, rubber, aluminium. In order to face these difficulties, the industrialists formed the Automotive Council for War Production, presided over by a representative of the firm of Packard and charged with organising and harmonising supplies. A certain standardisation of the principal components was sought, such as the Hercules RXC engine which equipped the Autocar 7144T and 8144T, the White 444T and the Diamond 4 Ton 6 x 6. Spark plugs, instruments fitted, batteries, tyres, etc, were also standardised as far as possible. Other changes intervened, notably in the structures and competences of the services of the US Army.

From the Quartermaster to the Ordnance

The responsibility for the management of motor vehicles was transferred from the QMC to the Ordnance Corps on July 25th, 1942, only effective as from September 1st. At the time, the responsible persons of the Ordnance Corps or Matériel Service did not grasp the vastness of the new tasks which were being entrusted to them. Compared with weapons, fighting vehicles, fire control systems, artillery and ammunition, the much simpler mechanics of lorries did not seem, at first sight, to present any acute problems to officers who were very familiar with the maintenance of equipment which was otherwise more complex. These same officers were not long in realising the immensity of the problems which they would have to overcome throughout the conflict. This was made more acute because they retained from their former duties repairs of all US Army material in the field, which in itself was already a Chinese puzzle. This decision had been taken in the interest of harmonisation. Indeed, previously the Quartermaster Corps, or staff corps charged with buying, managing, putting in place and transporting everything that kept the Army going, excluding only arms and ammunition, had the responsibility of acquiring all automobile *matériel* except fighting vehicles.

What was simple until the 1930s became, with the generalisation of mechanisation, a continual source of conflict between the two directorates. Was an artillery tractor a simple lorry or did it come within the competence of the Ordnance, as the latter maintained, since it replaced the former horse-drawn caissons and gun carriages? Should a Scout Car be considered an armoured 'car'—and in that case only the armour would come under the Ordnance—or a fighting vehicle?

To put a stop to these rivalries and these Byzantine discussions, the Ordnance thus assumed responsibility for designs, orders, parked storage before distribution and location of all automobile chassis. However, in terms of specialised bodies, the weapons directorates of the user services retained their prerogatives and issued notices expressing their needs in the matter, considering the Ordnance, in the same manner as the Quartermaster, as a mere administrative office of purchasing, when they did not themselves place orders directly, considering that the *matériel* was too specialised or that, as it concerned trailers or semi-trailers, and was therefore by definition without an engine, they could not be likened to motor vehicles. As for the maintenance and storage of this equipment, in units or assigned to the park, the question was treated on a case for case basis. The situation in each

Two photographs which illustrate the war production effort of one of the Yellow Coach workshops from where 562,750 GMCs would come off the lines, an absolute record (1943). Expertise acquired by the automobile industry allowed it to sustain the rhythm of production necessary to equip millions of combatants across the world.

branch of the service is indicated in the tables between pages 18 and 24.

War Production

The automobile industry and its sub-contractors made an unparalleled effort which, however, only partly satisfied the needs for motor vehicles for four primary reasons.

First, the big firms, like Ford, Chrysler and GMC saw entrusted to them a host of programmes, all having a priority greater than each other and all further and further removed from the motor vehicle: ammunition, artillery, radar, anti-submarine nets, aeroplanes, tanks, gyroscopes, propellors, torpedoes, etc. ad infinitum.

Secondly, the factories saw the rhythm of their manufacturing or their production programme constantly changing. Thus a company specialising in armour plating had to reconvert to manufacture components of axles for heavy lorries (Heavy-Heavy) production when it was in the middle of a crisis. This reorganisation took twelve months! In 1944 the War Ministry announced that no armament was now the same as at the declaration of war, having been extensively improved, or put into production since.

Thirdly, it was impossible to predict the need for spares. It was one thing to mass produce thousands of new vehicles, but it was necessary at the same time and on the same machines to manufacture hundreds and thousands of spare parts, all the more so since the production estimates for these had to be continually revised upwards (500 per cent increase at Chrysler at the end of 1942), because of the phenomenal rate of attrition through accident or bad maintenance—for the GI's only had scant respect for equipment—and conditions of transport by sea (submarine warfare, corrosion) and storage without precautions. Certain problems were real headaches and could never have been planned. Thus, because of the largescale use of mines in North Africa, vehicles lost their front wheels, which resulted in the workshops in an accumulation of rear axles recovered from vehicles destroyed, while during this period these same axles were 'consumed' in phenomenal quantity in the Pacific where the lorries were overloaded to reduce the turnrounds and the lengths of the convoys because of the permanent danger of Japanese snipers—but it was not possible, of course, to allow for such 'supply and demand'!

Fourthly, tyres, rubber and steel were in short supply and it was necessary to modify the workshops to revert to producing woodwork bodies, or remake the plans and bodywork pressings in order to substitute canvas cabs for sheet metal ones and even to launch the manufacture of synthetic or butyl tyres, a technology unknown in the USA.

The war effort was not only machines, factories and raw materials, but above all men and women, hundreds of thousands of women and men, at all posts, in industry and the arsenals, workers mobilised or not, and an immense training effort. General Motors alone initiated and trained seven hundred and fifty thousand new personnel.

The automobile industry also furnished cadres for the federal government agencies, like the president of General Motors, W. Knudsen, who was appointed by President Truman with the powers of a general as head of the War Production Board National Defense Council in May 1940. Knudsen, of Danish origin, then resigned from General Motors and accepted the post without asking for any remuneration to mark his solidarity and his patriotism towards his country of immigration. A difficult post where he had to oppose the conservatism of certain military men and face up at the start to the intransigent pacificism of Henry Ford, who at that moment refused to put his industrial potential at the service of the 'foreign' war and in particular of the British. The USA was still neutral at the time which led Knudsen to have Rolls-Royce Merlin aeroplane engines built at Packard's and not as he wished at Ford.

Fortunately, Knudsen's relations with the other leaders of American industry bore the stamp of confidence. Alarmed by the USA's weakness in the field of tank production, he called K.T. Keller, president of Chrysler, one Saturday morning in May 1940. The dialogue was concise:

'K.T., will you build tanks?'

'Absolutely! Where could I see one?'

From this brief exchange was born, seven months later, the gigantic Detroit Tank Arsenal, which remains the biggest centre of tank production in the western world.

It is to Knudsen also that we owe the design of the DUKW; the Cross Drive which revolutionised the driving of armoured vehicles, although more exactly, we owe this to his links with Duryea, one of the founders of the American motor car, who, at seventy-four years of age, invented the principle in one night and built a model of the device; and the construction by Ford of Willow Run, the biggest aircraft factory in the world, which produced 8,685 B-24 Liberator bombers, one per working hour!

The value of war orders for motor vehicles rose to 7 billion 1945 dollars. The automobile industry—which thanks to its production lines and its experience of mass production, was one of the key factors of American war power—also manufactured 5,947,000 weapons, 4,131,000 engines, 22,160 aeroplanes, more than 5,000,000 bombs, 3,000,000 rockets, 2,500,000 torpedoes and 12,500,000,000 rounds of ammunition. The American government spent 150 million dollars on armaments during hostilities, including 20 per cent with the automobile industry. A total of 2,600,887 trucks ($\frac{1}{2}$ to 45 Ton) and 529,647 trailers was supplied to the armed forces of the United Nations.

To recompense and honour the most deserving or the most productive firms, the War Ministry awarded the Army-Navy Excellence Award or more popularly the E-Award, in the form of a flag to fly over the factory and which could be represented on buttonhole badges to be worn by the factory's personnel. It became a very much sought after distinction.

However, from 1944, analysis of the war led the Americans to think that victory could no longer escape the democracies. Peace would mean a return to the forty-hour week and a 40 per cent reduction in the volume of orders. It was therefore becoming urgent to organise the deflation of war industry to allow its reintegration into a peacetime economy. This was all the more imperative because what had happened at the close of World War One had left damaging memories.

The problem was already more intrinsically difficult than passing on to a war footing. It was further complicated by the fact that, even if a large part of the contracts were to be cancelled or the pace of production slowed down, it was on the other hand necessary to negotiate other contracts for new *matériel* for use against Japan, the last theatre of war where the United States thought they would still have to make a major effort. General Motors for example, after the Normandy landings of June 6th, 1944, was notified of the cancellation of 1.25 billion dollars' worth of contracts. This policy was undertaken under the aegis of the Automotive Industry Advisory Committee. Full of wisdom and courageous to embark upon in the middle of a war, it made it possible to turn this difficult corner without too much heartbreak.

EXAMPLE OF EQUIPMENT

According to the Manual: *"Table of Organisation and Equipment of the US Army"* April 1943

Armoured Division (combat equipment):

79	Scout Cars
733	Half Tracks
126	Dodge M6 with 37 mm anti-tank gun
54	Half Track T19 or Sherman M7 with 105 mm howitzer
79	Armored cars M8
158	Light tanks M3 or M5
232	Shermans

Each of the two Armored Regiments comprised:

91	Jeeps
124	GMCs

Each Armored Infantry Regiment comprised:

61	Jeeps
58	GMCs

The disparities can be great. Thus, the establishment of a parachute regiment comprised two Dodge ambulances in order to permit security of the jump training zones, while these resources were normally concentrated at divisional medical company and battalion level in the other arms of service.

A 155 mm Howitzer Field Artillery Regiment received:

12	155 mm Howitzers, M17/18 or M1
9	¼ Ton trailers
8	1 Ton trailers
15	Jeeps
8	Dodge Command Cars
18	¾ Ton Dodges
13	GMC CCKW 353
9	GMC CCKW352
15	4 Ton Cargo Diamond-T
1	Wrecker Diamond-T
2	Piper Cubs (establishment)

An Engineers Dump Truck Company received forty-four GMC 2½ Tonners. On June 30th, 1945, 135

Eighty-one GMC AFKX 502s were bought in 1939 for the cavalry. These four-wheel drive tractors were coupled to a two-wheeled semi-trailer—combination Animals and Cargo, 6 Ton. This unit made it possible for the mounted cavalry units to move rapidly without having recourse to rail transport, whose loading and unloading operations were too long and necessitated military platforms which were not available at allstations.

The shortage of tankers obliged the US Army to resort to expedients, such as this makeshift mounting on semi-trailer platforms. The tractor is a M425 of the 3580th Transport Company, photographed in May 1945.

dump truck companies had been raised, including 112 solely composed of coloured personnel (to whom the Engineers denied any ability, while at that time 28 per cent of the Army Air Forces' mechanics were blacks!)

The Medical Regiment, an Army Reserve unit of the Medical Service which was not subdivided, comprised three companies of ambulances, or thirty-six Dodge ½ or ¾ Tonners per battalion, or seventy-two for the regiment, permitting the moving of 3,456 wounded lying down in turn, or the whole medical strength of the regiment and one hundred wounded.

The Infantry Division Medical Battalion, for its part, lined up:

- 30 Dodge ambulances
- 15 Dodge ¾ Tonners
- 7 1 Ton—250 gallon (946 litre) water tanker trailers
- 14 1 Ton Cargo trailers
- 16 GMCs
- 4 Dodge Command Cars
- 9 Jeeps

The personnel could only be transported at the same time as the equipment if the ambulances were used for this purpose, which was in any case a regulation procedure.

An infantry division numbered 2,537 vehicles during World War Two. It had only received 135 during World War One and a few hundred in the 1930s.

The Ordnance Evacuation Company received eighteen M26/40 Ton Tank Recovery Truck-Trailer M25 Combinations. An Ordnance Medium Maintenance Battalion possessed:

- 6 Jeeps

GMCs of the Red Ball prepare to set off again after refuelling in August 1944. Convoys were classed A1 and were only to yield priority to the medical services. It will be observed that the trucks are loaded right above the sides, a rare thing in the US Army which tended to underload, but the front was awaiting its supplies which were piled up in Normandy 300 miles (500 km) from the battle.

8	Command Cars
33	Dodge 3/4 Tonners
106	GMC 2½ Tonners, including workshops
32	Diamond-T Wreckers

One can compare this Table of Equipment with that envisaged for the same type of unit, at the time of the Louisiana motorised manoeuvres in 1941, which reveals a great disparity of models, a unit which was rather heavy and lacking in cohesion, as it had to fulfil several roles at the same time: repairs, maintenance, logistic support and even its own protection.

3	artillery repair workshop lorries
3	automobile repair workshop lorries
2	instrument repair workshop lorries
5	small arms repair workshop lorries
3	tank repair lorries
3	machine tool workshop lorries
3	workshop lorries for big repairs, all 23 on 4 x 4, 1½/3 Ton GMCs with cab set forward
32	Emergency Repair Trucks on ½ Ton Dodge or Chevrolet chassis
20	stores lorries for spare parts for various makes
5	welding lorries
1	1½ Ton cargo lorry
3	100 gallon fuel tankers
9	10 Ton M1 or Marmon-Herrington Wreckers
1	250 gallon water tanker
6	motor tricycles or Servi-Cars (under test)
4	Dodge ½ Ton Command Cars
12	motorcycles
2	saloons
9	GMC 2½ cargo lorries
6	Scout Cars for the protection of the unit

The Ordnance Heavy Maintenance Battalion consisted of:

31	6 Ton cargo semi-trailers
14	4 Ton Tractor semi-trailers
4	Jeeps
6	Dodge ¾ Tonners
4	Command Cars
14	GMCs
16	GMCs Lot 7
51	Diamond-T Wreckers
30	M1 Wreckers

The Quartermaster Truck Battalion ensured the daily transport of 2,016 tons of supplies using:

620	GMC CCKW353's: 576 assigned to transport, 46 to battalion duties or under maintenance
54	Jeeps
16	¾ Ton Dodge Carryalls
1	Command Car
54	Dodge ¾ Tonners
12	GMCs Lot 7

The whole of the means of transport, the motor vehicle fleet, the military railway service, and the very numerous coastal, river, harbour or ocean-going vessels either requisitioned or managed by the US Army, depended upon the employment of the Transportation Corps. In theory, these were mule or pack animal companies, notably for the mountain infantry divisions, but these had been dissolved at the time when they would have proved useful, during the Italian campaign. Then, the contribution of the French expeditionary corps with its Tabords was most fortunate. Some of the animal companies were reformed, in Luzon, with requisitioned animals and native muleteers. Its counterpart for the transport of fuel was the Gazoline Supply Battalion:

14	Jeeps
1	Command Car
21	Dodge ¾ Tonners
86	GMC tankers

The relatively modest scale of resources and capacities that this transported—430,000 gallons (244,200 litres) per battalion and 105,000 gallons (59,600 litres) per company, or 640,000 gallons (363,000 litres) per Army comprising two army corps or four divisions and its services—is explained first, by the role given to pipelines and to the railway in the American conception and secondly, by the underestimation of the needs which mechanised warfare and the extent and distance of the fronts to be supplied were going to entail. These conceptions and these *a priori* attitudes are explained by the facts that the Quartermaster, a very conservative branch of the service, had neither commissioned the study of nor ordered heavy tanker lorries or semi-trailers, (if one excepts twenty-five White 6 x 6s with trailers, acquired in 1943). This lack or underestimation was partly, but only partly, compensated for by the use of fleets of cargo lorries loaded with jerrycans and by the improvised mounting of makeshift tanks on the platforms of semi-trailers. Only the Army Air Force possessed large capacity semi-trailer tankers for refuelling its aeroplanes.

Finally, the Quartermaster Grave Registration Company had an establishment of:

5	Jeeps
12	Dodge ¾ Tonners
1	GMC

A Field Bakery Battalion (strength 701 men) could supply fresh bread for 160,000 men but did not possess any establishment means of ensuring the mobility of these field ovens and of its personnel. For other purposes, it disposed of:

5	Jeeps
1	Command Car
5	Dodge ¾ Tonners
5	GMCs

If one relates the number of men in the battalion to that of the vehicles on the establishment, the American army bakers were not overendowed as far as motor vehicles were concerned and certainly had to have recourse to 'borrowings' or to system D for their personnel movements.

This need to borrow is the case with nearly all the service and support units, whose specialised technical *materiel* was most frequently mounted on semi-trailers or trailers, but which did not possess their own means of traction, as they were considered as units of the rear echelon and therefore only semi-mobile. When he had drawn up his Tables of Organisation and Equipment, the Quartermaster had remained again too attached to the lessons of World War One, and had not integrated the needs of mechanised warfare. This did not pose too many problems in the Pacific or in North Africa, but was

M15 tank carrier semi-trailer (without additional ramps for passing the rear wheels) loaded with a 155 mm Long Tom with its M26 tractor belonging to the US Third Army in November 1944. Notice that the trailer is missing a wheel. The load not being too heavy, the suspension did not suffer too much and as supplies of tyres were in chaos, they kept moving all the same. Note also the number of jerrycans; in these times of scarcity it was better to hold than to run.

heavy with consequences during the race towards Germany. There, the specialised supply services only very imperfectly succeeded in pushing up forward (combat zone) the supplies and field rations which were, in theory, to be allocated to combat troops to replace those initially put in position by the service and support units of the rear zone (communication zone). One only needs to remember the fuel and tyre crisis (cf. *The GMC*), Patton's problems in the winter of 1944-1945 and the latter's angry outbursts, to understand the whole dimension of the problem.

The Quartermaster Sales Company existed to sell knickknacks and current consumer products, according to the canteen system for troops in the field. It was equipped with:

1	Jeep
3	Dodge ¾ Tonners
12	GMCs with specialised bodywork of "Bazaar" series
12	GMC cargo trucks

The Quartermaster Laundry Battalion could deal with the linen of 192,000 men per week. It was equipped with:

7	Jeeps
1	Command Car
6	Dodge ¾ Tonners
21	GMCs
64	laundry semi-trailers each with its 4-5 Ton tractor

One can see to what point cleanliness appeared important to the US Army when one finds that each semi-trailer has its own establishment tractor, an allocation rarely achieved by a service unit. At the time of re-equipment of the French army in North Africa, the Americans had the greatest difficulty in accepting the Tables of Establishment submitted to them and which were very different from their own. Indeed, the French command did not see the necessity of devoting an establishment of 1,243 men to laundry work, for each individual thus released would become a combatant who could quite well wash his linen by himself. Several weeks of bitter argument were necessary, going as far as breaking off negotiations, before the French could obtain what they wanted, and that unwillingly.

The same can be said of the Quartermaster Sterilization Battalion which, according to the *Official Organisation Manual* had the task of delousing the men and sterilising clothes, up to a capacity of 10,000 men per day. The unit was equipped with:

6	Jeeps
1	Command Car
5	Dodge ¾ Tonners
17	GMCs
16	steriliser semi-trailers with their 4-5 Ton Tractor

Note on the use of vehicles

One can observe the presence of the Dodge Command Car in service units with average or low motorisation owing to the dislike of this vehicle by the combatant units to which it was alone supposed to be assigned and which reproached it with being too heavy, too large and therefore too visible in comparison with the Jeep which was better able to fulfil the same functions.

The Carryall is mentioned only once for the Quartermaster Truck Battalion to whom it is supplied as a light field coach.

The GMC short chassis CCKW352 without a winch, if one refers to the General Table, was intended for the Field Artillery alone. Thus the two extra wheels, behind the cabin, were not as one might imagine spare wheels, but were intended to be twinned

Vehicle Production for the US Army During World War Two							
	Total 1939-1945	1939-1945	1941	1942	1943	1944	1945
Total	3,200,436	46,384	232,545	791,432	983,359	738,643	408,073
Light, 1 Ton and under	988,167	8,058	74,514	273,997	256,488	245,201	129,909
Medium, 1 Ton	428,196	14,153	37,139	140,375	133,523	80,888	22,118
Light-Heavy, 2½ Ton	812,262	9,589	62,123	182,049	193,177	220,012	145,312
Heavy, over 2½ Tons	153,686	804	9,838	23,314	38,314	50,862	30,554
Semi-Trailer	59,731	236	1,603	8,661	9,436	26,765	13,030
Trailer	499,827	6,494	33,311	81,881	241,450	79,188	67,503
Tractor	34,295	993	1,675	7,433	12,674	8,106	3,414
Other i.e. bicycles, motorcycles, cars, etc	224,272	6,057	12,342	73,722	98,297	27,621	6,233
Caterpillar tractors bought 'commercially' by Engineer units	82,099	–	–	–	–	–	–

Source: Whiting; Statistics, and Summary Report of Acceptances Tank Automotive Matériel 1940-45

Tank production in the United States During World War Two		
Tank Factories	Total December 31st 1945	Percentage
Total Tank production 1940-45	88,410	100.0
Detroit Tank Arsenal (Chrysler)	22,234	25.2
American Car & Foundry	15,224	17.2
Fisher Tank Arsenal	13,137	14.9
Cadillac Motor Company	10,142	11.5
Pressed Steel	8,648	9.8
Pullman-Standard	3,926	4.4
American Locomotive Works	2,985	3.4
Baldwin Locomotive Works	2,515	2.9
Massey Harris Company	2,473	2.8
Ford Motor Company	1,690	1.9
Lima Locomotive	1,655	1.9
Montreal Locomotive Works	1,144	1.3
Marmon-Herrington	1,070	1.2
Pacific Car and Foundry	926	1.0
Federal Machine	540	0.6
Rock Island Arsenal	94	0.05
International Harvester	7	0.05

with the front steered wheels on treacherous ground. In order to improve the grip still more, the vehicle could be fitted with flexible caterpillar tracks around the rear tandem and the front twin wheels (Hipkins system). Unfortunately, this system rather had the opposite effect. In addition, it greatly fatigued the personnel and the vehicle because it transmitted so much vibration, not to speak of the difficulties of fitting. In spite of that, with a fine stubbornness,, its use was regularly imposed, notably in desert warfare training sessions.

The planned distribution of the amphibian Jeep to fighting branches of the service (infantry, including airborne, cavalry and engineers, armoured units, tank destroyer) was far from being carried out.

Tank Destroyer Command was only to receive Command Cars with a winch and, with regard to lorries, only GMCs.

The presence of tipper lorries in the cavalry and not in the armoured units is explained by the fact that the cavalry, still possessing mounted divisions at the beginning of the war, needed this type of vehicle to clear away manure and that the allocation still bears the trace of it, even when this branch has been completely motorised. It is, besides, owing to the existence of these mounted units that eighty-one GMC AFKW502 4 x 4 tractors were ordered in 1940 to ensure the towing of the Combination Animal and Cargo 6 Ton semi-trailer (eight horses, eight men, saddles, equipment, etc) which was still classed as standard in 1943, and that ninety-three fodder racks (Stock Rack) were supplied by Perfection bodyworks in 1941 on GMC CCKW353 chassis.

The Chevrolet 1½ Ton Panel Delivery 4 x 4 had not yet been allocated to the Signal Corps according to the Table, while its tractor and semi-trailer version was to equip aviation and the armoured troops, but would in reality principally be allocated to the baggage train.

As for the Dodge 6 x 6, the Table shows clearly that it is a tactical vehicle for the infantry for which it was reserved, with a single exception for Tank Destroyer Command which had always favoured vehicles with three driving axles (cf. the affair of the tank destroyer on a Jeep 6 x 6 chassis in *The time-defying Jeep*). This explains why the Jeep was only built with a single type of body.

In order to permit a better adaptation of production vehicles to extreme traffic conditions, without having to resort to special vehicles, three adaptation kits were developed.

Desert—air compressor for the tyres making it possible to adapt their pressures to the carrying capacity of the ground, larger diameter tyres, expansion tank for the cooling liquid.

Winterization—high capacity batteries, protection of ignition and electric circuits, petrol heating, adaptation of the engine lubrication, to thick oils, etc, for extremely cold temperatures and a Fording Kit—watertight sealing and schnorkel for going throug h deep water.

The table of Tank Factories shows that of the seventeen specialised factories producing tanks in the United States, seven were factories belonging to an automobile group or were operated under its technical control, or were also building vehicles. A total of 1,038 factories, including 316 in the state of Michigan alone, belonged to the automobile industry participating in the war effort. The Pacific Car and Foundry also produced the M26 'Dragon Wagon'.

Theoretical Distribution of the Principal Vehicles of the US Army by Branches of Service
Source: US Army Handbook of Military Vehicles

Class	Type and Use	US Army Air Corps	Armored Command	Cavalry	Chemical Warfare	Coast Artillery	Engineers	Field Artillery	Infantry (Airborne)	Infantry Division	Infantry (Motorized)	Infantry (Mountain Division)	Medical	Military Police	Ordnance (Base Regiment)	Quartermaster (Heavy Maintenance)	Signal Corps	Tank Destroyer
¼ Ton	Jeep	★	★	★	★	★	★	★	★	★	★	★	★	★	★	★	★	★
4 x 4	Amphibian GPA		★	★			★		★	★	★							★
¾ Ton	Command Car	★	★	★	★	★	★	★	★	★	★		★	★	★	★	★	
4 x 4	Command Car with winch		★	★				★	★	★	★				★			★
(Dodge)	Weapons Carrier	★	★	★	★	★	★	★	★	★	★		★		★	★	★	
	Weapons Carrier with winch			★			★	★	★	★	★	★	★					★
1½ Ton	Cargo	★	★				★								★	★		
4 x 4	Cargo with winch	★	★							★								
(Chevrolet)	Panel Delivery	★			★													
	Tractor for semi-trailer	★	★															
1½ Ton 6 x 6	Cargo																	★
(Dodge)	Cargo with winch							★	★									
	Cargo	★	★	★	★	★	★		★		★	★	★	★	★	★	★	★
	Cargo with winch	★	★	★	★	★	★		★		★	★	★	★	★	★	★	★
2½ Ton	Short chassis Cargo					★												
6 x 6	Short chassis Cargo with winch			★					★		★	★						
(GMC)	Tipper with winch			★			★		★		★							
	Water Tanker (700 Gall.)						★											
	Petrol Tanker (700 Gall.)		★				★									★		
	15-Foot Cargo					★												
4 Ton	Cargo with winch			★			★	★	★		★	★						
6 x 6	Tipper						★											
(Diamond-T)	Wrecker			★		★	★	★			★					★		
	Long chassis Cargo with winch					★	★	★	★									
4-5 Ton 4 x 4	Tractor for Semi-Trailer		★			★					★				★	★		
5-6 Ton 4 x 4	Tractor for Semi-trailer with winch					★												
6 Ton 6 x 6	Tractor for Semi-Trailer with winch					★					★					★		
7½ Ton 6 x 6	Artillery tractor with winch						★	★										
10 Ton 6 x 6	Heavy Wrecker		★	★							★	★			★	★		
6 x 6	Tankl Recovery		★										★				★	

IDENTIFICATION OF VEHICLES

One of the first tactical recognition and identification signs used in North Africa were American flags on the windscreens or bonnets, often, as on the leading ½ Tonner, on both sides of the star.

Four letters and some figures were used to designate the series and sub-series of vehicles:

T: prototypes;
M: production vehicles;
E: a modification or improvement made to a vehicle;
A: sub-series within a type.

For example: Tank, Medium, M4 A3 E8 identifies the medium tank of the fourth type of tank to have been ordered in quantity, of the third sub-series of the model, and of the eight modification block—a Sherman. This identification principle was principally used for armoured fighting vehicles and less frequently during the war years for transport vehicles which received a designation comprising the weight class and use reserved for the vehicle. In principle, the proper names of the manufacturers were not employed. For example:

Tractor, High Speed, M5
Truck, Cargo and Personnel Carrier 6 x 6, 1½ Ton
Truck, Emergency Repair 4 x 4, ¾ Ton
Truck-Trailer, 40 Ton, Tank Recovery M25
Truck-Tractor M26, Semi-Trailer M15
Trailer, Full, Flat Bed, 16 Ton
Truck, Shovel-Crane 6 x 6, 6 Ton
Bus, Commercial type, 20-29 passengers, 4 x 2, 1½ Ton
Trailer, Cargo, Amphibian, ¼ Ton
Truck Tractor, Ponton, COE, 4 x 4, 5-6 Ton
Semi-trailer, Cargo 7 Ton (10 Ton gross)
Truck, Combination, Stake and Platform, COE 4 x 4, 1½ Ton
Car, Light Sedan, 5 passengers, 4 x 2.

The Signal Corps used its own letter, K, with a numbered indicator. The US Army Air Corps/Forces had a separate nomenclature, then followed the one in force:

F: semi-trailer and fuel-driven tractor, four-wheel trailer
D: (Dolly) two-wheel trailer converted for another use
C: semi-trailer, low platform with swan neck or recovery lorry
N: photographic semi-trailer
A: workshop semi-trailer or specialised two-wheel trailer

Dodge T 203, 4 x 4, 1½ Ton, of which 5, 369 were delivered in Iceland, in 1941. A tipper version was also built, totalling 390. The registration is preceded by a 'W' for War Department. The inscription partly hidden by the arm of the policeman indicates that the vehicle belongs to the 62nd Regiment of Coast Artillery, a branch of the service which, as its name does not show, was specifically charged with fixed anti-aircraft artillery (calibre above 40 mm). This Unit Identification Markings system used before the war permitted the identification of matériel by a combination of badges and abbreviations. It was officially abandoned on August 5th, 1942, in favour of the system described in the text.

A Chevrolet with stars of the regulation size and position (photograph taken from the 1943 manual of camouflage)

T: heavy caterpillar tractor with rigid metal tracks
J: airfield lighting
L: aviation oil tanker
G: vehicle for fighting aircraft fires on the ground

For example:

Trailer, Fuel Servicing, 600 Gallon, type A3
Semi-Trailer, Fuel Servicing 4,000 Gallon, type FIA
Truck, Tractor, Wrecking 6 x 6, 7½ Ton, C-2
Truck, Field Lighting, 4 x 4, 1½ Ton, J-5.

Classification of US Army Vehicles

The US Ordnance Corps proceeded to classify *matériel* in service in five big classes (Army Regulations 850-25):

'Standard' *matériel*: vehicles in this series are those which, after tests, were judged perfectly suited and subsequently were officially adopted. They were supplied and allocated in priority to the units.

'Substitute Standard' *matériel*: vehicles in this series complied in all essentials and in a still very satisfactory manner with the military requirements. When necessary, notably as a result of a shortage of vehicles of the 'Standard' category, these vehicles were supplied to the units.

'Limited Standard' *matériel*: vehicles in this class

Top right: The driver of this Diamond—T 972 tipper on Leyte decorated his door with a pin-up, a decoration more commonly applied to aeroplanes (Philippines, December 1944).

Middle right: Berlin Buster the nickname of this 203 mm howitzer towed by an Allis Chalmers M4. The custom of christening artillery pieces was very widespread. It is seen in Brittany in 1944.

Bottom right: Two motorcyclists of the Military Police, Boulevard des Italiens in Paris, in 1946.

were those, already old, whose own characteristics no longer fully comply with the requirements of the moment, but which could still be used if necessary in case of need. In general, these types of vehicle were no longer held in stock, but their spare parts were still in the stocks and can be supplied to ensure the maintenance of those in service.

'Limited Procurement' *matériel*: such vehicles had already undergone tests but had not yet been classified, most often because they were awaiting further tests. It is probable that a vehicle placed in this category would be subsequently adopted.

'Obsolete' *matériel*: old vehicles which were to be replaced or were totally outmoded technologically, were periodically placed in this class.

In the event of big repairs becoming necessary, or if a major spare part is lacking, the 'Limited Standard' or 'Obsolete' vehicles were simply scrapped or cannibalised to keep running vehicles which were still in running order.

Registrations

US Army vehicles carried a registration painted in grey-blue (blue drab) or white, most usually on both sides of the bonnet and at the rear. This number was preceded by a 'W' for War Department until 1942. The registration was composed of a prefix of one or two figures identifying the category of vehicle, followed by the individual registration number of the vehicle which was defined and laid down as the sequence number in the vehicle series at the time of awarding the purchase contract. The prefixes used were the following:

- **0** trailers and semi-trailers
- **00** maintenance vehicle workshops and recovery vehicles
- **1** 2 to 7-seat road liaison vehicles
- **10** mobile kitchens on trailers
- **2** light vehicles from $\frac{1}{2}$ to 1 ton
- **20** reconnaissance vehicles (notably the Jeep) and buses
- **3** vehicles of the $1\frac{1}{2}$ ton range
- **30** assault cars (all models)
- **4** lorries from $2\frac{1}{2}$ up to 4.5 ton
- **40** caterpillar and half-track vehicles
- **5** heavy lorries and tractors over 5 tons
- **50** fire-fighting vehicles
- **6** motorcycles

A Diamond – T Wrecker with the job of bringing back the lame ducks of the Red Ball.

British number preceded by the letters 'U.S.A.' for this Canadian Dodge allocated through Reverse Lease-Lend to the US Army. The word 'Good' indicates the general condition of the vehicle at the time of its sale at Marseille in 1945.

A field workshop of the Ordnance alongside the Red Ball Express. The vehicles belong to the 3621st and 466th Transport Companies under the Advance Section Communication Zone (ASCZ). From that moment, it became customary to paint warnings on the vehicle (pressure, anti-freeze, not to fill the tank right up to the top, etc.) when faced with the marked indifference of the drivers. It was hoped that they would read at least what they had in front of their nose. Notice that the vehicle in the left foreground has been fitted with doors at the rear, a sign that it is fitted out as a light workshop under the tarpaulin, a fairly common practice.

- 60 special vehicles: (radio, air compressors, etc machine-gun carriers and Scout Cars)
- 7 ambulances
- 70 amphibious vehicles
- 8 wheeled tractors
- 80 tankers
- 9 caterpillar tractors
- 90 old vehicles (obsolete) which have been kept
- S anti-parasite vehicles
- X captured vehicles or reconstructed ones (not regulation)
- U vehicles bought in Australia.

The last three letters were added to the registration number. Most often, after 1942, the letters 'U.S.A.' preceded or were above the registration.

TACTICAL MARKINGS AND PAINT SCHEMES

Regulation markings were most frequently placed on the bumpers; these markings permitted, by the use of code letters, recognition of the vehicles as belonging to such and such a unit (system of August 1942).

TACTICAL CODES	
Divisional, Regimental and Battalion Codes	
AA	Anti-Aircraft
AB	Airborne
C	Chemical
A	Armoured
E	Engineers
F	Field Artillery
I	Infantry
GI	Glider Infantry
M	Medical
P	Military Police
Q	Quartermaster
O	Ordnance
S	Signals
T	Transport
TD	Tank Destroyer
Support and Specialised Company Codes	
HQ	Headquarters
SV	Service Companies
AT	Anti-Tank Company
EVAC	Evacuation Hospital
GAS	Gasoline
S&B	Sterilisation and Bath (clothes & field showers)
AM	Ammunition
CONS	Construction
DP	Depot
DS	Direct Support
MR	Mortar
MT	Maintenance
RP	Repair
RMP	Transportation Motor Pool
Combat Companies	
A	Able
B	Baker
C	Camel
D	Dog, etc

A Truck Tractor 4 x 2, 5 Ton, 3719th Transport Company (TC) of the Quartermaster (Q), the thirty-fourth truck of the company (TRK-34) of the Communication Zone (CZ) of the Continental Advance Section (CAS).

The principal codes, preceded by a figure, employed at divisional, regimental and battalion level, and the letters which identified support or specialised companies are shown in the accompanying table. (After May 1945, a US Army vehicle driven by a prisoner of war was identified by the code PW Driver.)

In principle, the information was given in descending order of magnitude from left to right: division, regimental or battalion number, arm or service,

Tractors 4 x 4, 4/5 Ton, of the US Air Force wait to be sold in 1950. Although post-war, this curious decoration, with the recently adopted recognition mark of the US Air Force on the door, seemed to us to be sufficiently interesting to be included in this chapter.

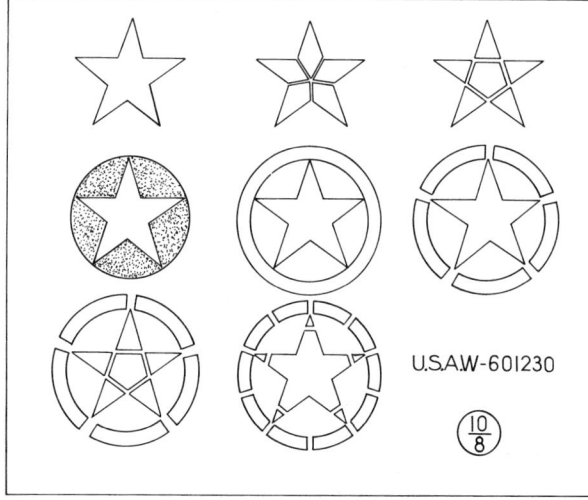

Different models of stars (yellow or white) with segmented circle or not, regulation registration and weight class plaque.

82 AB 320 F A 2: 82nd Airborne Division, 320th Field Artillery Regiment, second vehicle of A Company.
13 Δ 7011 135-0 C 1: 13th Armored Division, 135th Ordnance Battalion, first vehicle of C Company.
7 A 370 E HQ 3: 7th Army, 370th Engineer Battalion, third vehicle of the headquarters company.
28 229 F TRK 111: 28th Infantry Division, 229th Artillery Battalion, one hundred and eleventh truck.
82 ABX HQ 61: 82nd Airborne Division, sixty-first vehicle of the divisional headquarters company.
ABC 190 GI SV 6: Airborne Center (Camp Mackall), 190th Glider-borne Infantry Regiment, SV 6: sixth vehicle of the services company.

The non-divisional or service units were attached administratively to the commands of the rear or Communication Zone of the external operations theatre. The principal ones were for France:

AS Advance Section (zone immediately to the rear of the combat zone. C.Z. follows)
BBS Brittany Base Section
CAS Continental Advance Section (Atlantic coast to Switzerland)
CBS Channel Base Section (Channel coast region to Lille)
NBS Normandy Base Section
SS Seine Section (Paris and Parisian region)
OS Oise Section (region between Paris and Reims)
DBS Delta Base Section (South-east of France)

The mode of identification of the vehicles was then different. For, example, here is a registration of the Advance Section:

ASCZ 258 O 855 18: Advance Section Communication Zone, 258th Ordnance Battalion, 855th Repair Company, vehicle.

The marking 'Prestone', followed by a figure (42, 43, 44 or 45 according to the titration) in yellow or white, indicated the presence of glycol anti-freeze. A round yellow sheet-metal plaque, bearing one or two black figures separated by a bar (weight loaded in tons of the vehicle alone or with trailer) indicated the weight class for crossing military bridges.

The USA's five-pointed star was used to assist the identification of vehicles and armour from the air. It was retained as an air identification mark not only by the US Army, but also from the Italian campaign onwards as marking of the United Nations, adopting the definition adopted after the Moscow declaration.

company, serial number of the vehicle within the company. If one of the elements did not exist, for example in the case of a vehicle coming directly under a divisional or army general staff, the missing step was replaced by an 'X'.

A code and/or horizontal bars carried most frequently on the bumpers made it possible, through the combination of their different colours, to identify the units and their order of loading in the landing craft. For example:

Jeep ¼ Ton, 82nd Airborne Division, 504th Parachute Infantry Regiment, fourth vehicle of C Company.

`82 AB  504-1                    C 4`

Jeep ¼ Ton, 13th Armored Division, 135th Ordnance Battalion, first vehicle of C Company (Germany, 1945).

`13 △ 135-0                      C 1`

Jeep 1¼ Ton, 7th Armored Division, sixth vehicle of the Divisional Command Company (France, 1944).

`7 △-X           ★            HQ 6`

Dodge 1½ Ton, 84th Infantry Division, 333rd Infantry Battalion, tenth vehicle of the Anti-Tank Company (Ardennes, 1944).

`84 333-1                       AT.10`

GMC 2½ Ton, Advance Section Communication Zone, 3886th Transport Company, truck No 19 (Red Ball Express, 1944).

`ASCZ 3886 TC                  TRK-19`

GMC 2½ Ton, 2nd Infantry Division, 23rd Infantry Battalion, forty-sixth vehicle of the Service Company (Korea, 1952).

`2-23-1         ★              SV 46`

Pacific Car and Foundry M26, Normandy Base Section, 457th Material Evacuation Company, thirty-seventh vehicle. 4/32h

`NBS    457★ EVAC                  37`

GMC 2½ Ton, Seine Section, 3619th Transport Company, forty-seventh vehicle (Paris, 1945).

`SS 3619 TC                     TRK 47`

To attract the attention of British drivers to the specific features of US vehicles on the road in Great Britain, the absence of direction indicators and the left hand drive, were systematically brought to notice on all American vehicles.

CAUTION NO SIGNAL LEFT DRIVE

It was yellow or white according to the period and was applied only on vehicles in the combat zones or the Communication Zones overseas. Made by spraying through cut card stencils often created by Corps workshops, the form of the stars varied greatly. They could be surrounded by a segmented circle of variable width, in which case the background was the colour of the vehicle.

For the landing in North Africa Operation TORCH of November 1942, the star was inscribed in a circle with a blue background, accentuating its resemblance to the US aeroplane to the national marking used on aeroplanes. Moreover, some stars had a red spot in the centre. Until 1942, the Armored Corps used as a recognition mark a white star with a blue roundel in its centre, the whole inscribed in a circle with a red background. Their positioning and their size often depended on conditions of local use.

Also in North Africa, marking by stars was complemented by the use of American flags printed on paper and on the bodywork, the bonnet, the bumpers or the windscreen. This last arrangement was also used on vehicles during the Normandy landings.

In the Pacific, the stars were most often fairly discreet and rather the province of the US Army than of the US Marines. However, in Tunisia, the presence of the star in a circle and/or framed by a bar of white paint on the turret of the Shermans or on the side of the half-tracks was criticised by the crews because they gave German anti-tank gunners a perfect aiming point.

During the Italian campaign, the star was surrounded by a yellow circle of great width, or even entirely yellow, reminding one of an earlier instruction of 1942. With star removed, the vehicles coming under the different Service Commands (non-operational commands in the USA principally) were marked instead with geometric identification figures for a few months from March 1944 onwards.

A matt ochre paint (Paint Liquid Vesicant Detector M 5) could be painted on the bonnet as the background of the circled star, rectangle, etc. This paint had the peculiarity of changing colour in the presence of chlorine compounds and therefore served as an alarm device for the crew in the event of unexpectedly encountering combat gas. This system was already old and had been used by the French and British (horizontal metal plate in front of the driver's seat for the latter). Its effectiveness was fairly limited, for it gave a late warning of detection which left the crew of a vehicle too little time to put on individual

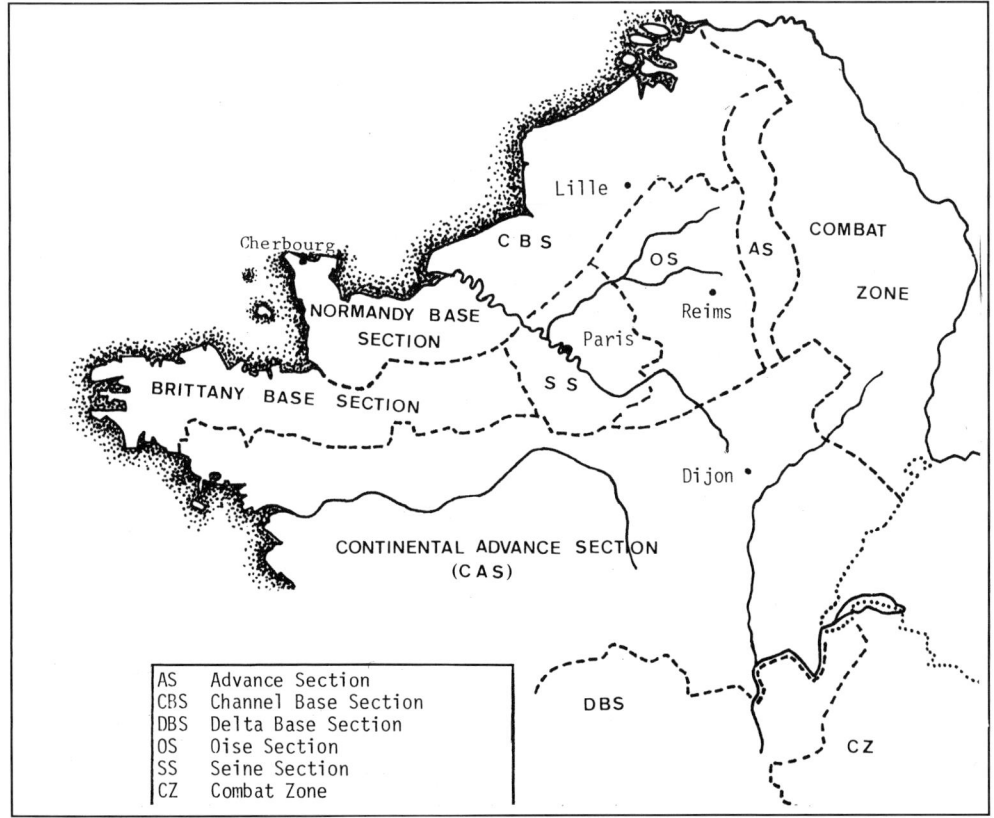

Situation and division of the Communication Zone in January 1945.

protective clothing before encountering a lethal concentration. It was nevertheless used on certain occasions, notably during the campaign in Europe.

The basic colour throughout the whole of the American armed forces, including the Navy and Marines, for all tactical vehicles was Olive Drab (glossy or matt according to the paint batches). These latter two services also used glossy forest green on a large scale.

Manual FM 5-20 B, devoted to the camouflage of vehicles, indicates a number of shades and their application according to the theatres of operation and the seasons. These regulations were not very often followed. Instances of camouflage, at least in Europe, were not frequent. Exceptions were a daubing of white paint which was fairly general during the Alsace and Ardennes campaign in 1944-45, and the use of three-tone paint schemes in Tunisia and Sicily.

On the other hand, the Marines in the Pacific very often had recourse to camouflage paint, showing in this area as in many others, their spirit of independence. The shades varied according to the landing places and the opinions of the unit as to what best matched the environment. Rationality often gave way, as everywhere in the world to such subjective considerations as personal taste, the sense of harmony and sometimes taboos attached to certain colours.

Administrative vehicles of the US Navy and the Marines were painted 'battleship grey'. The registration numbers and marking were black. The Coast Guard also used grey, but of a lighter shade, for all its fleet. The four letters 'U.S.C.G.' were painted in white very discreetly on the bonnet or more often on the door. Vehicles of the US Army were Olive Drab, or black for general officers' cars.

Apart from very rare vehicles of general officers, the chromed parts of private cars or lorries—radiator grilles, bumpers, door and boot handles, light and window surrounds—from requisition or purchased directly from American dealers were painted like the rest of the bodywork to avoid reflections. In the case of Cadillacs and Packards—according to some wags of the time—it was to give them, in spite of everything, a little look of wartime austerity!

Vehicles intended for driving on snow in Alaska or the Aleutians for example, were white.

On aerodromes of continental America or on those which could not be within range of enemy action, the service vehicles were painted bright yellow or in red and white or yellow and black checks. In that case, the nationality stars would be black, a foretaste of Vietnam and the present period.

Firefighting and medical vehicles, except in the US Navy, were most often, since peacetime, painted Olive Drab.

All vehicles of medical formations, whatever their use, ended up by carrying a red cross, either painted on the bodywork or on the canvas hood or on an added cloth. In principle, according to the Geneva Convention, only ambulance vehicles had to carry it.

Chaplains' Jeeps frequently bore the word 'Chaplain' surrounded by two white crosses on the windscreen.

The custom of christening one's vehicle was very widespread. Generally, there was less emphasis in the Army on sexual fantasies then there was in aviation units. There was much more reference to personal and familiar memories or the usual GI jokes. The use of allegorical figures such as pin-ups, film actresses, strip cartoon characters and so on, if it did exist, was fairly limited, High Command prohibitions being easier to enforce on vehicles than on aeroplanes.

Motorcycles

The motorcycle was put into service in the US Army as a liaison, convoy escort and police vehicle. The motorised manoeuvres of the spring and summer of 1941 were, for the Harley-Davidsons of the cavalry, the last occasion on which they were employed on reconnaissance, full-scale experience having finally proved that the Jeep was much superior to the motorcycle in this role. In general, and that in spite of large production, the motorcycle did not appear to the US Army to have capital importance and was relegated to service missions.

Chain-driven road motorcycles

Two prestigious makes, Indian and Harley-Davidson, shared the monopoly of the manufacture of motorcycles for the US forces. Their military machines were based on their civilian models. All American motorcycles were of chain type with three-speed gearbox, except for two models, the Harley-Davidson 42XA and the Indian 841 which had shaft transmission and four-speed gearbox built in small series.

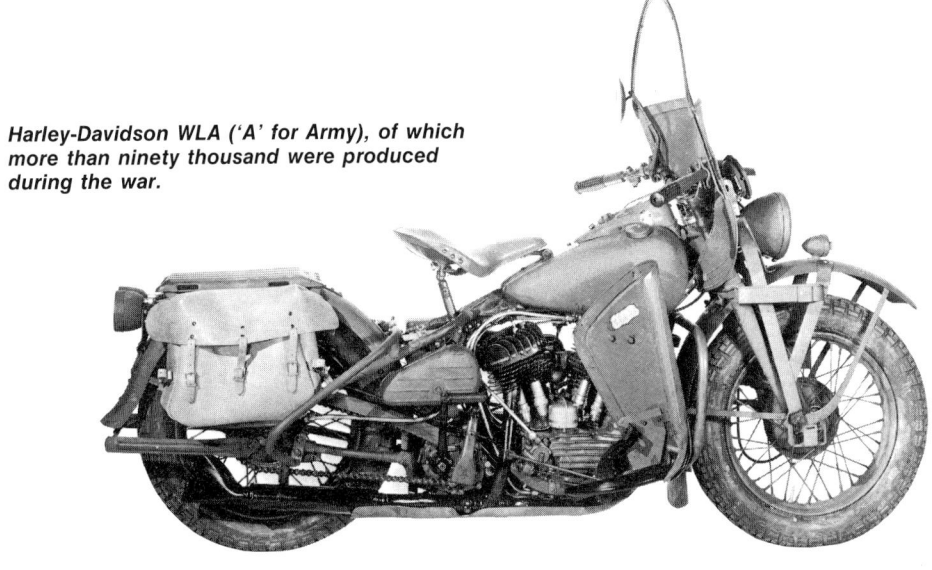

Harley-Davidson WLA ('A' for Army), of which more than ninety thousand were produced during the war.

The most widely used model was the Harley-Davidson WLA (A for Army), derived from the civil model WL which had come out shortly before the war. It was produced for the Canadians under the designation WLC. Notably, it had a different lighting system, rear black-out lights consisting of two small tubes; the clutch control was on the left handlebar grip, that of the brake then going over to the right; interchangeable front and rear wheels, which was not the case for the WLA; a different fork with longer, external struts, (whereas there were internal ones on the WLA) owing to the big front wheel hub, the 'Canadian brake', springs which served to spread the stresses and filter the oscillations of the fork; and a three-rivet saddle. The WLC was produced in three models: Model 42 with rear pillion seat on the mudguard; Model 43 'Export' single-seater and Model 43 'Domestic' with pillion seat fitted with spring suspension putting it in a raised position.

Harley-Davidson 45 x 4 shaft-drive.

The WLA conformed to the civil model of the make and only received very few extra military items of equipment. It is true that a motorcycle leaves little choice and possibility in this field. The modifications comprised:

    bigger and more robust baggage-carriers which could take two large leather bags;
    a leather gun case which could be fixed to the left front fork;

A Harley-Davidson first model containing elements of the civil range like the headlight in a high position (1940).

As far as shaft-transmission motorbikes are concerned, the Model 841 was Indian's reply to the Harley-Davidson. Tested in 1941, it was produced in small series until 1942. The two-cylinder (90°) 'V' engine developed 28 hp for a cylinder capacity of 750 cc. With the Harley-Davidson XA, it was the only American motorbike to have a four-speed gearbox.

the attachment to the front fork of a metal box with two compartments, a large one for ammunition and a small one for papers;

different types of windshield, including one made of strong fabric with a transparent upper part, which could be complemented for winter by fabric flaps for the legs;

a protective plate for the crankcase;

mudguards without sides in order to facilitate the removal of mud and avoid the clogging of earth between the tyres and the mudguards.

The first series, built with parts in stock, had retained the position and support of the civil headlights before these were repositioned under the horn in a less exposed location. In addition, a second seat could be fitted.

The Indian 640 B, 741 B and 644 followed the same evolution, although their conversion was more limited since they did not, in principle, receive gun cases and ammunition boxes. On the other hand the windshield was much larger than that of the Harleys, but with a very small transparent surface. It proved to be more 'comfortable' but less practical than the rival arrangement. As in the case of the Harley, the engines were 750 cc two-cylinder 'V' types. The gear lever was fixed either on the front (640B) or on the back of the fuel tank (741B). The forks were either of the spring model (Indian 741A, Harley-Davidson WLA), or of parallelogram type. American motorcycles did not possess any suspension at the rear, so the rider's comfort only depended on the wide saddle and its two spiral springs. Sheet metal leg shields were provided both for Harley and for Indian, but very frequently removed, as they were considered dangerous by the motorcyclists.

More than 90,000 Harley-Davidsons, including more than 60,000 WLAs and nearly 20,000 WLCs, honouring contracts of January 1st 1943, contract W398 QM 11 782 for 20,313 motorcycles and contract 271 ORD 2849 for 7,275 WLA's were produced! The spare parts produced by Harley-Davidson corresponded to 30,000 extra motorcycles. Only the WLAs were retained by the US Army after the war. It is estimated, according to the manufacturer's archives, that some five hundred Harleys were sent to Europe. In total, only a few less Indians were built.

The Harley-Davidson as it was never to be seen employed during the war—as a mount for a reconnaissance platoon (1940). The badge borne on the fuel tank is that of the US Cavalry, which served as Unit Identification Markings. In theory, an armored division had 250 motorcycles, but in practice this establishment was only rarely allocated.

Shaft-driven road motorcycles

Two models were manufactured again by Indian and Harley-Davidson. They are shown by the September 1941 edition *TM 9-2800,* as being on test. A total of one thousand test vehicles was ordered in 1941 and 1942 from the two manufacturers. Mention must be made however, of the efforts of Crosley who designed numerous prototypes notably, with a single telescopic rear shock absorber offset to the left.

More highly developed than previous models, one can readily sense that it was for the US Army a matter of testing in a military unit a modern motorcycle suited to its specific use and not a fairly classic civil model simply equipped with the indispensable for turning it into a military vehicle One can also see there, to a certain extent, the influence of British tests carried out on captured German machines, whose evaluation reports were passed on to the Americans.

The Harley-Davidson CXA or 42XA had a shaft transmission which in theory could not be put out of adjustment and was more robust than the chain type, a 740 cc 2-cylinder horizontally opposed four-stroke engine type XA, a foot-operated gear change and a suspension by telescopic shock-absorber at the rear.

The motorcyclists' instruction manual (Armored School, Motorcycle Department) 1943 edition explains at length on the advantages of these new motorcycles—end of the nightmare of maintenance and tensioning of the chains, better suspension, greater flexibility of the engine, and so on. The manual does not conceal the fact that the armoured branch of the service was a warm partisan of this transmission. As a result, it received eight hundred of the thousand shaft-driven Harleys built.

The Indian 84 was identical to the Harley in terms

Motorcycles of General Leclerc's 2nd Armored Division on their Harley-Davidson WLAs prepare to embark for France in August 1944. Note the mixture of French, British and American helmets worn by the men of this unit. In the middle background, a Claytrac tractor and self-propelled M8s also wait to go aboard the landing craft.

of design, but had a 750cc two-cylinder 'V' four-stroke 841 engine. A certain fragility, the fact that foot controls had not been among the driving habits of the American motorcyclist, and the small need for motorcycles when it came to the point did not encourage the US Army to press matters any further.

These were the last motorcycles to have been designed by the US Army, which lost interest in this category of vehicle after the war, except for those for the Military Police which received Harley-Davidsons up to the 1960s and, occasional machines for tactical trials in the 1970s.

Motorcycle sidecars

Considered in Europe as the typical reconnaissance vehicle, at least at the beginning of World War Two, the motorcycle sidecar combination was, on the other hand, for the Americans a vehicle solely used for liaison duties (Messenger Service).

Indian's model 340, very easily recognisable by its plate half-springs above the mudguard between the two forks, had gone into service in the French army from 1938 in the reconnaissance units under the name of Indian Cav (cavalry). The commercial name, Chief, recalled the Indian's head decorating the horn. It was also used by the British.

Besides the Indian, the Americans also used the Harley-Davidson ELA and UA. Experimentally, a Harley-Davidson 42 XA was fitted with a sidecar (model XS). The use of the sidecar by the United States was very limited, not to say rare.

Motorcycles for airborne troops

According to the staff manual giving the composition of the different formations of the US Army Airborne division was to include in its regulation equipment 246 motorcycles. Harley-Davidson presented, without success, its model 125 for airborne roles.

The models retained were either the Indian 148 (Standard, December 1944) or the Simplex Servi-Cycle (Limited Standard, April 1943). The Simplex was more a large autocycle with drive by two V belts. Two gear ratios (normal and reduced) could be selected by a foot control. Starting was effected by pushing. The engine was a Servi-Cycle single-cylinder 1.6 two-stroke. It was not much use for anything.

Although it was the most widely used, and was still classified as standard equipment in 1947, the

Left top: Indian model 640.

Left middle: The Indian 148 or Motorcycle, Solo, Extra Light, M1, was built at the end of the war for the airborne troops. The engine was a single-cylinder 225 cc four-stroke. It weighed 215 kg.

Motorcycle Solo, Extra Light M1 Indian Model 148 is a rare model. In any case, it was not much used and then only for communications in the camps in the United States and not for combat by airborne troops. It weighed 108 kg and could tow a light two-wheel cart (2 Wheels, Cart Airborne). Its ignition was by magneto, which permitted the elimination of battery, lights and dynamo, reducing its weight to 100 kg. Its Indian single-cylinder four-stroke engine developed six hp. It was fitted with parachute attachment rings.

In this application, the motorcycle proved perfectly useless. It was heavy, with no useful load, noisy, of poor performance on bad terrain, voluminous to transport and difficult to parachute. To remedy these inconveniences, the design of a scooter was put in hand (Scooter Motor 2 Wheels, Airborne Cushman 53) with 16M71 single-cylinder four-stroke engine with magneto ignition and chain drive. Standardised in March 1944, it was low, but hardly lighter (101 kg), parachutable, fairly fast (70 km/h), but still as useless to parachutists, who did not use it much. It is, besides, already reclassified "Limited Standard" in the 1947 edition of *TM 9-2800*.

Indian, after the war, succeeded in having an improved model of the 148, the 149 M, standardised in 1951 under the designation T-3. Practically none of them was ordered.

The Cushman chain-driven scooter, Model 53, had been designed for the parachute units. It was fitted with a single-cylinder 250 cc four-stroke engine developing 4.6 hp.

Use of motorcycle engines for the Lightened Jeeps Programmes

This ultimately unsuccessful programme (see *The Jeep: A Challenge to Time*), experimented with using motorcycle engines amongst other things, to reduce the Jeep's weight. It was hoped that the relatively high powers that could be obtained from a motorcycle engine for its weight would give adequate power without exceeding the 750 kg top weight limit. Chevrolet turned to Indian and Jeep to Harley-Davidson (Willys Air Cooled), using engines from the shaft-driven motorcycles then under test.

A postal orderly riding a Harley-Davidson ELA sidecar distributes the mail at the beginning of 1942 in a training camp in the USA.

	US Army Motorcycles and Motorcycle-Sidecar Combinations 1939-1945					
	Motorcycles				Motorcycle-Combinations	
	Harley-Davidson WLA	Indian 640N	Harley-Davidson 42 X A	Indian 841	Harley-Davidson ELA	Indian 340B
Length (metres)	2.33	2.28	2.28	2.30	2.42	2.48
Width (metres)	0.92	0.825	0.914	0.933	1.76	2.25
Height to top of Handlebars (metres)	1.04	1.17	1.02	1.03	1.08	1.12
Wight Empty (kg)	243	244	238	244	386	384
Weight Loaded (kg)	333	334	375	347	567	564
Ground Clearance (cm)	10	12.7	16.5	15.2	10.5	12.7
Fording (cm)	46	48	48	48	–	–
Climbing Gradient (%)	55	33	55	55	30	35
Turning Radius (metres)	2.13	1.83	2.51	1.83	2.28	2.74
to left	2.28					
Speed (km/hr)	105	105	105	105	90	105
Range (kilometres)	200	250	250	300	180	170
Fuel Capacity (litres)	12.6*	13.2	17	20.8	–	–
Engine Make	Harley-Davidson	Indian	Harley-Davidson	Indian	Harley-Davidson	Indian
Capacity (cc)	750	750	750	750	1,000	1,210
Configuration	V-2	V-2	Flat-2	V-2	V-2	V-2
Cooling	air	air	air	air	air	air
Ignition	6-Volt battery	6-Volt battery	6-Volt battery	6-Volt battery	6-Volt battery	6-Volt battery
Tyres	400 x 18	400 x 18**	400 x 18	400 x 18	400 x 18	4.50 x 18
Brakes	Mechanical	Mechanical	Mechanical	Mechanical	Mechanical	Mechanical
Transmission	Chain	Chain	Chain	Chain	Chain	Chain

* two-part tank; filler caps for oil & petrol
** option for sand: 500 x 16

Indian 340 fitted with a 1200 cc two-cylinder V engine, recognisable by the half-spring which holds the suspension of the front wheel. This model was known in Europe under the name of Chief because of the Indian's head adorning the horn of the pre-war models.

Harley-Davidson sidecar, Model UA, with a 34 hp 1230 cc two-cylinder V engine. This vehicle replaced the model ELA, whose engine was of lower cylinder capacity (1,000 cc) in all sub-divisions of the US Army.

Tricycles

Motortricycles or Servo-Cars, an American speciality, could not fail to interest the US Army. Crosley, Indian, Harley-Davidson and even General Motors made test vehicles for equipping the infantry, cavalry or ordnance with liaison and reconnaissance vehicles, but the Jeep, once more, got everyone's agreement.

Let us also mention a curious Harley-Davidson motorcycle with twin rear wheels, tested by the Desert Warfare Training Centre at Indio. The existence of this vehicle was revealed by Fred Crimson in *US Military Wheeled Vehicles*.

The load of the Indian 340 sidecar was 180 kg. This one was supplied to the British Army.

LIAISON AND COMMAND VEHICLES

Like all armies, the US Army possessed a fairly large fleet of motor cars (saloons, estate cars) for ensuring command liaisons. Quite obviously the United States' entry into the war necessitated the purchase of tens of thousands of vehicles. Three resources were tapped: first requisition, which was fairly limited but was put into operation all the same; secondly, direct purchase of 29,000 Ford, Chevrolet and Plymouth saloons from the dealers where they were stored after stoppage of manufacture in February 1942; and thirdly, purchase from the manufacturers. No standardisation was possible, all the more so because it was necessary to buy what was available, for the stoppage of the lines producing these vehicles hardly left any choice. The US Army classified its cars as follows:

Light Field Sedan (four-door body, five passengers): Chevrolet KB Master, or Special De Luxe series 1500 or 2000 (AG 1503, BG 1503), Ford De Luxe 1 GA and 2 GA 73 B, and Fordor O IA, Plymouth P 11, P 9, P 14.

Medium Field Sedan (four-door body, seven passengers): Buick, Chrysler Custom, Packard, Pontiac.

Heavy Field Sedan (four-door body, five or seven passengers): Buick, Cadillac 74, Chrysler, Packard 160, 180, 190 and 2000, Clipper Custom. Ford thus supplied 12,116 Special Fordor Sedans in addition to the De Luxe ones, or: 600 (model 11 A273) in 1941, and 11,516 (type 2G A73C and 21A73C) in 1942, including 9,384 in a single order. Heavy Field Sedans, corresponding to the class of luxury saloons or limousines, were reserved for general officers.

Light and Medium Station Wagon (estate car): Ford, Chevrolet, Buick with wood or metal bodywork.

A seven-seat Field Sedan with a lengthened body was called a Limousine. Models directly acquired from the industry corresponded to two specifications MCM 17 for Light Sedans. and MCM 18 for Medium Sedans.

The conversions required:

eliminating or painting all chrome parts;
painting the body standard Olive Drab, except for the cars of high rank general officers in the United States or those assigned to diplomatic missions whose cars were painted black;
fitting black-out lights at front and rear in place of civilian lights;
armoring the ignition and anti-parasiting;
reinforced bumper and shock absorbers;
a fire extinguisher;
sometimes a weapons rack;
air conditioning.

The model years were 1940, 1941, 1942 and sometimes, as in the case of the Packards, 1943. The Packard 1083, 1903 and 2003 were the only vehicles dating from the war (1940-43) to benefit still from a classification Standard in 1953, thanks to their universally recognised robustness.

The US Army also bought Airport Limousines, vehicles produced by lengthening the wheelbase and fitting four doors on each side and four windows, to permit the carriage of about twenty passengers. It was especially Chevrolets and Packard Clippers (100 of the 487 Clippers of the US Army were thus converted) which were used.

In England and Australia (Holden, Oldsmobile), locally-built cars were also used. The US Navy, whose cars were light grey or black, bought Buick Specials, Chevrolet Fleet Lines and Fords, including by direct purchase from local dealers. A not insignificant number of cars captured from the Germans or Italians was also recovered and put into service again.

Ford Special Fordor of the US Army, photographed in 1945 during a car safety test for military drivers.

A Cadillac put at the disposal of General de Lattre de Tassigny. If the US Army used the Cadillac or the Packard, the US Navy chose the Lincoln.

Chevrolet BG 1503, 1942 model, 'Airport Limousine' or 'Bus Sedan, Converted', able to transport fifteen passengers. A similar vehicle was also made on a lengthened Ford or Packard 110 'Clipper' chassis.

Chevrolet series 1500 of 1942, powered by a 3500 cc engine, Model 2 AA.

Packard Heavy Sedan (seven passengers).

TACTICAL VEHICLES

Light-Heavy: between $2\frac{1}{2}$ and 4 Tons;
Heavy-Heavy: above 4 Tons.

This chapter examines the basic tactical chassis. The reader should refer to the appropriate chapters for the bodies, equipment and specialised uses.

During World War Two, almost the whole of the American tactical fleet was composed of vehicles with drive to all their axles, which was far from being the case with the other belligerents. In spite of the initial difficulties and hesitations, the effort had been able to be concentrated on a fairly small number of models, which permitted a certain degree of standardisation.

The Jeep

The Jeep was born of the need, arising from World War One, to supply the US Army with a light vehicle of small dimensions, capable of good performance on bad terrain, which could at the same time serve as a liaison vehicle and as 'maid of all work' for the combat troops. On May 27th 1940 after numerous tests, a long gestation and many uncertainties, the services of the US Army defined the characteristics

A Bantam 40 BRC of the British Army, captured by the Afrika Korps in Tunisia in 1942.

A tactical vehicle in the US Army is defined as any vehicle intended to ensure transport for the direct benefit of forward units, whether this transport is by the orders of the Quartermaster (supplies, petrol, ammunition, personnel) or is intended for the services of the combat units proper, such as the artillery or the engineers.

According to a particularly simple typology of classification, the US Army categorised its motor vehicle assets into four major classes of *matériel*:

Light: up to $\frac{1}{4}$ Ton;
Medium: between $\frac{1}{4}$ and $2\frac{1}{2}$ Tons;

Ford GP in the Burmese jungle.

The first 25,808 Jeeps produced by Willys differed from the model subsequently built by their cubic fuel tank, the absence of the jerrycan carrier and especially by their cast radiator grille.

To stabilise this Jeep for transverse anti-aircraft firing, a strut was fitted on either side of the vehicle (New Caledonia, 1943).

of the future vehicle as follows:

    maximum weight of 1,300 pounds (590 kg)
    useful load of 600 pounds (272 kg)
    wheelbase: 2.032 m
    four-wheel drive
    two or four-wheel steering
    armed with a .30-cal. machine-gun

On July 11th, 1940, 135 companies were contacted but only two sent a submission: Willys-Overland Inc. and American Bantam Co. To be honest, one really had to like taking up challenges to launch oneself into such an adventure. To design a vehicle which was as light as this and was also capable of travelling over any terrain with a good performance and a satisfactory robustness was attempting the almost impossible. Moreover, the administrative conditions imposed incredibly short time limits: forty-nine days for the design, construction, transport and presentation of the prototype at the Holabird depot of the Quartermaster Corps, in Maryland, seventy-five days in all for the realisation of the complete programme, or seventy vehicles including eight with four-wheel steering.

Two men stamped their mark on this period: Probst at Bantam, and Ross at Willys. The opening of tenders on July 23rd, 1940, provisionally gave the advantage to Bantam, Willys having asked for a prolongation of the time limit of 120 days, fearing interruptions of supply from certain of its subcontractors, in particular Spicer for the drive axles. On September 23rd, shortly before 5 o'clock in the evening, the Bantam driven by Karl Probst himself was going into the camp and on the very next day was beginning its contractual 5,500-km test drive, including 500-km along the potholed tracks of Holabird. On December 17th, 1940, the delivery of the seventieth test vehicle was completed. Called Model B60, they had a simpler body shape and redesigned wings, but retained the 45 hp Continental Y-4112 engine of the first prototype.

The contract had been respected from end to end, to the satisfaction of the US Army which had, besides, placed a first firm order for 1,500 Bantams, 40 BRCs, a developed and improved version of the pre-production Model 60s. This was an ephemeral success for Bantam, for although absent from the opening of the bids in July, Willys had continued to work on the project, knowing quite well that the size and production capacities of the company would be weighty factors when it ultimately came to going into

These American soldiers are all of Japanese descent of whom a large colony resided in San Francisco and Los Angeles. They were not used in the Pacific and were only sent to Europe in a special unit. Here they serve in Italy.

mass production. At Ford, they worked upon the same reasoning. Although they had not even replied to the request for offers, they had studied the programme, even sending a price offer on their own initiative on October 16th. Thus, on November 11th the Willys Quad and on November 23rd the Ford Pigmy also arrived at Holabird.

The submissions may have been late, and inspired by the Bantam which the engineers of Willys and Ford had been authorised to examine in detail, but in the end, all that mattered to the US Army, who had only limited confidence in the industrial capacity of Bantam, was the reassurance that two larger manufacturers had joined the programme.

Tests showed that the Willys, thanks to its Go Devil engine, performed better in spite of its weight of 1,090 kg. Nobody, in any case, had been able to keep to the 1,300 lb required by the first programme specification and the weight had had to be raised to 2,160 lb (980 kg). Even after this redrawing of the specifications, the Willys still weighed 119 kg too much.

To encourage the two new competitors to do better, as from November 14th—that is to say, before the prototype tests—the principle was declared of ordering 1,500 pre-production vehicles from them also, on condition that their prototypes should satisfy the technical and administrative requirements of the programme, certainly the least that one could ask. The decision, one imagines, hardly pleased Bantam.

Ford produced the GP, which followed the Pigmy, without great enthusiasm, for the company engineers knew that its engine, which came from a Ferguson tractor, was too low-powered and that its gearbox was badly graded. The 1,500th GP was delivered on May 7th, 1941. But it was thought that the company's connections were powerful and that such a giant would not be set aside without looking twice at the programme if the latter expanded.

On the other hand, Willys, while still building the first MAs, launched into a great attack on superfluous weight, even going as far as to weigh the paint and saw off the bolt ends in order to attain the critical 2,160 lb, for Ross refused to envisage the fitting of a less powerful and therefore lighter engine, convinced that it was precisely the power of the Go Devil that would give him final history. His obstinacy and General Knudsen's perspicacity proved him right, since the first series contract for 16,000 vehicles was finally allocated to Willys.

The Jeep MB or ¼ Ton Utility Truck had just entered history at the price of 1,000 dollars apiece.

A total of 638, 245 of them was built, including 277, 896 GPWs under Willys licence at Ford, to which should be added 2,675 Bantam 40 BRCs, 3,650 Ford GPs and 1,500 Willys MAs. The first 25, 808 Jeeps had a cast iron radiator grille, a fuel tank of rectangular shape with right-angled corners, a unique dash-board, and the name of the manufacturer stamped on the rear panel. After this, a different dashboard was fitted; and, from March 1943, a jerrycan was fitted at the rear.

The Jeep is still classified 'Standard' in the 1953 edition of *TM 9-2800*, (see *The Jeep, A Challenge to Time*).

Dodge ½ Ton, ¾ Ton

During World War Two, the Dodge company participated extensively in the effort of production of military *matériel*: aircraft components, precision instruments for air navigation, armoured cars, industrialisation of the 40 mm Bofors gun, proximity fuses, etc. The core of its activity was nevertheless that of producing vehicles, of which 437, 892 were built. Among these the Weapons Carrier, 4 x 4, ¾ Ton

Command and reconnaissance vehicle Model VC-1.

Command Car, Model WC 6. The WC 7 had a Braden winch and the WC 8 was wired to receive a radio set.

Dodge WC 1 4 x 4, ½ Ton.

Dodge WC 10, ½ Ton Carryall.

Dodge Model VC 3 of which eight-one were built. The VC 3, like all the other vehicles of the VC series, is equipped with the Chrysler T 202 6-cylinder in-line engine of 3300 cc cylinder capacity.

Dodge ½ Ton, WC 11, sheet-metal van body, of which 353 were built.

Dodge WC 4 fitted with a Braden winch.

WC 41 light repair vehicle. 7/63

Elements of the US Ninth Army in Dodge WC 52s cross the Rhine on a bridge built by the 17th Engineer Battalion during March 1945.

Workshop vehicle, Model WC 60, Emergency Repair M2.

Weapons Carrier modified as a cinema during the campaign in North Africa, in June 1943. The vehicle was hastily painted beige, as the spread of the paint over the wheels proves. Notice the registration characters in Arabic figures at the rear.

remains the most famous.

At the end of the 1930s the US Army, which was at the centre of the process of motorisation, expressed the need for a tactical vehicle with a useful load of 500 kg, such as was proposed by Marmon-Herrington (Ford International chassis). At the end of comparative tests and a few small scattered orders, the Dodge model was approved by the Quartermaster Corps and was finally built. This model, designated T 202 by the manufacturer, still retained a very civilian appearance. Series production, which began in 1939, finished in 1940 after 4,640 had been produced. It was built with a tarpaulin-covered platform, as Command Car, Carryall.

In 1940, this model was replaced by the series known as T 207, then T 211 and T 215 (WC 1 to 27 and WC 40 to 43). Global production of these different models was 77,678 (tarpaulin-covered platform, Command Car, Carryall, ambulance, van, etc.). It was also built in Canada (T 212-D8A, 8 CWT) with a less powerful engine of 74 bhp. It was only in 1942 that the series T 214, whose useful load had been brought up to $\frac{3}{4}$ Ton, appeared.

Production of the Dodge 4 x 4, $\frac{3}{4}$ Ton, or series WC (Weapons Carrier) totalled 255, 196. Like the $\frac{1}{2}$ Ton, it was also built in Canada (D3/4APT-T 236), this time with a somewhat larger capacity engine (3880 cc as against 3780 cc). Weapons Carriers types WC 51 and WC 52 had a transport capacity of ten men or 750 kg of ammunition or small *matériel*. Certain models (WCV 52) were fitted with a Braden winch at the

Dodge M6 armed with a 37 mm cannon.

Dodge WC 52 transporting soldiers of the Thai contingent of the United Nations forces, in Korea.

On a bridge constructed by the US Engineers, a Jeep of the 239th Transmissions Battalion passes in front of a GMC air compressor and a Dodge ¾ Ton Carryall, Model WC 53.

front, of 2.2 tons capacity.

Numerous versions of the ¾ Tonner were built including WC 53 Carryall (two-door glazed estate car with sheet-metal body), WC 54 Wayne medical which could transport four wounded on stretchers or six wounded sitting, WC 56 and 57 Command Car (command liaison and reconnaissance), and WC 58 radio version of the Command Car. More specialised workshop (WC 60) and telephone line maintenance vehicle (WC 59 and WC 61) versions were also built, but in relatively limited numbers.

A large percentage of Command Cars and Gun Carriers (WC 52 equipped with a 37 mm anti-tank gun used by Tank Destroyer Command), having no further use, had their specific bodywork removed or were disarmed in 1944 to become simple Weapons Carriers again or to receive ambulance bodies, or with a folding body made of wood and non-strategic materials

Dodge 4 x 4, ¾ Ton, WC 56.

Dodge 4 x 4, 1½ Ton, derived from the 4 x 2 commercial model of 1939. A thousand were built with a 4.5 ton capacity winch. The 3958 cc T203 engine developed 99 hp.

Tests on difficult terrain of a Dodge, 4 x 4, 1½ Ton (1940).

(WC 64 KD), or, after the war, with a sheet-metal body with sliding doors (S7 MA 51 Boyertown) on a lengthened chassis and fitted with extra shock absorbers.

The Command Cars with winch and Weapons Carriers were still classified as 'Standard' and the Command Cars without winch 'Limited Standard' in the 1947 edition, and both as 'Limited Standard' in the 1953 edition of *TM-9-2800*, as well as the whole series of ¾ Tonners. The series of ½ Tonners is classified for the last time as 'Limited Standard' in 1947 (see *Dodge, Five Generations of Off Road Vehicles*).

1½ Ton lorries

This weight class was one of the favourites of the US Army, as it corresponded to a chassis category which was in very widespread production by the manufacturers.

In the 1930s, Marmon-Herrington had done pioneering work in the range of 4 x 4, 1½ Ton tactical vehicles, modifying commercial chassis, principally Fords, but also Dodges or Internationals to off road vehicles. From 1939, GMC supplied ACKX 353s with tarpaulin-covered platforms or as tippers, a vehicle model which was also ordered by France under the designation ACK 353 (the X indicating for the USA alone a wheelbase which was not a production one at General Motors) and 82 AFKX 352 with Heil body in 1940. Chrysler's Fargo division, which was

GMC tipper 4 x 4, 1½ Ton, Model ACK 353, built during the period 1939-40.

Chevrolet 1½ Ton panel delivery, of the Austrian Army. A total of 3,658 was built.

GMC 1½/3 Ton AFKX 352, with Heil metal cargo body, of which seventy-nine were built in 1939-40.

responsible in the group for sales to the administration and to the armed forces, in 1940 supplied 6,472 T203 chassis in the series VF 400 (VF 401 to 407). Like the GMC it was also put into production for France and, in consequence, it was used by the British because they took over the supply contracts after the fall of France to the Germans in June 1940 (see *The GMC: A Universal Truck*).

This vehicle was derived from a road-going truck (TE 30), by the simple addition of a front-driving axle designed by Dodge and a protective grille for the radiator and headlights, and was fitted with mudguards which had large cut-outs in them to avoid clogging, and allowed a better travel and favoured oversized tyres. Some one thousand chassis received a winch and 390 a tipper body. The cargo version was still classified 'Standard' in the 1947 edition of *TM 9-2800*, while the tipper was 'Substitute Standard' and had been deleted in that of 1953.

It was, however, Chevrolet, part of the General Motors group, which virtually monopolised the production of four-wheel drive vehicles of this tonnage from 1940 onwards. Numerous versions were built:

drilling vehicle K 44 (Signal Corps) or M1 (Engineers), 1,659 vehicles

vehicle for construction and maintenance of telephone lines K 42 and K 43, 4,229 vehicles

long-wheelbase cargo, 303 vehicles

cargo with and without winch (steel or wood

Chevrolet 1½ Ton Truck Prefixes

1941	1941	1942-3
Y	Z	N
A Telephone with winch	A Telephone with winch	–
B Telephone without winch	–	–
C Telephone with winch and drill	–	–
E –	chassis alone	chassis alone
F –	–	Searchlight Carrier
G Van	Van	Van
H Tipper	Tipper	Tipper
J Cargo	–	Cargo
K Tractor	Tractor	Tractor
L Tipper with winch	Tipper with winch	Tipper with winch
M Cargo with winch	Cargo with winch	Cargo with winch
N forward cab	–	forward cab
P –	–	long-wheelbase Cargo
Q long-wheelbase Cargo	long-wheelbase Cargo	Bomb Transporter
R –	–	Telephone with winch and drill
S –	–	Telephone with winch
X –	–	Firefighting Truck with forward cab
Z Bomb, AAF	–	Aviation Fire Fighting Truck

Examples:
1. NH is a Chevrolet Tipper Truck of 1942-43;
2. YJ is a Cargo Truck of 1941;
3. ZQ is a long-wheelbase Cargo Truck of 1941.

Chassis/Body Combinations

Series G 4100	Series G 7100	Bodies
Years before 1942	Years after 1942	
	G 7163	K 42 Drillers
G 4112	G 7173	Telephone K 42/3
G 4174	G 7127	long Cargo rear cab
G 4112/41	G 7107	Cargo without winch or Airborne (towable for air-transport)
G 4163	G 7117	Cargo with winch
	G 7105	Van and K51
G 4112, 4152	G 7106	Tipper without winch
G 4162	G 7116	Tipper with winch
	G 7113	Tractor
	G 7128	Bomb Transporter M6
G 4103	G 7123	Forward-cab Cargo
G 4112	G 7143	Searchlight Carrier
	G 7153	Fire fighting Truck (forward cab)
	G 7133	Fire fighting Truck (rear cab)
	G 7133	Gunnery Trainer E5
	G 7107-7103	Bare chassis to be equipped

Chevrolet 4 x 4 1½ Ton Trucks 1939-1945

	Cargo Chassis with Tarpaulin	Long Chassis Cargo	Forward Cab
Length (metres)	5.69	7.53	7.26
Width (metres)	2.19	2.21	2.50
Height to top (metres)	2.65*	2.74	2.50
Wheelbase (metres)	3.68	4.45	4.45
Weight Empty (kg)	3,420	3,678	3,887
Useful Load (kg)	1,360	1,360	1,360
All Up Weight (kg)	4,780	5,038	5,247
Ground Clearance (cm)	25	–	–
Fording (cm)	81.2	–	–
Climbing Gradient (%)	65	–	–
Angle of Approach (°)	45	–	41.5
Angle of Departure (°)	30	–	29
Speed (km/hr)	77**	–	70**
Fuel Capacity (litres) ****	113.5	–	–
Fuel Consumption on road (litres/100 kilometres)	36	–	42.8
Engine	Chevrolet BV-100 UP Type 235	Chevrolet BV-100 UP Type 235	Chevrolet BV-100 UP Type 235
Cylinders	6, in-line	6, in-line	6, in-line
Ignition	6-Volt Battery	6-Volt Battery	6-Volt Battery
Tyres	7.50 x 20 twinned rear	–	–
Brakes	Hydraulic	–	–
Axles	Banjo only	–	–
Winch	4,530-kg 5.87-metres long	None	None
Body	Wood (height: 2.72 metres) or Steel	Wood (height: 2.72 metres) or Steel	Wood (height: 2.72 metres) or Steel

*   To tarpaulin
**   At Regulation 3,100 rpm
*** At 2,850 rpm
**** Tank mounted between chassis beams

Chevrolet G 7016 tipper, of which 5,133 were built.

A Chevrolet 1½ Ton G 7017 of the Soviet Red Army transports French prisoners in Germany.

Chevrolet NJ G 7107, converted in 1944 so as to be able to be transported by air in the Douglas C-47. The driver's cab roof has been removed, only the windscreen has been retained. The cargo body is of wood. The chassis separates into two parts by simply unbolting it.

Only 338 of this version with platform with sides of 15 feet (4.572 metre) (Models G 4174 or G 7127) were built.

body), 113,077 vehicles
 van, some equipped as radio vehicle K 51 (Signal Corps), 3,658 vehicles
 tipper with and without winch, 14,141 vehicles
 tractor for semi-trailer with electric braking control for the Warner semi-trailer
 bomb transporter M6, 2,175 vehicles
 forward-cab cargo, 598 vehicles
 searchlight carrier vehicle
 fire-fighting vehicle (forward cab or rear cab)
 gunnery training E5

The model built in the greatest numbers was of course the cargo version—with 86,871 vehicles without winch and 26,206 with winch. The tipper version had a capacity of 1,520 kg, and was equipped with Heil or Hercules equipment. A total of 9,008 tipper vehicles without a winch and 5,733 with winch was produced. Its performance off road was considered rather mediocre, but the truck had rather a reputation of being pleasant to drive on the road.

In the 1953 edition of *TM 9-2800*, the Chevrolet cargo and the tractor for semi-trailer were still classified 'Standard', while the bomb transporter, the long cargo truck, with or without forward cab were 'Limited Standard' and the tippers 'Substitute Standard'.

The similarity of shape to the GMC often makes one think that the Chevrolet is only a shortened CCKW. This is of course incorrect: the vehicle being perfectly original. On the other hand, Chevrolet as Yellow Truck, a company in the GM group then building the CCKW, had designed the vehicle's sheet-metal military cabs on the basis of the pressed parts of the civil range. It is not surprising that the final result was alike: for economic reasons, construction was simplified while at the same time, commercial

considerations dictated an effort to present a range of vehicles which was not unified but which resembled each other enough to produce an effect of a 'family of vehicles' and thus the shape of their cabs was very alike. However, the overall dimensions and methods of fixing on the chassis (three points on the Chevrolet) are different.

Chevrolet, in order to standardise production, made several prototypes based on the shortened GMC $2\frac{1}{2}$ Tonner, with one driving axle less, whose useful load was brought down to $1\frac{1}{2}$ Tons. The Dodge 6 x 6, much lower in silhouette and much superior in performance, was selected by the US Army, so the matter was not followed up.

Except for the bomb transporter M6 (short wheelbase of 3.175 m) and the dismantleable air portable Airborne versions, the Chevrolet was not fitted with an open cabin. The long version was characterised by its transmission shaft being in two parts supported by an extra attachment point and a lengthened body known as '15 Feet'.

The forward-cab model conformed with Chevrolet's civil production, but with two driving axles. It was principally used for the transport of antennae by the Signal Corps (K33 and K34), although it was also used in the transport units as a cargo truck. It was fitted with only a single type of body, which had high slatted wooden sides (Stake and Platform), very typical of the American bodywork. The most handsome and rarest of the Chevrolets remains the sheet-metal bodied van (Panel Truck $1\frac{1}{2}$ Ton) of which the majority was in fact directed towards the Signal Corps (K51) to transport a powerful radio set. Its body came from a road model (4 x 2, $1\frac{1}{2}$ Ton, Type MR) used as a transport vehicle or rather spartan ambulance. The MR chassis also served as a basis, even if the result

A Chevrolet $1\frac{1}{2}$ Ton tipper (Heil or Hercules Steel Products body) is unloaded in India. Besides their normal employment, these tippers could be fitted with tarpaulin, the hoops for which can be seen stowed behind the cab, and be employed as a cargo lorry or troop transporter.

Chevrolet $1\frac{1}{2}$ Ton, forward cab, of which 598 were built. This vehicle was a purely civil model.

On the Red Ball Express routes, a convoy of Chevrolet G 7113 tractors of the 3014th Transport Company refuels.

Chevrolet 1½ Ton Panel Delivery, of the Austrian army. A total of 3,658 was built.

was very different, in the last resort, for the design of an off road chassis.

When the infantry group was changed from eight to twelve men in 1942, the leaders of this branch of the service asked Dodge to extrapolate from the 4 x 4 ¾ Tonner a vehicle permitting the transport of the new elementary combat formation. By lengthening the chassis and the body and adding a third driving axle and gearbox, the manufacturer produced a new vehicle of which ninety-six per cent of the parts were common with its predecessor. The T223 (series WC62 and WC63 with winch) did not have, in production models, any variant of equipment. In the same weight class as the Chevrolet (1½ Tons), it was quickly preferred mainly because of its much lower silhouette and its excellent performance off road.

The rather modest production total of 43,278 built at Mount Road is explained by a first big reduction of orders at the end of 1942 and a second in February 1944 which further reduced the remaining quantity by a third. In addition, the sea transport crisis was slowing down the despatch vehicles to the fronts, while

Dodge 1½ Ton 6 x 6 WC 52 and WC 53 (with winch)	
Length (metres)	5.46
Length with winch (metres)	5.70
Width (metres)	2.10
Height to top (metres)	2.17
without canvas roof (metres)	1.59
Wheelbase (metres)	3.18
Weight Empty (kg)	3,138
with winch (kg)	3,274
All Up Weight (kg)	4,498
with winch (kg)	4,634
Ground Clearance (cm)	27
Fording (cm)	86
Climbing Gradient (%)	60
Angle of Approach (°)	54
with winch (°)	37.5
Angle of Departure (°)	33.5
Speed (km/hr)	87 at 3,200 rpm (regulation)
Engine Make and Type	Dodge T 223
Capacity	3,800
Cylinders	6
Fuel	petrol
Ignition	6-Volt Battery
Tyres	9.00 x 16, singles

Dodge 6 x 6, 1½ Ton, during tests at the manufacturer's.

A Dodge 1½ Tonner of the Free French forces, fitted with a ring mounting for a 50-cal machine gun and towing a 57 mm anti-tank gun, passes through Ostheim during operations to reduce the Colmar pocket (February 1945).

A convoy of Dodge 6 x 6, belonging to the 35th Division, crosses a flooded zone in the Puttelange region in December 1944.

ACKWX 353 of the US Army, photographed in September 1939. It is a development of the AC civil range. Several thousand were used until the end of the 1940s by the US Army, then the US National Guard, but were not sent outside the United States.

Bare CCKW and AFCKWX chassis waiting to have bodywork fitted.

the difficulties in the supply of raw materials and the very noticeable losses during transport owing to the safety of sea convoys both had effects on total production.

Its replacement, in spite of a few attempts and the pressing demands of the users, was provided from other classes of vehicles, either by the $2\frac{1}{2}$ Ton class trucks or by armoured personnel transports, such as the WC 62/63. Its performance, mobility and flexibility, had at the same time the characteristics of transport vehicles but also, and perhaps especially, for the infantry it had those of the tactical manoeuvre or even combat vehicle. It was still 'Standard' in 1953.

The French army, which still uses some and is going to replace them by Renault TRM 2000's, was after the war the only Allied army to receive some directly from the USA (Mutual Assistance Pact, then NATO). Sweden also bought some directly from US Army stocks. Along with the chassis from International, it remains an exception, vehicles of the $1\frac{1}{2}$ Ton class not in theory justifying three driving axles.

The GMC 6 x 6, $2\frac{1}{2}$ Ton and other $2\frac{1}{2}$ Ton trucks

The most brilliant symbol, along with the Jeep, of American automobile production of the 1940s, the GMC $2\frac{1}{2}$ Ton model CCKW also constitutes a record of operational longevity. Indeed, more than forty years after its conception, this truck still remained in service in several armies, not to mention the thousands still employed through the world, notably by civil public works companies or recovery services.

Nicknamed 'the workhorse of the army', or even more familiarly 'Jimmy' or 'Deuce and a half', the CCKW 6 x 6, $2\frac{1}{2}$ Ton was designed by the firm of Yellow Truck. This company was created in 1921, and was under the control of General Motors from July 1st, 1925, before becoming a mere department of General Motors on September 30th, 1943.

In 1938, the British and French Governments were busy trying to find, principally in the United States, new sources of supply. The Yellow Truck company was approached at that time by France. It then received large orders for road and off-road lorries, all derived from the commercial range then in production. Among these there figured the ACKWX 353, a 2.5 ton 6 x 6 lorry, of which 2,000 was ordered. Owing to the events of June 1940, these vehicles were

On this short chassis GMC, Model CCKW 352, under test, the front axle has been fitted with a twin mounting using the two spare wheels stowed between the cab and the platform. Furthermore, all the wheels have been fitted with chains (Hipkins system).

delivered to Great Britain. The vehicle had kept its civil cab.

To gain time in design, when the US Army presented its equipment plan, and to accelerate production, Yellow Truck worked with what it possessed, namely the ACKWX 353 already put on the production line for France. It was christened CCKWX 353, the letter C, reference symbol for the year 1941 in the manufacturer's nomenclature, replacing the letter A, representing the year 1939. The vehicle had been given a 'military' radiator grille and bonnet, that is to say with simpler geometric forms, both to facilitate repairs and to improve the cooling by increasing the heat exchange surface of the radiator. The letter X indicated a wheelbase which was not a production one at GMC. It was to be abandoned when the CCKW became the only product to come off the production line.

From January 1941, the first of the 13,186 trucks of the two initial contracts (W398 QM 8266 and 8275) came off the production line. Among those first deliveries were thirty-four trucks equipped with a water purification unit and 276 750-gallon (2,835 litres) Columbian tankers. The vehicle gave such satisfaction that, rapidly, new orders were placed, bringing the total production for the year 1941 to 56,397. In total, 562,750 GMC 6 x 6 2½ Tonners had been built when production was stopped in 1945, an absolute record for a truck, civil or military, which only the Chinese Jay-Fong, a copy of the International K, has beaten. The most widespread chassis was the CCKW 353 cargo without winch, which accounted for 231,352 vehicles.

The GMC was built in long chassis (CCKW 353) or short chassis (CCKW 352) versions, with sheet-metal or canvas topped (from July 1943) cab, with or without winch, with tarpaulin-covered wooden or

The short chassis version of the GMC 6 x 6, 2½ Ton was originally designed for towing artillery guns of up to 105 mm calibre. This one is in Normandy, in June 1944.

GMC 6 x 6 2½ Ton Truck			
	CCKW 353 with winch	CCKW 352 with winch	AFKWX 353
Length (metres)	6.864	6.220	6.769
Width (metres)	2.235	2.235	2.235
Height (metres)	2.362	2.362	2.692
Wheelbase (metres)	4.166	3.683	4.166
Weight Empty (kg)	5.103	5.012	4.900
Useful Load (kg)	2.427	2.427	2.427
All Up Weight (kg)	7.530	7.439	7.327
Climbing Gradient (%)	65	65	65
Angle of Approach (°)	31	31	45
Angle of Departure (°)	36	44	32
Speed (km/hr)	72	72	72
Range (kilometres)	480	480	480

A convoy of GMC 2½ Tonners on the Red Ball Express pushing towards the front the supplies disembarked in Normandy in 1944.

GMC reassembly line installed in the Norman countryside in August 1944. The GMC petrol tanker is fitted with tarpaulin-carrying hoops, with the intention of camouflaging this vehicle as a simple cargo lorry.

700-gallon (2,645 litres) water tanker with motor pump. Although designed initially for the transport of drinking water, this vehicle was often used as a fire fighting vehicle. It is seen in Morocco in 1947.

700-gallon water tanker built by Columbian, mounted on a CCKW 353 chassis.

GMC CCKWX 353 fodder wagon, intended for the transport of hay for the mounted cavalry units. In total, 119 was built in 1941. The 'X' was abandoned in 1943, when only the CCKW chassis was in production.

metal platform with slatted sides and with either Split or Banjo axles. A 6 x 4 version was also built, as well as Airborne (tipper and cargo) versions which were dismantleable for transport by air; these were on chassis with three driving axles.

A version with semi-forward cab, the AFKWX 353 was also put into production with a tarpaulin-covered wooden or metal platform with slatted sides, 15 feet (4.5 m) or 17 feet (5.1 m) long and a sheet-metal cab originally used on civil products of GMC and already used on other models by the Army. A canvas-covered cab replaced it during production. The first 671 models only came out in 1942; these had Split axles, replaced from 1943, by Banjo axles. A total of 7,232 was built.

In 1940, three examples of a version fitted with a less powerful engine, the AFKWX 353, had been built. These had a cargo body and a twin wheel mounting. One was converted into a tipper with wheel mounting in single version for the engineers (Split axles from Timken, engine type 256). A few vehicles were tried out in 1940 with open or semi-open cabs (fixed windscreen and canvas hood).

In 1953, all the GMCs were still Standard, except the AFKWX 353 with 15-feet platform and the CCKW 352s and 353s with sheet-metal cab and cargo body which were classified 'Limited Standard', as the war in Korea and gifts to Allied armies had caused stocks to fall.

From 1941, need for the $2\frac{1}{2}$ Ton range of trucks appeared particularly great. The Yellow Truck company being faced with the material impossibility of meeting the development of production, the Quartermaster Corps contacted other manufacturers, first of all the Studebaker company of South Bend, then later International Harvester and Reo. The latter assembled under licence long-chassis Studebakers, without winch and with sheet-metal cab. Initially, it had been envisaged that Studebaker would produce a copy in conformity with the Yellow Truck model. However, this idea was rapidly dropped, for it would have required too extensive modification of Studebaker's production lines. Such a solution would only have lengthened the production times and entailed extra costs estimated at several million dollars. From March 1942, Studebaker produced four thousand a month, while it had only built 4,424 in the whole of 1941 for its civilian customers.

Although some parts were common to the vehicles produced by Studebaker and General Motors, most of the mechanical components were not interchange-

Forward-cab version of the GMC 6 x 6, 2½ Ton, Model AFKWX 353, fitted with a 15-foot (4.57-metre) body.

AFKWX 353 with sheet-metal cab. Only 671 had a sheet-metal cab and a small number of these received Banjo axles instead of split ones because of problems of supplying parts.

Studebaker 6 x 6, 2½ Ton			
Designation	Year of Manufacture	Wheelbase (metres)	Type
US 6-U1	1941	3.759	Cargo without winch
US 6-U2	1941	3.759	Cargo with winch
US 6-U3	1941-44	4.115	Cargo without winch
US 6-U4	1941-44	4.115	Cargo with winch
US 6-U5	1941-42	4.115	5,000 US Gall. Tanker without winch
US 6-U9	1943-44	4.115	Special chassis, including Engineering Workshop
US 6-U10	1943	3.759	Tipper with winch
US 6-U11	1943	3.759	Tipper without winch
US 6-U12	1943	3.759	Side Tipper with winch
US 6-U13	1943	3.759	Side Tipper without winch

able. Thus, Studebaker trucks were fitted with a Hercules JXD engine while the GMCs were fitted with a General Motors type 270 engine. The JXD was so good that the Russians copied it and built it for more than fifteen years. The sheet-metal cab, apart from the 'military' front, came from the M civilian truck.

The annoying consequences which this duality in the 2½ ton range of trucks could have entailed were in fact very limited because Studebaker trucks were principally intended to equip Allied forces under Lend-Lease arrangements (China, Great Britain, Brazil, and the USSR which, on its own, received more than one hundred thousand). A total of 197,678 was built, the priority production of the Weasel having upset the production rhythms of the vehicle.

The so-called US 6 had either a sheet-metal or canvas-hooded cab, and appeared with or without winch, and in both short and long chassis versions. Some sheet-metal cabs had a 'manhole' as a mounting ring for a 12.7 mm machine-gun.

In *TM 9-2800* of 1947, the rear tipper and tanker versions, the latter identical to that of GMC assigned to the Air Force, are classified 'Standard', while the 6 x 4 long cargo is 'Substitute Standard'. They no longer appear in later editions.

International Harvester, although essentially given the task of producing 2½ Tonners for the US Navy and the Marines, received an order from the US Army for 525 M-5-6, 450 short chassis without winch, twenty-five short chassis with winch, twenty-five long chassis with winch and twenty-five long chassis without

The firm of Evans Product Co. of Detroit fitted both GMCs and Chevrolets or FWDs with its adapter for travelling on rails, Autorailers.

After the end of hostilities in Europe, thousands of vehicles were overhauled and cleaned in order to be sent to the Pacific. Two GMC AFKWX 353s, a CCKW 353 workshop and a 6 Ton heavy lorry are steam cleaned in late 1945.

International M-5-6. 2.743-metre short-chassis, with Budd Body cargo body.

International M-5-6 3.658-metre long-wheelbase, with Budd Body cargo body.

The Stilwell road in the Paoshan region; a convoy of 113 vehicles, consisting of Studebaker 6 x 6, 2½ Tonners, heads for Kunming in February 1945.

Studebaker 6 x 6 filing past at Harbin to mark the act of unconditional surrender of Japan. This vehicle is equipped with one of the famous 'Stalin organs' (Model M13).

Short-wheelbase version of the Studebaker 6 x 6, 2½ Ton lorry, Model US 6 U2. The version not fitted with a winch was designated US 6 U1.

Test of a Studebaker US 6 U4 at the testing ground.

French prisoners in the Heidelberg region being repatriated on board FWD HAR 1 trucks. The vehicles have been fitted with headlights of various models to improve their lighting system which is in fact reduced to a mere black-out light on the left mudguard in accordance with British practice.

winch, with Budd metal cab, in 6 x 6 version, all with sheet-metal cabs. Under Lend-Lease, all were sent to Russia (see *The GMC, A Universal Truck*).

FWD 4 x 4, 4 Ton

The Four Wheel Drive company was created shortly before World War One. During the conflict, it had built a large number of off-road trucks, including thousands of class B for the Allies. When peace had returned, the company, established at Clintonville in Wisconsin, specialised above all in public works vehicles. In 1940, it built the first bridging trucks for the US Army.

The first orders received by FWD at the beginning of World War Two were placed by the British Government, for the models SU and HAR. The SU series was of the 4 x 4, 5-6 Ton type with forward cab. The four wheels offered the special feature of all being permanently driven, according to the company's technique, which used a central differential-transfer box, conical-torque floating axles. The HAR series, also permanently 4 x 4, comprised three types of vehicles:

HAR 01: military version of a civil lorry equipped with a Gar Wood winch placed behind the cabin
HAR 03: derived from the HAR 01, without winch, and tractor for a semi-trailer
HAR 1: with canvas-hooded cabin and front-mounted winch.

The HAR 01 was a vehicle of the 4 x 4, $3\frac{1}{2}$ Ton class. It was supplied to Canada and Great Britain (814 vehicles). The chassis built in the USA were sent bare to the factory which FWD possessed in Canada at Kitchener in Ontario. There they received their bodies made by the firm of Brentford Coach and Body Ltd. The HAR 03 was a tractor for a semi-trailer, of which 1,524 were ordered by Canada. The wheelbase of this version was shorter (3.454 m) than that of the HAR 01 (3.962 m).

Mechanically similar to the two preceding models, the HAR 1 had a very different external appearance. Built from 1943 to 1944, the FWD HAR 1 was essentially supplied under the Lend-Lease Law. The US Army nevertheless used some in Iran and on the Alcan road (Alaska-Canada), for example.

During and after the war, France and Great

Diamond-T 968A with wooden cargo body, in its classic role of tractor for the 155 mm gun, seen in Indochina in 1954.

The Diamond-T 970 was mechanically identical to the Model 968A, but had a 4.369 metre wheelbase as against 3.835 metre for the 968A. The winch at the front is a Gar Wood of 6.8 tons capacity. This model is fitted with a metal body.

Truck 4 x 4, 4 Ton, FWD HAR 1	
Length (metres)	6.76
Width (metres)	2.45
Height (metres)	2.82
Wheelbase (metres)	3.98
Weight Empty (kg)	5,187
All Up Weight (kg)	9,187
Ground Clearance (cm)	28
Fording (cm)	78
Climbing Gradient (%)	40
Angle of Approach (°)	35
Angle of Departure (°)	30
Fuel Consumption on road (litres/100 kilometres)	43
Engine Make and Type	Waukesha BZ
Capacity (cc)	4,860
Cylinders	6
Fuel	petrol
Ignition	6-Volt Battery
Tyres	9.00 x 20, twinned at rear
Brakes	Hydraulic
Winch	6,000-kg, mechanical, front-mounted

Britain used HAR 1s. The British Royal Air Force used some until the mid-1960s, converted to snowploughs by the Bros company. Holland (HAR 01 and 03), Australia and Iran also received some, this last country in consequence of the numerous HAR 1s which had been supplied to Russia using the Persian corridor.

The HAR 1 was a 4 x 4 4-Tonner, the only truck of this tonnage bought by the US Army with two driving axles. One of its particular features was its very frugal lighting, a single headlight mounted either on the right or on the left according to which side of the road the traffic drove on in the country for which it was intended, and two position lights with black-out device. The production orders totalled nine thousand but were brought down to seven thousand after cancellation of some contracts. The HAR 1 was often called 'Hari' or 'Ari' because of confusion between the numeral 1 and the letter i whose typographical form in the manuals was very similar. Some people thus thought that it was the name or nickname of the vehicle in English, especially in France where the name of 'Ari' was commonly used.

Fifty HAR 1s of the 36th Transport Company of the French army were sent to Marseille in August 1945, at the request of M. Defferre, to ensure the restarting of the local bus network. They were simply equipped with a metal ladder fixed to the rear. These 'Auto-Trams' remained in service until 1947.

6 x 6, 4 Ton lorries

Before 1941, the White and Autocar companies supplied a small number of 4-ton 6 x 6 trucks. Thus it is that Autocar supplied eleven of its vehicles, including three recovery vehicles (model C 7066), and White seventy-nine vehicles, including six recovery vehicles (model 950 X 6). However, in this range, the most

Transporting German prisoners, a Diamond-T 968A, fitted with a ring mounting for a 12.7 mm machine gun, passes Sees cathedral.

usual model was the one designed and produced by Diamond-T Motor Car Co., of Chicago, from 1941 to 1945. This company, which had been created in 1905 by C. A. Tilt, at first only produced touring vehicles before devoting itself, fairly rapidly from 1911 onwards, exclusively to the building of trucks. In 1958, Diamond T became a subsidiary of the firm of White.

Diamond-T's first 6 x 6 4-ton model, supplied to the US Army in 1941, was the Type 9676 of which 976 of the cargo version and twenty-two recovery vehicles was produced. The principal other models produced subsequently were:

Type 968: 4.369-metre wheelbase cargo
Type 968 A: 3.835-metre wheelbase cargo
Type 969, 969 A and B: recovery vehicle with Ernest Holmes Company lifting equipment
Type 970 and 970 A: bridging material transporter, on long chassis (Pontoon Truck), most often used as a simple cargo type
Type 972: tipper
Type 975: chassis supplied solely to Canada (about 2000)

The total production of Diamond-T trucks was 12,748 units, including 2,197 chassis supplied to US Army Engineers for the making of specialised vehicles such as a 3,790-litre water tanker for sprinkling the workshop, a bitumen spreading transport of 3,030 litres capacity, a cartographic reproduction vehicle and a pipe-line transport vehicle. This truck was of very harmonious lines, C. A. Tilt attaching a very great importance to the aesthetics of his products which he supervised himself. The truck rapidly acquired a

Diamond-T 6 x 6, 4 Ton Trucks Principal Characteristics				
Models	968A	969A	970A	970
Length (metres)	6,817	7,191	7,534	6,721
Width (metres)	2,438	2,527	2,438	2,388
Height (metres)	3,000	2,946	2,950	2,873
Wheelbase (metres)	3,835	3,835	4,369	3,835
Weight Empty (kg)	8,187	9,684	8,527	7,802
Useful Load (kg)	3,786	Residual 160	3,629	3,786
All Up Weight (kg)	11,973	9,844	12,156	11,588
Fording (cm)	60	60	60	60
Climbing Gradient (%)	68	68	68	68
Angle of Approach (°)	37	37	37	48
Angle of Departure (°)	46	46	39	67
Max. Authorised Speed (km/hr)	65	65	65	65

A Diamond-T, 6 x 6, 4 Ton, positioned at the end of the runway, supplying the power for the radar and communications instruments installed in a trailer. This model is fitted with a wooden body.

This Federal tractor, supplied to the French air force under the Mutual Defense Assistance Program (MDAP), unloaded from the LST 546 of the United States Naval Service, belongs to the first series built, which were characterised by the sheet-metal cabin and the presence of the manufacturer's mark, a metal flag in the middle of the bonnet (North Vietnam, 1954).

reputation for remarkable reliability and did not jib at the load, even an excess one, to be transported.

The majority of Diamond-T 6 x 6 4 Tonners were equipped with a front winch of 6,800 kg capacity. All were powered by a Hercules RXC engine of 8.7 litres, developing 120 hp at 2,200 rpm. The transmission had the particular feature of being practically "flat", which improved its terrain-crossing qualities.

All categories of Diamond-T were 'Standard' in 1953.

4 x 4, 4/5 Ton tractors

In the category of 4 x 4 4/5 Ton tractors for semi-trailers, three companies participated in production: White, Autocar and Federal.

White and Autocar produced models which were identical in all points, the White Model 444 T and the Autocar 7144 T. Federal supplied its Model 94X43 which kept its own cab and, although quite closely resembling the other two models, had numerous different mechanical elements such as the steering gear case. Not only were they very similar externally, but these vehicles were also powered by the same engine, an 8,670 cc Hercules RXC engine developing 112 hp at 2,200 rpm. This engine was also found in the Diamond-T 4 Tonner—the two chassis are in any case very similar in design.

These tractors were, like most other American vehicles of the time, first built with sheet-metal cabs of civilian type. These were replaced by canvas-roofed cabs, making it possible to reduce the height of the vehicle with windscreen lowered to 2.337 m (White and Autocar) or 2.26 m (Federal). Kenworth and Marmon-Herrington assembled 4 x 4, 4/5 Ton tractors with open cab, based on complete sub-assemblies supplied by Autocar and White.

The pneumatic feed system also feeds the windscreen wiper motor. The red rear light is also controlled by the pneumatic braking circuit. The Federal was designated K 32 by the Signal Corps. The White/Autocar

A Federal 4 x 4, 4/5 Ton tractor, Model 94X43, refuels on the Burma road. It is followed by a relatively rare vehicle a Dodge T234, 4 x 2, 2½ Tonner, used predomin antly on this famous artery which was the Chinese forces from India.

vehicles were used concurrently in the US Army Air Forces. In 1953 they were still classified 'Standard'.

The first series of 4 x 4, 4/5 Ton tractors were fitted with a sheet-metal cab (White 444T).

4 x 4, 4/5 Ton Tractors		
	Autocar U-7144 and White 444T	Federal 94 x 43B
Length (metres)	5,169	5,156
Width (metres)	2,423	2,426
Height (metres)	2.84	2.66
	2.74 with metal cab	2.77 with canvas-roof
Wheelbase (metres)	3.42	3.42
Weight Empty (kg)	5,307	5,420
Ground Clearance (cm)	30	29
Fording (cm)	61	59
Climbing Gradient with semi-trailer (%)	30	30
Angle of Approach (°)	54	55
Angle of Departure (°)	50	52
Max. Speed (km/hr)	70	65
at Regulation rpm	2,400	2,300
Fuel Consumption on road (litres/100 kilometres)	73	94
Engine Make and Type	Hercules RXC	Hercules RXC
Capacity (cc)	8,670	8,670
Cylinders	6	6
Fuel	petrol	petrol
Ignition	two 6-Volt batteries	two 6-Volt batteries
Tyres	900 x 20 twinned rear	900 x 20 twinned rear
Brakes	Pneumatic	Pneumatic

An Autocar, Model U 7144 T, fills up in a transit camp at Saint-Denis, near Paris (13th Traffic Regulation Group).

The severity of the Korean climate led the drivers to improvise wooden cabs to replace the canvas-roofed cabs. The Autocar tractor in the foreground bears the maker's plate; this practice was abandoned during 1942.

Embarkation of an 18-ton river tug on a semi-trailer, 12½ Ton, Model C2, Wrecking 40 Foot, towed by a 4 x 4, 4/5 Ton tractor. In theory, this semi-trailer was intended for the transport of aeroplanes in the dismantled state or after an accident, but where necessity dictated it could be used for other tasks (March 30th, 1945).

Produced in 1936, the 6 x 6, 6 Ton Corbitt was designed as an artillery tractor, and was the progenitor of this class of vehicles.

The production line of the White 6 x 6, 6 Ton in 1942.

Heavy trucks

In the Heavy-Heavy category, problems date from the summer of 1943. In July 1943, the Ordnance Corps asked for annual production of Heavy trucks effectively to be doubled, from thirty-five thousand to sixty-seven thousand units. Until this point, Heavy truck construction had been accorded a somewhat low priority and this attitude was now belatedly seen to be a grave error whose consequences were serious. In fact, experience gained particularly in North Africa had made it readily apparent that it was essential to have trucks of this category for transporting supplies and towing artillery.

The demands made by the Ordnance Corps bordered upon the impossible, not just because there was inadequate manpower available but especially because such a programme required an initial investment estimated at several million dollars.

Nevertheless, the Ordnance Corps applied itself to making the best of the situation and approached constructors who specialised in heavy trucks. However, the large corporations like GMC, Ford and Chrysler could not become involved, because of their commit-

A 6 x 6, 6 Ton lorry, towing a 90 mm anti-aircraft gun, passes through the Vosges town of Rambervillers. This vehicle is camouflaged, which is relatively rare on the European front (US Seventh Army, November 1944).

ment to and specialisation in Medium and Light-Heavy trucks as a result of their commercial series and their specific expertise.

Among the companies concerned in production were Brockway, Corbitt, Diamond-T, Kenworth, Ward La France, White, FWD and Mack. These manufacturers, however, did not produce the entire range of mechanical parts which went into their vehicles. The majority of them indeed, in accordance with the American custom, did not manufacture their engines, axles or transmissions, but had to obtain supplies of them from firms like Continental, Hercules or Waukesha for engines, or Timken for axles. From this situation production bottlenecks arose, as these companies were already working to full capacity. Fortunately, other companies till then orientated towards manufacturing other products joined the specialised industrialists in the production of transmissions and axles, under the war diversification programmes.

A special committee for the harmonisation of production of heavy lorries was set up in the autumn of 1943. In 1943, 38,314 heavy trucks came off the production lines; the following year production rose to 50,852 units. The ambitious objective of 67,000 lorries was therefore never attained. At the beginning of 1945 requirements were brought down to 60,000 vehicles. The fall of Germany and then of Japan caused contracts to be interrupted in August 1945, after 32,014 heavy trucks had been produced in the last eight months of activity.

6 x 6, 6 Tonners

Two families of vehicles very largely dominated the range of 6 x 6, 6 Ton trucks, the series NM produced by the Mack company and the White series of lorries (Type 666). The production of these was supplemented by other manufacturers such as Brockway, Corbitt, Ward La France and FWD.

The 6 Ton tractors built by Mack were derived from a first model christened NM1, which appeared in 1940. This vehicle powered by a 6-cylinder in-line engine from the firm of Allentown (Model EV) developing 160 hp, had an empty weight of 9,825 kilos. The production of NM1s totalled eighty-seven vehicles. The NM1 was followed in 1941 by that of an identical model, NM2, of which a total of 107 was built. The NM3, the third of the series, on which a few modifications had been made, especially with regard to the lighting and to fitting a pair of strong recovery or towing lugs on the front bumper, was equipped with a noticeably more powerful EY engine, developing 170 hp at 2,100 rpm. In total, 104 NM3s was built. In 1942, the model NM5 appeared, which was characterised by the installation, for the first time, of a canvas-roofed driver's cab; a total of 801 was built. The NM6, built from 1943, was the most widespread version with a production of 3,240 units. This model was followed by two other versions NM7, of which 1,944 was built between 1944 and 1945; and the NM8, of which 1,057 came off the production lines of the Mack company in 1945 and which had regained a sheet-metal cab.

The Macks used a Wisconsin two-ratio transfer box and Timken axles common to the 6 x 6, 6 Ton class. A Gar Wood D 545 winch was mounted in a central position behind the cab and driven by chains from the power take-off (power 13,610 kg).

The other 6 x 6, 6 Ton Standard model, better known under the name of White 666, in fact owes its origin to Corbitt who, starting from their Model 50 SD6 of 1939, continually developed the vehicle. Designed originally principally for towing anti-aircraft guns, which were then among the heaviest and largest in the American arsenal, the 6 x 6, 6 Ton Standard was in general use in the engineers, ordnance and infantry and was put into production at White and Corbitt. Brockway, White, Ward La France, and rather late in the day, FWD manufactured the bridge-carrying and crane-carrying versions. Although similar, the White 666 and Corbitt 50 SD6 differed a little in their dimensions and weight, the maximum permissible axle load, and in lower gearbox reduction ratio on the White, the presence of winches behind the cabin (6,750 kg on some 50 SD6s), and in other details. Corbitt built 3,211 vehicles and White 3,446 in the basic version, artillery tractors (Prime Mover).

Besides the basic version (platform with wooden or metal slatted sides with tarpaulin cover), the White 666 existed also as a van for the Signal Corps transporting SCR-545-A radio sets with Superior or Thomas bodywork, and as a tractor for a semi-trailer (112 vehicles). A few rotary-cutter snowploughs were built, and twenty-five as fuel transporters with a 7,600-litre Heil tank, towing a trailer of the same capacity with four twin wheels. The tractor for the semi-trailer was equipped with Timken 'heavy' axles, 14.00 x 20 tyres and a front winch identical to that of the bridging truck.

During operations for crossing the Rhine, in March 1945, two 15-ton cranes place a 'sea mule' on the platform of a 6 x 6, 6 Ton truck. A 'sea mule' was a motorised craft for pushing vehicle transport barges.

White 666 equipped with a 2,000-gallon (or 7,580 litres) petrol tank. The vehicle was intended to tow a four-wheel trailer of the same capacity.

Corbitt 50 SD 6 tractor for semi-trailer of the Austrian army, converted from the artillery tractors. In 1945, the firm of White built 112 tractors for semi-trailers fitted with bigger tyres (14.00 x 12), an 11.3-ton winch at the front and Timken reinforced axles.

During the offensive against Cologne, a 6 x 6, 6 Ton lorry of the US Ninth Army goes through the town of München-Gladbach on March 1st, 1945.

6 x 6, 6 Ton Trucks		
	Corbitt 50 DS6	White 66
Length (metres)	7.25	7.27
Width (metres)	2.44	2.44
Height (metres)	3.00	3.00
with lowered hood (metres)	2.74	2.64
Wheelbase (metres)	4.70	4.70
Weight Empty (kg)	10,024	10,387
Ground Clearance (cm)	28	27
Climbing Gradient (%)	50	50
Angle of Approach (°)	52	59
Angle of Departure (°)	43	47
Max. Speed (km/hr)	60	56
at Regulation rpm	2,200	2,150
Fuel Consumption on road, no trailer (litres/100 kilometres)	78.5	62.5
Engine Make and Type	Hercules HXC	Hercules HXC
Capacity (cc)	12,800	12,800
Cylinders	6	6
Fuel	petrol	petrol
Ignition	two 6-Volt batteries	two 6-Volt batteries
Tyres	10.00 x 22*	—
Brakes	Air	Air
Winch	11,340-kg	11,340-kg
	behind cab**	behind cab

* First models: 3.75 x 22
** 6,750-kg Winch on some Corbitts

The Corbitt's radiator contains 68 litres of water! The 6-cylinder Hercules HXC 202 hp engine was common to the whole series. The cab, of sheet-metal at first, became open from 1943.

The 6 x 6, 6 Tonners, including the tractor for semi-trailers, were 'Standard' in 1953. The crane and tanker versions are indicated as still existing in the inventory, but without classification. The Mack NM1, NM3, NM5 and NM6 were without classification, although still entered in the inventory of vehicles.

Mack 6 x 6, 6 Ton, Type NM 5	
Length (metres)	7.19
Width (metres)	2.44
Height, sheet-metal cab (metres)	**2.92**
open cab, canvas removed	2.24
Wheelbase (metres)	4.50
Weight Empty (kg)	10,840
All Up Weight (kg)	16,283
Ground Clearance (cm)	26
Climbing Gradient (%)	36
Angle of Approach (°)	45
Angle of Departure (°)	45
Speed (km/hr)	55
at Regulation rpm	2,100
Engine Make and Type	Mack EY
Capacity (cc)	11,600
Cylinders	6
Fuel	petrol
Ignition	6-Volt Battery
Tyres	10.00 x 22 twinned rear

Above: Eighty-seven of the series of Mack 6 x 6, 6 Ton trucks were built in 1940.

Right: A Mack NM 5 equipped with a Gar Wood US 11.3 Tonne winch. The sheet-metal cab is of the civil type and was replaced by an open cab.

Below: A Mack NM 6 equipped with a British Radar Set T132 in French *Armée de l'Air* service in Germany in 1952. An NM chassis was specially modified for the carriage and operation of the Radar aerial.

Below right: In 1945, on its final production model of the NM series, Mack reverted to the original sheet-metal cabs which offered greater comfort to the driver. A total of 1,057 of this model, the NM 8, was built. The example shown here was part of a batch offered to France by Canada under NATO air schemes.

Mack NM 7 of the Austrian army. A total of 1,944 vehicles of this model, characterised by the absence of the winch behind the cab, was built in 1944 and 1945.

Mack NM 6 of the French army towing a 155 mm twin-trail 155 mm gun, Model 50.

Display of military vehicles in a small town of the United States with a view to developing the spirit of defence and collecting the famous War Bonds necessary for financing the immense war effort. The 6 x 6, 7½ Ton tractor, Mack's Model NO, was intended for pulling heavy artillery guns.

This rear view of a Mack NO enables one to see the manual hoist used to lift the trail of artillery guns up to the towing hook. While still towing a 15-ton gun, the Mack NO could transport 5 tons in its body over any terrain.

Mack NO 6 x 6, 7½ Ton

The idea of the Mack NO 6 x 6 7½ Ton artillery tractor was born in 1940 during the manoeuvres at Alexandria in Louisiana. Indeed, on this occasion, officers of the Ordnance Corps noticed the lack of mobility of the heavy artillery guns pulled by caterpillar tractors and the traffic hold-ups caused by their slow, majestic movement. The officers exchanged ideas about the best means of overcoming these inconveniences. A few Mack 6 Ton 6 x 6 trucks which were parked nearby inspired them with the idea of using these vehicles as tractors for the 155 mm guns. Tests were carried out which proved this solution to be suitable with the sole reservation that a slightly more powerful vehicle was needed.

Things evolved favourably for, at the same period, Mack was designing on its own initiative a tractor complying with the requirements of heavy artillery. The Directorate of Field Artillery asked for three prototypes to be built, christened NQ, for towing 155 and 240 mm guns. Two tractor 'cargo' trucks and one tractor towing the gun in the manner of a semi-trailer were tried out at Aberdeen Proving Ground in November 1940. These vehicles were to give rise to the family of NO 6 x 6 7½ Ton trucks.

The Mack NO, powered by an 11,600 cc 6-cylinder in-line engine Model EV developing 157 hp at 2000 rpm was equipped with a rear door and a hoist for lifting and hooking on the 155 mm 'Long Tom' gun which weighed about 15 tons, when the latter was fixed directly to the tractor's hook without using its front bogie. An 18,140-kg capacity winch was mounted at the front of the vehicle. On this vehicle, for the first time, were fitted as a production feature double-reduction arch-type axles in front. These made it possible to increase the ground clearance without raising the centre of gravity.

This vehicle, the biggest ever produced by Mack till then, gave full satisfaction and on November 3rd, 1942, a first production order comprising 403 vehicles was signed. Two subsequent orders, placed on February 23rd, 1943, and August 31st, 1945, brought to 2,053 the total number of NOs supplied to the US Army and the Allies. The numerals 2, 3, 6 and 7 which follow the letters NO characterised the years of production, especially for the accessories. Its use was reserved for artillery units (Field Artillery and Coast Artillery). The vehicle was managed by the Ordnance. The versions NO 2, 3, 6 and 7 were 'Standard' in 1953.

Presentation at Aberdeen Proving Ground of a Mack 7½ Tonner towing an M1 155 mm gun; this model, as on a quarter of the vehicles produced, had a ring mounting for the 12.7 mm machine-gun. The Jeep, in the foreground, is towing a 37 mm M3 anti-tank gun and gives the scale of this enormous creature.

This Mack NQ tractor for semi-trailer, built in 1940, and along with it two cargo versions, were the true prototypes of the series NO of which 2,053 was built altogether. The Mack NQ did not get past the prototype stage.

Mack NO 2 6 x 6, 7½ Ton Truck	
Length (metres)	7.55
Width (metres)	2.58
Height (metres)	3.09
with hood lowered (metres)	2.39
Wheelbase (metres)	3.96
Weight Empty (kg)	12,000
All Up Weight (kg)	19,257
Ground Clearance (cm)	36
Climbing Gradient (%)	65
Angle of Approach (°)	35
Angle of Departure (°)	45
Speed (km/hr)	50
at Regulation rpm	2,100
Fuel Capacity (litres)	605
Engine Make and Type	Mack EY
Capacity (cc)	11,600
Cylinders	6
Fuel	petrol
Ignition	two 6-Volt batteries
Tyres	12.00 x 24
Brakes	Air
Mechanical Winch	18,140-kg

WORKSHOP AND REPAIR VEHICLES

In the immediate pre-war period, the *matériel* services of the US Army, the Ordnance instituted a new generation of repair and workshop trucks, on GMC forward-cab chassis, which came to replace or supplement older vehicles, notably Marmon-Herringtons. This was only achieved after a long administrative battle in the 1930s when some services carried away by their partisan spirit quite simply denied the usefulness of repairs in the field.

In 1940, seventy-eight AFKX 352s with a Superior body very much inspired by the school buses made by this coachbuilder, were bought for the repair of small arms, as well as three with a Heil metal body whose spars and side panels could be lowered to the horizontal to increase the working surface. A further 135 were bought from Marmon as machine tool workshop trucks (Metal Shop Body), but the biggest order was allocated to Wayne from 1941 to 1942 for 1,912 units of a workshop van, in seven different internal arrangements:

artillery repair (M2)
car repair (M2)
equipment repair (M1)
workshop (M4)
small arms repair (M1)
tank maintenance (M1)
spare parts store (M2)

Truck 1½/3 Ton, GMC AFKX 352, with Wayne body.

AFKX with Heil body with panels that could be raised.

GMC AFKX 352 4x4, 1½-3 Ton Workshop Truck	
Length (metres)	5.97
Width (metres)	2.36
Height (metres)	2.96
Wheelbase (metres)	3.33
Weight Empty (kg)	4,404
All Up Weight (kg)	5,896
Ground Clearance (cm)	25
Climbing Gradient (%)	65
Angle of Approach (°)	46
Angle of Departure (°)	21
Speed (km/hr)	72
at Regulation rpm	2,870
Range (kilometres)	290
Fuel Consumption on road	
(litres/100 kilometres)	31
Engine Make and Type	GMC Type 248
Capacity (cc)	4,100
Cylinders	6
Fuel	petrol
Ignition	6-Volt battery
Tyres	7.50 x 20 twinned rear
Brakes	Hydraulic

CCKW 353 with ST 6 body. The grille panels can be raised and lowered.

CCKW 353 with equipment for repair of tyres in the field.

A Workshop for analysis of fuels in the field on AFKWX 353.

Some of these vans were supplied to Great Britain and, during re-equipment in North Africa, to France.

This type of classification, Class 1½ Ton (off road)/3 Ton (road), was only re-used for the FWD HAR 1 which was, for a while, classified 2½—4 Ton, and for the 6 x 4s derived from the GMC or Studebaker tactical trucks which were 2½—5 Ton.

Considering the loads and volumes to be transported, the AFKX proved to be too small; moreover, it corresponded to a class of vehicles which was not retained for war construction. Naturally, it was the CCKW 353 2½ Ton truck which was principally used to meet the needs of this weight class.

Two models of CCKW 353 were built: the rigid ST 5, declared 'Limited Standard' in November 1942, and the ST 6. The body was a metal van with six-side grille-covered windows, which could be covered by black-out curtains for night work. The ST 6's height could be lowered by 60 cm by removal of the section of bodywork comprising the windows and of the double rear door to save space during sea transport. On the opening of the rear door at night, the interior lighting was automatically switched off. The ST 5 body could be fitted with hoops and a tarpaulin to conceal the function of the truck from air observation.

Only the CCKW chassis was used with, indiscriminately, Banjo or Split axles and sheet-metal or canvas-roofed cabs. The bodies were built by Hicks, P. A. Thomas, Superior and Krieger. In this field, the Americans practically realised their dream of standardisation of vehicles. The engineers had their own model. The fleet was completed by a large number of models of trailers and semi-trailers with technical or commonplace body (can or platform with sides) carrying machines (textile, wood, mechanical, etc.)

The ST 6 workshop vehicles were redesignated M535 in the new nomenclature of the US Army. They were still 'Standard' in 1953.

ST 6 Workshop Body	
Length of Body (metres)	3.76
Width of Body (metres)	2.44
Height of Body (metres)	2.06
Volume of Body (cubic metres)	18.00
reducible to	13.40
All Up Weight of Vehicle (kg)	7.665
Overall Length of Vehicle (metres)	6.47
Overall Width of Vehicle (metres)	2.44

Designation of Workshop Bodies On CCKW 353 Chassis	
ST 5 Body	**St 6 Body**
Small Arms M7	Small M7 A1 and A2
Auto M8 (LA, LB)	Auto M8 A1 (LA, LB)
Welding M12	Welding M12 A1
General Mechanics	General Mechanics
M16 (LA, LB, LB1, LB2, LC, LD, LF)	M16 A1 (LA, LB, LB1, LB2, LC, LD, LE, LF)
Electricity M18	Electricity M18 A1 and A2
	Transmissions M30 and M31
	Tyre Repair M32 (LA, LB)
Artillery M9 and M9 A1	
Optical Instruments M10 (LA, LB) and M10 A1 (LA, LB)	
Tools and Lathes M13	
Spare Parts Store M14 (LA and LB)	

RECOVERY VEHICLES

Sergeant John Kurtz, from Rochester, USA, of the 3091st Ordnance Services Company, monitors the traffic at the entrance to the Sissone camp (Aisne), rechristened Camp Washington. The vehicles, including a CCKW 353 Series 7, are being regrouped in view of their subsequent despatch to the Pacific (June 19th 1945).

In this area, the Americans also applied their expertise and equipped their armies with assets which, to the present day, have remained unequalled.

Light Recovery Vehicles

The simplest US recovery vehicle, but not the least effective, was the recovery unit Set No 7 for 2½ Ton vehicles, composed of a gantry and a Yale 500 kg hoist permitting the towing of vehicles of the 2½ Ton class. This unit was simply mounted on a CCKW 353 or 352 chassis with platform and sides, and having, apart from rare exceptions, a front winch. The basic equipment, often supplied by the users, included tool chests, workbench, compressor and welding set.

The intermediate class was represented by Holmes equipment on a Diamond-T, 6 x 6, 4 Ton, 969, 969A or 969B. The Holmes crane was of the mechanical type with cables with opening double jib. The movement of the towing winch was controlled by the vehicle's auxiliary power take-off. The rotation of the jibs could and other tow hooks were manual. The jibs could work for lifting or towing integrally and jointly in the axis of the chassis (lifting power 4,540 kg), or singly up to 260° on each side of their axis. Their

A Ward LaFrance 1000, Series 5, in service in Austria.

Diamond-T 969 with Ernest Holmes Co. of Chattanooga (Tennessee) equipment.

power in this case did not exceed 2,800 kg with the use of the mechanical supporting legs fixed on the jib-bearing structure. Diamond-T was a vehicle with a deservedly very good reputation. Very flexible, of very good performance and light, and could recover a vehicle wherever it lay, due to the orientation of its jibs.

Although less powerful, a well trained crew could obtain results which were almost identical to those of a Wrecker M1 (see below). Its equipment also comprised a De Vilbiss or Kellog air compressor with Briggs and Stratton single-cylinder engine and a welding set. The body consisted of a short metal platform with two tool chests. The rear of the platform was closed by a flap which could be lowered, of the same model as that of the cargo type. It could be fitted with, although this equipment was rarely used, hoops and a tarpaulin to make it appear commonplace to enemy observers.

Diamond-T 969 Wrecker with 5-Ton Holmes Crane	
Length (metres)	7.42
Width (metres)	2.33
Height (metres)	3.00
Wheelbase (metres)	3.84
Weight in Running Order (kg)	9,842
Ground Clearance (cm)	28
Fording (cm)	21
Climbing Gradient (%)	65
Angle of Approach (°)	46
Angle of Departure (°)	37
Speed (km/hr)	65
at Regulation rpm	2,300
Fuel Consumption on road (litres/100 kilometres)	200
Engine Make and Type	Hercules RXC
Capacity (cc)	8,700
Cylinders	6
Fuel	petrol
Ignition	two 6-Volt batteries
Tyres	9.00 x 20
Brakes	Air
Front Winch Capacity (kg)	6,800
Crane	
Capacity along axis (kg)	4,540
Jib Opening (°)	260 (two side support rams)
Operation	Manual, except mechanical winding/unwinding of manoeuvring and lifting cable. Some models all-mechanical.

Probably the best Wrecker of the US Army, at least in the matter of flexibility of use, the Diamond-T 969 had Holmes equipment with opening jibs. Men of the 3547th Repair Company of the Ordnance change the Hercules engine of another Diamond-T seen in Camp Brooklyn at Suippes, in June 1945.

Diamond-T 969B equipped with an M36 ring mounting for 12.7 mm machine gun in Indo China in 1951.

Some had an M36 ring mounting for 12.7 mm machine gun. Like all the Diamond-T 6 x 6, 4 Tonners, its desert conversion kit comprised a high-capacity water pump and 124.00 x 20 tyres mounted singly. A total of 6,420 was built and the type was still 'Standard' in 1953.

Heavy Recovery Vehicles

The US Army and its Allies used a large number of heavy recovery vehicles. They were models M1 and M1 A1, according to the nomenclature of the US Ordnance Corps, built jointly by the firms of Kenworth and Ward LaFrance.

The origin of these vehicles, intended to tow and recover motor vehicles which had broken down or been in an accident, went back to the end of the 1930s, a time when the US Ordnance received its first heavy recovery vehicles. These were lorries designed by Marmon-Herrington on the basis of a 6 x 6 chassis, model TL 31-6, with Hercules engine. On 1937 this vehicle was officially standardised under the designation M1 and production was entrusted to the firm of Corbitt of Henderson in North Carolina.

In 1940, when the needs in respect of this specific category of *materiel* had increased, Ward LaFrance, a company established at Elmira in the state of New York, received a first order relating to a batch of sixty-nine vehicles christened Model 1000 by the manufacturer. Subsequently, new supply contracts were placed and, in total, the production of M1 recovery vehicles by Ward LaFrance rose to 1,554 units.

An order for 300 units was also allocated, at the end of 1941, to Kenworth, a small local company established at the time in Seattle, whose two principal shareholders—hence the name of the firm—were Messrs H. W. Ken and E. K. Worthington. This order was the opportunity for John Helmstrom, who managed the company, to introduce the practice of production line manufacture, the vehicles being until then assembled one by one by hand! However, Kenworth also received contracts to manufacture bomber forward fuselage Boeing B-17 and B-29 sections, to such an extent that the truck factory had to leave Seattle and install itself in the amusement park buildings of Yakima in the state of Washington. This first order was supplemented by a second for thirty. These recovery vehicles were designated by the manufacturer Model 570. In 1942, a further order for one hundred, which had become Model 571 which only differed in a few minor details, was placed.

On the first models of M1 recovery vehicle the lifting system, designed by Gar Wood and comprising a telescopic jib, was operated manually. All these vehicles were powered by the same engine: an 8,210 cc 6-cylinder in-line Continental 22 R, developing 145 hp at 2,400 rpm.

In 1943, a new model, whose external appearance was profoundly modified, made its appearance as the Ward LaFrance Model 1000, Series 5 and the Kenworth 573. The differences between the vehicles built by Ward LaFrance and Kenworth were minor. The

M1 heavy recovery lorry, Ward LaFrance, Model 1000, Series 2, of the French army, fitted with 14.00 x 20 tyres mounted singly. It is seen in Germany in 1957.

Kenworth 572. The mudguards of the vehicles built by Kenworth are semi-circular.

M1 heavy wrecker truck, Kenworth, Model 570.

most characteristic feature of the new model was the canvas-roofed driver's cab. The engine remained that of the M1 but the lifting system of the crane, though still built by Gar Wood, was now driven by the vehicle's engine. The vehicle was declared 'Standard' *matériel* in 1944 under the designation Truck, Wrecking, Heavy M1 A1.

After the war the heavy recovery vehicles were very much appreciated by civilian users and it was not unusual, forty years after their construction, to see some along the roads in specialised heavy truck garages.

According to Kenworth's production figures, the company produced 709 military trucks and 87 civil ones in 1943, 716 and 217 respectively in 1944 and 484 and 427 in 1945. The civil vehicles were allocated to the priority sectors of the mines and forestry work sites. Thus, since 1941, 2,339 vehicles were built for the US Army. Comparing this figure with the orders (1,853 Wreckers and 1,100 M426 tractors, a total of 2,953 vehicles) indicates that 614 vehicles were 'victims' of the cancellations of war programmes, or

Manufacturer	Type	Production	Year of Manufacture
Production of M1 and M1 A1 Heavy Wrecker			
M1			
Ward LaFrance	Model 1,000 Series 1	69	1941
Ward LaFrance	Model 1,000 Series 2	720	1941-42
Ward LaFrance	Model 1,000 Series 3	365*	1942
Ward LaFrance	Model 1,000 Series 4	400	1942
		(1,554)	
Kenworth	Model 570	330	1941
Kenworth	Model 571	100	1942-43
Kenworth	Model 572	100	1943
		(530)	
M1 A1			
Ward LaFrance	Model 1,000 Series 5	3,500**	1943-45
Kenworth	Model 573	1,323	1943-45
		(4,823)	
* Only for Lease-Lend Nations			
** Estimates			

A small series, limited to a hundred, of Ward LaFrance recovery vehicles, Model 1000, Series 2 (chassis numbers 422, 624 to 422, 723), was equipped with this type of front bumper and towing triangle. On the front mudguard, which slopes gently away, a characteristic of the Ward LaFrance models, a siren is installed (1947).

The Ward LaFrance, Model 1000, Series 4, was fitted with a jib which was curved at its end.

a fifth of the production envisaged—and that without taking account of 4 x 4, 4/5 Ton tractors, assembled from White sub-assemblies.

There are several differences between the M1 models built by Kenworth and Ward LaFrance which assist in identifying one from the other. They are as follows:

> radiator protection grille: upper part flat on the Kenworths; angled on the Ward La Frances;
> air intake orifices on the sides of the bonnet on the Ward LaFrances; absent on the Kenworths;
> semi-circular front mudguards on the Kenworths; sloping gently away on the Ward LaFrances;
> different driver's cabs.

There are several differences between the M1 A1 models built by Kenworth and Ward LaFrance which assist in identifying one from the other. They are as follows:

> the tool storage chests installed behind the running board are shorter on the first models of Ward LaFrance, but this feature disappeared in the last series;
> the triangular lifting tackle (bar) fixed on the front bumper is different on the two models.

Performance of the Vehicles

The vehicles were fitted with two mechanical winches of Gar Wood manufacture (9 tons in front, 21 tons at the rear). The front winch was controlled by a shaft actuated by a chain-driven intermediate cut-off box. The tractive power for both front and rear winches came from the transfer box, therefore from the vehicle's engine. The rear winch, which had the benefit of a special independent gearbox with two forward and reverse ratios whilst the front winch was controlled by that of the vehicle, was equipped with a pneumatic servo control of the clutch. It was set up so as to be able to pull along the vehicle's axis and also, which is of prime importance in recovery, sideways, thanks to transmission pulleys and cable guides and two anchoring legs.

A Sherman M32 B1 tank being recovered is hoisted on to an M9 trailer by means of the rear winch of a Wrecker M1 A1. The vehicle is provided with an M2 ring mounting for a Browning 12.7 mm machine-gun (Algeria, 1957).

Two models of Gar Wood cranes were used. The first, the 9-ton US 5, shorter and curved at its end, equipped the M1s. Its operation was called manual, since the orientation of the crane, the central articulating pivot and the adjustment of its working height, were effected by arm power. Of course, the operations of lifting the load were mechanical, through an independent winch situated under the central tubular frame controlled by a special gearbox with one reverse gear and two forward gears, and pneumatically assisted clutch.

The second model US 6 was called mechanical, as the operations of pivoting (180°) was effected by a worm screw and adjusting the height of the jib was controlled by a cable actuated by a winch. Its maximum capacity of 7,264 kg on the hook could only be attained after positioning two supporting legs situated 4/5 of the way along the jib and permanently mounted on the latter.

The vehicle was also fitted with two supporting rams level with the rear of the platform and two jib struts attached to the central tubular frame. These last two were more particularly used for the rotation of the crane. Finally, two spade-shaped anchoring legs used for tilting the vehicle when using the winch, might also be used to stabilise the whole vehicle.

In spite of its qualities, the vehicles showed considerable limitations. It could not work on a slope exceeding eight per cent without damaging its mechanics. It was complicated to put into operation, and it was heavy and expensive. It had a high fuel consumption; in practice, it exceeded on average 1 litre per kilometre and, in theory 94 litres per 100 kilometres. Considering its weight, the power of its engine, its mechanical transmissions and the torques which had to be transmitted, its use had to be closely supervised if one did not wish to damage it, which assumed specialised personnel. In particular, the use of the front driving axle had to be an exception rather than the rule in view of wear and tear and overload. It had not to be engaged when the front winch was operating.

In spite of its shortcomings, it was a powerful vehicle, capable of carrying out manoeuvres far beyond the limits envisaged by the manufacturer. It has always been in favour with the users. Its performance on irregular terrain was good, except on treacherous terrain, owing to its high ground loading.

The data may vary according to the manufacturer, the type of technical manual and its year of manufacture, as will also the extra recovery equipment transported on the vehicle. Thus, the majority of M1 A1s in service were in fact operating at a weight of over 19,000 kg. Armour-plating was experimentally fitted to the cab of an M1 A1 of Ward LaFrance (Model 13) in 1943 to allow it to intervene on the battlefield.

Front view of the two versions of the M1 A1 heavy recovery lorry. The model on the left, built by Kenworth, Model 573, and that on the right, built by Ward LaFrance, Model 1000, are distinguished by their towbar fixed to the front bumper. In addition, the radiator protection grille of the Kenworth is flat, while that of the Ward LaFrance is slightly triangular.

Prototype of Ward LaFrance armored heavy recovery lorry, Model B, produced in 1943.

A single example of this Mack 7½ Ton NO 5 heavy recovery truck was built for the artillery. A similar model, but fitted with a tow attachment saddle for a semi-trailer, was also designed for the US Army Air Forces and christened NO 4.

A mock-up of it had previously been made on a Ward LaFrance 1000 Wrecker (Series 1) at Aberdeen Proving Ground, the Mecca of American motorisation during the Second World War.

The series Ward LaFrance Model 1000 (Series 1, 2, 3, 4) and Kenworth (570, 571, 572) were 'Limited Standard' in 1953, while the Ward LaFrance Model 1000 Series 5 and Kenworth Model 573 were classified 'Standard'.

An M1 Wrecker cost the US Army nearly 14,000 dollars.

Two prototypes of Mack heavy recovery vehicles, NO 4 and NO 5, were tested in May 1943, but did not give rise to any production order. The model NO 4, intended for the US Army Air Forces, differed from the NO 5, which was intended for the artillery, by the installation of a tow attachment saddle for a semi-trailer in accordance with the customs of this service.

M1 A1 (Kenworth 573) Data	
Length (metres)	7.137
Width (metres)*	2.559
Height (metres)	3.091
Wheelbase (metres)	4.597
Loaded Weight (kg)	17,252
Ground Clearance (cm)	28
Fording (cm)	100
Climbing Gradient (%)	54
Angle of Approach (°)	50
Angle of Departure (°)	50
Turning Radius (metres)	10.675
Speed on surfaced road (km/hr)	78
Fuel Capacity, total two tanks (litres)	378.5
Fuel Consumption on road (litres/100 kilometres)	
Engine Make and Type	Continental 22R
Capacity (cc)	8,210
Output (horsepower)	145
Cylinders	6
Fuel	petrol
Gearbox	five forward, one reverse
Transfer Box	two ratios
Ignition	12-Volt battery
Tyres	1,100 x 20
Axles	Timken, 8.27:1 reduction
Front Winch	Mechanical, 9,080-kg
Purpose	Hauling or anchoring a vehicle along longitudinal axis
Rear Winch	Mechanical, 21,563-kg
Purpose	Recovery work, towing in axis or sideways by transferring cable via pulleys and cable-guides on rear platform
Crane Type	Mechanical, fixed jib, cable
Maximum Capacity (kg)	7,264**
Nominal Capacity (kg)	4,994 with struts

* Postwar, the width was reduced 'administratively' in France to 2.50 metres to allow civil registration
** Capacity varies as a function of slope of the jib, the use of supports and the position on the jib of the two-position lifting pulley. The lifting force of 7,264 kg is only possible if the supports are in place, the lifting pulley is in the intermediate position and the slope of the jib corresponds to a deployed height of the supports of 3.3 metres

8 x 8 HEAVY TRUCKS

Powered by a Continental engine, Model R 6602, of 9,866 cc developing 240 hp at 2,600 rpm, this 8 x 8, 8 Ton heavy cargo type, christened T20, was designed by the firm of Cook Brothers.

The more wheels a vehicle has in contact with the ground, the more the ground pressure decreases and the more, in theory, its mobility on treacherous and difficult ground is improved. This technical observation, coupled with a certain attraction for giant size, was to lead the manufacturers and the US Army to design and test heavy 8 x 8 trucks.

In June 1942, a first experimental vehicle, christened 'Experimental Desert Vehicle' started its test in a centre specialising in studies of combat conditions in a desert zone, established at Indio in California. This vehicle had been designed by Cook Brothers, a Los Angeles company specialising in the conversion of production road vehicles to 6 x 4, and thereby a rival to Marmon-Herrington, Hendrickson and others. Like many American products of the time, the transmission was by chains.

Other models, none of which ever reached series production, made their appearance. Thus the firm of Cook Brothers, doubtless rich with the experience acquired from its first vehicle, proposed towards the end of the war an 8 x 8, 8 Ton vehicle designated T20, of which two were built, one as a cargo type, the other as a tractor for semi-trailer. This vehicle, of an empty weight of 16.8 tons (cargo version), was powered by a powerful Continental R 6602 engine of 9,867 cc, developing 240 hp at 2,400 rpm. The tractor for semi-trailer version had a Gar Wood double-drum winch, of 27 tons capacity. On both versions, the two front driving axles, combined in a bogie, were steerable.

In the heavier range of 8 x 8, 12 Tonners, the firm of Sterling of Milwaukee (Wisconsin) proposed its T26. This vehicle, with an empty weight of 23.1 tons

semi-trailer was also built. The T58 E1 tractor and its semi-trailer unit with its maximum load had an all-up weight of 81.6 tons, which did not prevent it from travelling on the road at 56 km/h. At the end of the war, Corbitt also designed an 8 x 8, 12 Ton heavy vehicle designated T33. The tests only took place after the end of the war. Only one cargo version weighing 23 tons was built, it was powered by a 9-cylinder Continental R 975-C4 radial engine.

The Corbitt T33 of the 8 x 8 class, fitted with four steerable wheels in front, was powered by a 9-cylinder Continental radial engine developing 450 hp.

and a fully loaded weight of 34 tons, was tested at Camp Bullis (Texas), where it proved perfectly suitable for moving over difficult terrain. The T26 was powered by a 12,358 cc 12-cylinder 'V' type American LaFrance engine developing no less than 275 hp at 2,800 rpm. A tractor version for a tank-transporter

From 1943, Sterling tried out this 8 x 8, 12 Ton heavy truck. Christened T26, this vehicle was powered by an American LaFrance V12 engine, developing 275hp.

LOW SILHOUETTE TRUCK SERIES

Rather unorthodox prototype proposed by Studebaker, Model LC, in the 4 x 4, 1½ Ton range. Access to the driver's position is gained from the front and the driving position is placed in the centre of the vehicle.

Even for those who were not endowed with particularly sharp observation, it became clear than it was easier to camouflage a Jeep or a Dodge ¾ Tonner than a GMC 2½ Tonner. Therefore, the idea of making tactical vehicles more discreet, particularly by lowering their height and making their silhouette more compact, was developed at the request of the military authorities, the concept formed the basis for a host of designs from the main transatlantic manufacturers. This research, although it gave rise to numerous prototypes, did not result in the adoption of trucks or vans complying with the 'Low Silhouette' concept.

The reasons for this setback were many; first of all, in spite of a certain originality but also a certain complexity in the design and shapes of the 'Low Silhouette' types, the savings in height remained relatively modest. By way of example, the low silhouette GMC, Model DCKW, with a height of 1.880 m, was only 5 cm lower in comparison with the classic standard GMC CCKW 352 or 353. Furthermore,

'Low Silhouette' Vehicles		
Model	Height (metres) Canvas Cover	Minimum
CCKW 353	2.743	1.930
DAKW	2.413	1.930
DCKW	2.794	1.880
DOKW	2.438	1.930

putting these new vehicles into production would have necessitated more or less major modifications of the assembly lines, and redesign of the special bodies for those which would have replaced the 'normal' chassis equipped as workshop vehicles or tippers, for example. Such a policy would have necessarily entailed too heavy budgetary costs in proportion to the objectives and to the improvements of the characteristics. Finally, a redeployment of production would have necessarily caused difficulties with the production of standard vehicles of classic manufacture. Such a slowdown of supplies was unthinkable at such a time.

However that may be, all these low silhouette vehicles were given lengthy tests by the US Army at its specialised establishments from 1943 to 1944: Aberdeen Proving Ground, Fort Holabird and Fort Knox. The majority of the reductions in silhouette were obtained by putting the engine further back,

'Low Silhouette' Vehicles Tested 1943-1944	
Class	Vehicle
4 x 4, ¼ Ton	Dodge T 225
	Dodge T 226
	Ford GCA
	Ford GLJ
4 x 4, 1½ Ton	Ford GAT
	Ford GTB
	Chevrolet G 7129
	Reo LS 30 F
	Studebaker LC
4 x 4, 3 Ton	International DOB M-6-4
	International DF M-6-4
	Reo LS-30F
6 x 6, 2½ Ton	GMC DCKW
	CMC DAKW
	GMC DOKW
	Studebaker LA 005
	Studebaker LB
6 x 6, 3 Ton	Studebaker LD 148
	Studebaker LD 162
	International DF M-5-6
	International DOB M-5-6

Left: The only version of 'Low Silhouette' to have been produced in series (6,000 built), the Ford GTB 4 x 4, 1½ Tonner, was used by the US Navy and the US Army. Beside the radiator, the tool chest forms an integral part of the radiator grille.

International 6 x 6, 3 Ton, Model DOB M5 6. The driver is seated outside the framework of the chassis.

Below: The fitting of a ring mounting on this version of the International DF M5 6 of the 'Low Silhouette' programme seems at least paradoxical! The driver's access to his seat does not seem to be among the easiest. All this is due to the fact that the engine is mounted in a very far back position behind the front axle and therefore only leaves very little space available.

4 x 4, 1½ Ton Ford GTB

Length (metres)	5.730
Width (metres)	2.235
Height (metres)	2.667
Weight Empty (kg)	3.289
Useful Load (kg)	1.360
All Up Weight (kg)	4.649
Climbing Gradient (%)	42
Angle of Approach (°)	40
Angle of Departure (°)	21
Speed (km/hr)	75
Engine Make and Type	Ford Model G 8T
Capacity (cc)	3,700
Output (horsepower/rpm)	91/3,400
Cylinders	6, in-line
Fuel	petrol

inverting the suspensions, putting the axles above the springs and by placing the driver's seat outside the framework of the chassis or actually in the cargo compartment.

In the final analysis only one model entered production, but nevertheless on a relatively modest scale. It was the Ford model GTB 4 x 4, 1½ Ton truck, of which a total of 6,000 were built and used both by the US Navy in a bomb transporter version and by the US Army in a cargo version. The driver was seated alongside the engine. The front retained a false appearance of Ford's Jeep prototypes. The metal plate beside the radiator grille gave access to a tool chest.

A 'Low Silhouette' version of the standard CCKW was also made by General Motors. The modifications concerned the design and shape of the cargo body, the positioning of the fuel tank behind the cab and a new transmission. Thanks to these elements, a saving in height of 10 cm was realised; beside this, the 5 cm wide cargo body enabled it to transport fourteen men.

Most of the prototypes thus designed were kept by the US Army until about 1949, when they were finally scrapped.

TRAILERS

A 1 Ton Ben Hur trailer seen here with electric generating unit for the Signal Corps. Each Chevrolet K51 and each GMC radio vehicle towed one for supplying power to its sets. The unit's motor was the Go Devil of the Willys Jeep. In this use, it was designated K52 or K63. twenty-six companies participated in the construction of the 1 Ton, including Bantam, Checker, Gersten Lager, Nash-Kelvinator, Willys and Winter-Weiss. A little known fact, its body was made indiscriminately of steel or wood.

The 2 Ton Four-Wheel Tilting, Tandem by Fruehauf. The presence of a manual winch on the trail and of two small loading ramps at the rear makes it possible to identify the specialised version for the transport of electric generator units on skids (M18).

In this rather thankless and very often forgotten area, the Americans were able to create a few fine classics. Whether it be the ¼ Tonner in the cargo version, or the tipper converted from it by Converto (Trailer Dump ½ Ton), or the 1 Tonner, whose largest manufacturer was called with a certain aptness Ben Hur (Model 41-120), or the 250-gallon (946 litres) water tanker trailer on the same chassis. There were so many incontestable successes. They were all slavishly copied after the war when stocks were exhausted, usually identically, which means that one often has to look closely in order not to be mistaken. It remains difficult, not to say impossible, to do better today in designing trailers than what was done in 1943.

It is quite clear that the Americans were responsible for popularising the semi-trailer using fixed ball-mounting hitches, a vehicle which had certainly been known for a long time, but which really took off in their wake. The tandem hitch, very much used on airfields, was practised for some time after the war, notably in France.

of course, the trailer and semi-trailer fleet included an impressive number of special vehicles (workshops, refrigerators, bomb transporters, transmissions and so on) and low loaders for transporting heavy vehicles (Low Boy 20, 40, 16 and 8 Ton, La Crosse, Steel Products, Roger Bros, Fruehauf, Winter-Weiss), as well as a series of caterpiller trailers intended for operations in difficult terrain (20 or 6 Ton BT 898, ET 1076, Athey Truss Wheel), and even amphibian trailers for the DUKWs (Cleaver-Brooks WT CT-6).

Special mention should be made of the most ingenious trailers produced in the United States, the 2 Ton, Four Wheel, Tandem Tilting produced by Fruehauf. It was very low, yet it was capable of travelling on the road at a good speed as well as on bad terrain. It was stable thanks to its four tandem wheel layout, its low attachment point and its droppable trail and resting on four stabilisation rams when at a standstill, and could be fitted with small rear ramps or with a low spar back to allow *matériel* to be loaded easily. It would tilt backwards on its axles to facilitate loading. It was widely used in many applications:

M14, M22: a closed body, Central anti-aircraft artillery fire control point (Brill, Fruehauf).
M7: electric generator unit (Brill, Fruehauf, Kreiger).
M13: identical to the M14 but canvas-covered (Brill).

M15 A2 trailer of the tank transporter unit M25. This widened version permitted the transport of heavy tanks, like the Pershing and the Patton. This version was fitted with extra ramps, overcoming the necessity for the caterpiller vehicles to pass directly over the wheels.

A 7 Ton semi-trailer with wooden slatted sides, with Studebaker 6 x 4 tractors in the Iranian mountains on the way to the USSR.

Winch loading of an M5 light tank on a Rogers or Winter-Weiss 45 Ton trailer, forming, with the Diamond-T, the M19 tank transporter unit. The M19 trailer was also built by Fruehauf, Pointer Willamette.

A convoy leaves the cover of a wood in Normandy Chevrolet 1½ Ton tractor with Stake and Platform 3½ Ton trailer semi-trailer. Twelve manufacturers joined Checker, a company specialising in the building of taxis, to produce this semi-trailer which was standardised for all 1½ Ton tractors.

M1: transporter for searchlight
M7: transporter for smoke generator
M17: platform for quadruple Maxson mounting for 12.7 mm machine-gun
M18: transporter of electric generator units on tubular skids (two small ramps at the rear, loading winch in front on the trail head, Fruehauf)
K84: antenna transporter

Athey Truss Wheel 6 Ton BT 898-4 caterpillar trailer. A 6 Ton model with low slatted sides also existed (BT 898-1) and a 20 Ton one (ET 1076-1), all intended for transport in difficult terrain and hitched to heavy caterpillar tractors.

GMCs towing M14/M22 trailers, central fire control posts of an anti-aircraft artillery unit, followed by an M17 trailer for electric generator unit, landing in Normandy.

The Mercy Tank, with Donald Roebling at the controls, plunges into Lake Webb (Clearwater, Florida, May 1936).

AMPHIBIOUS VEHICLES

Caterpillar landing vehicles: LVT

In 1924, J Walter Christie perfected an amphibious vehicle which the US Marine Corps used during manoeuvres and tested satisfactorily on the Hudson and Potomac. In 1927, six modified versions were also used in China by the Marines who were stationed there for the protection of the internal concessions and missions. Things remained at that stage until in 1935, an engineer, Donald Roebling, who had retired to Florida, designed an amphibious caterpillar-tracked vehicle specifically intended for rescue operations in the swamp zones of the Everglades, where access by traditional vehicles was difficult. One of the originalities of this vehicle, built of aluminium, lay in the manner that propulsion in water was by caterpillar tracks fitted with 'buckets'.

In 1938, the US Marine Corps became interested in the question and sent Major J.W. Raluf of the Vehicle Committee of Quantico to visit Dr. Roebling. The Envoy of the US Marine Corps was very favourably impressed by what he saw. In September 1939, Major E. Linsert, who had replaced Major Raluf at Quantico, accompanied General Moses to Florida. The two officers saw the fourth model in action. They succeeded in convincing engineer Roebling of the military value of his machine. He himself, who had until then been reticent about a military use for his vehicle, agreed to revise the design of the tractor to incorporate military characteristics.

In January 1940, Roebling drew up plans of a machine possessing the desired characteristics; he agreed to build one for twenty thousand dollars. The Marines' budget not having credits available for land vehicles, the question was settled by assigning the expense to a line of credits allocated to landing craft. Roebling immediately set to work. At the end of October 1940, the vehicle was completed.

The demonstration before the authorities was a success and the building programme for the vehicle, now designated Landing Vehicle, Tracked, was launched on November 5th 1940. An order for one hundred vehicles was sent to Roebling. The first battalion of amphibious tractors of the Marines was constituted in August 1941.

The firm of Food Machinery Corporation of San Jose (California) was contacted and agreed to put its

From prototype to prototype, the vehicle evolved and is beginning to approach its definitive shapes. The engine is still at the rear, the transmission at the front, with a curious system of screws engaging in the vanes of the caterpillar skids.

The first LVT Mk 1s are tested by the British Royal Marines. The vehicles are not yet fully assembled; in particular, the shutters are not put in place.

Dunedin (Florida) factory at the disposal of production of these amphibious tractors. Subsequently other firms, Graham-Page of Detroit, Ingersoll of Kalamazoo and Saint Louis Car Company, participated in the production.

Termed LVT 1 Alligator (Amphibian Tractor T 33), this vehicle was exclusively designed for the transport of loads during landing operations and was not armoured. A total of 1,225 was built. The engine and the transmission formed a block at the rear. With a very high performance on water thanks to its 'bucket' and caterpillar track and capable of passing over coral reefs, the vehicle was not very comfortable on land. Moreover, its large size made it a choice target.

Rapidly the US Marine Corps, in liaison with the Borg-Warner company, sought to improve the LVT 1 which suffered in addition from a certain number of faults: rapid corrosion of certain parts, frequent detrackings, lack of armour. In 1943, the LVT 2 appeared, equipped with caterpillar tracks consisting of forty-seven elements with removable axles and therefore easily replaceable: the transmission and the engine were those of the M3 light tank. The LVT 2 (Amphibian Tractor T34) received its baptism of fire at Bougainville and Tarawa in November 1943. It was given the nickname of Water Buffalo, thereby marking the fact that it was a question of more than a simple evolution of a vehicle, but was indeed a new design.

At the request of the US Army and following the experience of the first amphibious landing assaults, a certain number of LVT 2s, instead of being manufactured of plain steel sheet, were built with armour plates. These vehicles, of which 2,963 were built, designated LVT(A) 2, were engaged in battle for the first time at Arawe in December 1943. Some LVT 2s received improvised armour plates.

Parallel to the development of the LVT 2, a version fitted with the 37 mm gun and turret of the M3 tank was designed to support the waves of amphibious tractor transport vehicles. It was designated LVT(A) 1. The 37 mm gun proved insufficient and a new version with the 75 mm howitzer as on the M8 self-propelled gun was built. Designated LVT(A) 4, 1,890 were built. The first operational use of the LVT(A) 4 came at Saipan in June 1944, while the LVT(A) 1 had gone into service at the end of 1943.

Until then the LVTs had their engine at the rear and from the LVT 2s their gearboxes at the front, which had made it necessary to install a bulky and heavy transmission, running almost the whole length of the

Rear view, engine side, of the LVT Mk 1, in operation with the Marines. Its range at sea was about 45 nautical miles.

Stowed on the deck of a cargo boat, these LVT 2 Alligators prepare to leave the port of Los Angeles bound for the Pacific. This photograph gives one an idea of the arrangement of the transport compartment and of that of the engine at the rear.

vehicle. This arrangement reduced the space available for transport and did not particularly help loading and unloading operations. A prototype, derived from an armoured support model, made by Borg-Warner in April 1943, gave rise to the first version fitted with a rear access ramp. In this, the Cadillac engines were moved forward to clear space for the ramp on each side of the hull. The transmission was the Hydramatic of the M5 tank. This vehicle was nicknamed Bushmaster, and designated LVT 3. A total of 2,962 was built. It is considered the best of them all.

For its part, Food Machinery Corporation modified an LVT 2 in August 1943 by adding a rear ramp also, after installing the Continental engine at the front. This modification resulted in the LVT 4, which could transport a Jeep or thirty fully-equipped men, as against only eighteen in the LVT 2. The LVT 4, used operationally for the first time at Saipan in the Marianas on June 14th, 1944, was the model built in the greatest numbers (8,343).

From 1947, the LVT 4 and the LVT 4(A) were classified 'Standard' and 'Limited Standard'. The LVT 3s were modernised in 1949 at Long Beach and San Francisco by the addition of an armoured roof above the cargo compartment; in addition, a small machine-gun turret was fitted to the vehicle.

These vehicles were used in Korea, notably during the Inchon landing in 1950. Similarly the LVT(A)5 designed in 1945 and identical to the LVT (A) 4 but fitted with a turret stabilisation and aiming system, were modernised. The turret, which was uncovered, was blanked off by an armoured panel and the hull was modified, notably in front, to improve the seagoing qualities.

For the Marines, the LVTs were known as AMTRAC, a contraction of Amphibian Tractor.

The British, within the famous 79th Armoured Division, made several conversions of the LVT, either for deck transport of artillery guns, in particular 17-pounder anti-tank guns, or as support vehicles for assault troops; they also used it (LVT 2 and 4) as commando transport vehicles, notably for the assault on Walcheren in Holland. Known as the Buffalo in the British Army, they were only made available to it during operations in the Netherlands, in September and October 1944. None had been able to be allocated soon enough for the Normandy landing. Of course, General Hobart's men hastened to convert them to support in strength divisional units during the crossing of the Meuse and of the Rhine. Some were

The LVT 2 with its regulation armament one .50-cal machine-gun in front and one .30-cal at the rear.

LVT 4 of the French navy in the streets of Port Fuad during the Franco-British operation of November 1956 on the Suez Canal. The land forces also used LVTs during the operation.

LVT 3 of the Argentine navy. It was the first LVT to be equipped with a lowerable door at the rear.

A Water Buffalo—the British name for the Alligator— plunges into the Rhine in March 1945.

While awaiting the arrival of the LVT (A) 1s, LVT 2s were armed—three .50-cal machine-guns, one Colt 37 mm cannon at the rear and two rocket launchers in the compartment. These are seen in the Pacific during 1943.

fitted with ground carpets on a tubular superstructure, which were unrolled to enable amphibian Sherman DDs to come out on muddy slopes. Others had their armament increased by a Poltsen 20 mm cannon. After the war, the specialised establishment of the British army equipped an LVT M with a flame thrower, and named it Sea Serpent.

Five LVTs were sent, for tests, to the USSR.

Right: Equipped with the light tank turret with an M6 37 mm cannon and a co-axial M 1919 A5 .30-cal machine-gun, this LVT (A) 1 is carrying out night-fire training. The extra armament of this first version of the Alligator also comprised two other .30-cal Model M 1919 A4 machine-guns, and occasionally a .50-cal Browning M2 HB.

LVT Armament
Transport LVT models: one 12.7 mm machine gun in front, two 7.62 mm machine-guns at the side. This regulation armament was very often increased by units.
LVT (A) 1: one 37 mm cannon M3 tank turret, two 7.62 mm machine-guns on a Scarf ring mounting (identical to those on the landing craft transport models) behind the turret. Firing positions were provided in the hull to shelter the gunner.
LVT (A) 4: one 75 mm short barrel gun (M8 howitzer tank turret).
LVT (A) 4: one 75 mm gun (M24 Chaffee tank turret). Designed in January 1945 to increase the fire power, the project abandoned at the end of the war.
Rocket Launcher: Type T45, two rows of ten rockets were mounted at the rear of the vehicle, firing forward (LVT(A) 2, LVT(A) 4 and LVT 1).
Rocket Launcher: Type T54, twenty 7.2-inch rockets in a firing pod were mounted in the cargo compartment, firing forward (LVT modified 4).
Rocket Launcher: Type T89, same equipment as the T54, but with ten rockets (LVT 3).
Flame thrower: Type E7: the equipment could replace either the 37 mm cannon (LVT(A) 1) or the 75 mm gun (LVT(A) 4) or be mounted behind a shield above the driver's position (LVT 4). It was introduced in 1944.
E14-7R2: this kit replaced the 37 mm cannon on the LVT(A) 1. Ten were built.
Ronson: Canadian flame-thrower. The weapon replaced the cannon or gun on the LVT(A) 1s and 4s, or could be installed on the left in the driver's compartment.
LVT(A) 2 bridge-layer: a modification to carry an ARK light assault bridge above the superstructure on deck, intended to permit the crossing of coral reefs. Used at the Tinian landing (August 1944), it was a local conversion by one unit.

Landing Vehicle Tracked Specifications							
	LVT 1	LVT 2	LVT 3	LVT 4	LVT (A) 1	LVT (A) 2	LVT (A) 4
Length (metres)	6,553	7,976	7,468	7,950	7,950	7,976	7,976
Width (metres)	2,997	3,251	3,404	3,251	3,251	3,251	3,251
Height (metres)	2,475	3,502	3,023	2,404	2,464	2,502	3,111
Weight Empty (kg)	7,847	11,000	12,066	12,429	13,177	12,519	17,900
All Up Weight (kg)	9,888	13,720	17,510	16,510	13,600	15,990	18,600
Engine make	Hercules	Continental	Cadillac	Continental	Continental	Continental	Continental
Type	WXLC 3	W670 9A	2XV-8	W670 9A	W670 9A	W670 9A	W670 9A
Cylinders	6	7	16	7	7	7	7
Speed							
water (km/hr)	10	12	10	12	12	10	11
land (km/hr)	20	32	27	32	32	27	26
Range							
water (km/hr)	100	160	120	120	120	120	160
land (km/hr)	240	240	240	240	240	240	240
Production Total	1,225	2,963	2,962	8,348	509	450	4,890

A Sikorsky S-51 and two Piaseckis fly over an LVT (A) 4 of the US Marine Corps in 1950.

This top view of an LVT (A) 1 shows the two .30-cal machine-gun positions behind the turret. The 37 mm gun has an elevation of —10/+25°.

In January 1945, the LVT (A) 4 was tested with a Chaffee turret to increase fire-power during landing operations.

Mounting of the T54 rocket launcher

The LVT (F), christened 'Sea Serpent', was equipped by the British with two flame-throwers and a small turret for a .303-inch machine-gun. The vehicle on which it was based is the LVT 4.

In June 1954, the French forces regrouped in the Delta and evacuated villages and isolated posts. The LVT (A) 4s and Crabs finish the sweep through the rice fields. In the foreground is a radio Crab with its 24/29 sub-machine-gun. It bears on the side plate the inscription MDAP, indicating that it formed part of a batch of American matériel sent after the De Lattre mission to Washington.

Crabs and Alligators in Indochina

The Weasel M29Cs, or to give them the nickname under which they became famous, Crabs—came mainly from a depot in Manila where they had been discovered by a French purchasing commission which was seeking American surplus equipment for Indochina.

Very much at ease in the marshes, they were not good in water courses with a strong current which they tackled with difficulty. Their caterpillar tracks were fragile and did not stand up well to long-distance journeys on hard roads, where the vehicles had to be transported by trucks like the Dodge T110, GMC Diamond-T, 6 x 6, Ton. In addition, the fairing around the caterpillar tracks often clogged up in the grass. Maintenance was finicky and constant; in particular the running gear had to be lubricated every day—no less than fifty-eight lubrication points.

From their arrival, during 1945, they were equipped with a universal plate behind the engine, which could carry different armaments: 24/29 sub-machine-gun, 7.5 mm machine gun, 57 mm recoilless cannon (two per platoon). The Americans had also carried out tests in 1944 for arming the Weasel (.30-calibre 57R machine-gun, etc.) but had not pursued the matter.

In French service, the crew was three men, because one of the three rear seats had been removed and replaced by an ammunition box.

Overloaded, the vehicles consumed a great deal of fuel (12 litres an hour and more in the water) and their freeboard was very limited. Some were fitted with a tarpaulin on raised hoops to fit them to serve as command vehicles.

In the very difficult terrain of the rice fields of the Cochinchina delta, the crews were often forced to set foot on land and haul their Crabs by arm power across tricky passages—mudfields without grip, bank exits, too low water level, freeboard obstacles more than 35 cm high—as the caterpillar tracks did not have much grip. But as 'White-Cap' says in the series of articles on amphibious vehicles in Indochina: 'a Crab squadron will always reach its objective. How long it takes is determined by the terrain, and the determination of the crew!'

Crabs seen during Operation CLAUDE to the south of Haiphong, reveal a number of the conversions or customs of Indochina—front plate raised and windscreen sloping forward, one supporting the other; universal weapons mounting plate permitting the use of a .30-calibre machine-gun, of a Bar of 24/29 sub-machine-gun or a 57 mm recoilless gun with or without shield, removal of the caterpillar track fairings to avoid the clogging which caused frequent detrackings.

The biggest problem with the Crab besides the weakness of its caterpillar tracks, was the necessity of daily maintenance. Every day, as here, these legionnaires had to lubricate no less than fifty-eight points on their vehicles.

To operate with the Crabs, the first Alligators arrived from the amphibious operations centre of Arzew, in Algeria. Some others were also in service in the naval troops in Madagascar (Gagneron escadron). They were also entrusted to the 1er Group d'Escadrons du 1er Étranger de Cavalerie which became the 1er Règiment Autonome de 1er Régiment Étranger de Cavalerie on September 1st, 1951. The 1er Régiment de Chasseurs would also form an amphibious subgroup.

The Alligators—only this nickname would be used by the French army, who ignored the name Water Buffalo—were either LVT 4s for the transport of troops or LVT(A)4s with a turret-mounted 75 mm howitzer. Several LVT 4s were modified, either being fitted with a 40 mm Bofors or Holmes recovery equipment from a Diamond-T Wrecker.

An LVT 4 mounted, equipped with the short 75 mm turret of the M8 support tank. This version was used by the Foreign Legion in Indochina. The vehicle is equipped at the rear with a system permitting its being pushed by another vehicle in this very difficult terrain. The transport LVT 4s in the background are equipped with 75 mm and 57 mm recoilless guns.

Support Alligators of the amphibious sub-group of the 1er Étranger de Cavalerie, with their 40 mm Bofors cannon, with twin mounting of co-axial 12.7 mm mounted behind an armoured shield.

Very much at ease in the water thanks to their sea-going shape and their 'bucket' caterpillar tracks, they were much less so on treacherous ground where their narrow caterpillar tracks were a disservice to them, and most of all on roads where the tracks broke and wore out, as did the track-carrying pulleys which became oval in shape. Therefore they had to be transported on tank transporters, which was no easy matter, or brought to the scene of operations by sea or river in landing craft. In addition, their Continental engine reserved many surprises if the crew did not take certain precautions such as the unsticking of the cylinders by hand before starting up, so as to avoid accumulation of oil in the lower cylinders, and buckling of the connecting rods. Any trench more than 1.50 m wide stopped it permanently. In spite of its limitations, the Alligator brought powerful support in combat, carrying infantry platoons or, for the support vehicle, that of its 75 mm 'spud thrower'.

As for the LVT 4s, armed with the 40 mm and with two co-axial 12.7 mm machine-guns, they had been converted, according to the ideas of Captain La Chapelle, by the amphibious sub-group of the 1er Régiment de Chasseurs. Very successful vehicles, they were of great value and proved irreplaceable, notably for cutting down the particularly tough bamboo palisades and thick vegetation surrounding the native villages. They served in the Legion d'Étranger from 1952.

The armament of some transport LVT 4s was augmented. Some were fitted with a 75 mm recoilless gun and these vehicles were issued two per platoon in addition to the normal four collective weapon supports, either 7.65 or 12.7 mm machine-guns.

The extra armament was added because it was felt that the LVT 4 was too weak to withstand an ambush.

The Alligator rendered great services in spite of its weight and size. One account of operations noted: 'It was recognised that an amphibious group composed of a Navy tender, an LST and a platoon of LVTs and its commando, constitutes a perfectly adapted force on the coast. It is sufficient to permit a fairly deep raid into the interior.'

Each platoon had eight vehicles, as in the case of the crabs. They comprised a command vehicle with back-up radio support, four transport LVTs, two support LVT 4s and one for assistance and recovery which was sometimes equipped with the Holmes opening double jib.

Although originally intended for use in the Delta, the amphibians were also be employed in the North,

An Alligator LVT (A) 2 of the 1er Étranger de Cavalerie. The front machine-gun on a ball and socket was as a general rule removed (Operation CRACHIN [DRIZZLE], Tonkin, March 1952).

where platoons of nine Crabs were put into operation transporting five men each, including a land combat party, or 'carried platoons' (*pelotons portés*), equipped with five to six Crabs without a collective weapon on board, manned by native personnel who also fought on land. These variations, far removed from those original classic cavalry traditions, were popular with the Crab crews since they avoided becoming embroiled in protracted sealing-off operations.

At the end of the war in Indochina, the LVTs were transported to Arzew in Algeria, to the Centre pour Opérations Amphibies Intervention (CIOA: Centre for Amphibious Operations Intervention), and were not used again as such, other than for training purposes. The CIOA was relocated in Lorient in 1962 and served as a pivot for the Force Amphibie d'Intervention (FAI: Amphibious Intervention Force), an inter-service and inter-army unit (naval commando, landing craft, air support, beach companies of engineers and amphibious squadrons of naval troops, signals etc.) It is interesting to examine the motives put forward at the time for the creation of the FAI:

'It has therefore appeared necessary for France to have permanently available a specialised amphibious force whose structure—very flexible—can be tailored to the different forms of action which circumstances might require.'

These are the beginnings of the concept which would lead to the creation of the Force d'Action Rapide (rapid action force) twenty years later.

The amphibious squadron of naval troops was stationed in the old fort of Penthievre (Quiberon Peninsula), where the émigrés landed to their misfortune during the Revolution. Its composition was one command platoon and two combat platoons with seven transport LVTs and four howitzer LVTs per platoon. In theory, the LVTs were transported and launched facing the beaches by an LST.

If nearly ten minutes were needed at sea to man each vehicle going in reverse, by means of the stern ramp (45 cm clearance on either side of the opening!), and that only if the swell were not too strong, on the other hand the LVTs with troops on board entered the water at the rate of one every twenty to thirty seconds.

Old and rusty, the LVTs were withdrawn from French service in the 1970s.

Termed GPA, for General Purpose Amphibian, 12,774 of the amphibious Jeep were supplied.

Amphibious Jeep

The National Defense Research Committee (NDRC), was a body composed of civilian engineers and researchers who were given the job of finding practical solutions, even if they were not very orthodox, to the manifold technical and scientific problems connected with modern warfare, including the amphibious Jeep. This committee among many other things, was given the task of designing amphibious vehicles.

P. C. Putman, of the NDRC, therefore made contact in 1941 with Roderic Stephens Jr, boss of the Sparkman and Stephens Naval Yard for the sea-going hull of the "Jeep", and with Marmom-Herrington for the mechanical side. The prototype designated QMC 4 (for Quartermaster Corps) carried out its first tests at the end of 1941.

This hybrid vehicle used fairly diverse components including some taken from a Bantam. As a result of the close links maintained between Ford and Marmon-Herrington and of the very big work load of the latter manufacturing thousands of drive axles and transfer boxes for Canada and the Commonwealth forces, the pre-production design work was undertaken by F. G. Kerby and C. L. Kramer at Ford.

The Ford prototype, which then only had three seats side by side in the front compartment, was presented on February 18th, 1942. After a few alterations (crew of five, incorporation of stiffeners in the hull, exhaust on the front segment, and others), a first contract for 7,896 vehicles was signed on April 10th, 1942. In total, 12,785 General Purpose Amphibians were built according to Ford but 12,774 according to the contracts issued by the US Army up to June 1943.

The mechanical components came of course from the GPW. 606 kg heavier than the Jeep, with largely the same components, lacking in freeboard, and like any amphibian, difficult and expensive to manufacture and maintain, the GPA did not find great success in the American army. Further, its interest as an amphibious reconnaissance vehicle was fairly limited, as the majority of rivers in Western Europe had canalised banks and the GPA needed gentle slopes to come out of the water. Its lack of effective load capacity and its lack of height above the water made it practically unusable in landing operations.

The Russians, on the other hand, found it useful and well suited to their rivers which had sandy banks or vast marshy zones. Not content with receiving the greater part of the production, they copied it at the beginning of the 1950s under the name of GAZ-46 MAV, although with substantial modifications.

France also received a fairly large quantity of GPAs, notably during the re-equipment of her forces in North Africa, and unlike other Western users, kept a certain number of them after the end of hostilities.

The GPA was also nicknamed 'Seep', a contraction of Sea Jeep.

Driving lessons in Morocco on a GPA supplied to the French army following the Antra accords.

The GMC DUKW 353 amphibian goes into production. The first models were characterised by a straight windscreen with folding protective metal plate fitted with two forward-vision portholes and by unfaired rear wheels (until chassis 2006).

GMC DUKW 353 'Duck'

Probably one of the most original vehicles of the period, the GMC amphibian, Model DUKW 353, rapidly nicknamed 'Duck' through phonetic analogy, was designed in spring 1942, when the Quartermaster Corps approached the National Defense Research Committee and requested it to develop an amphibious lorry capable of transporting the supplies necessary for the forces engaged in combined operations from cargo boat to shore. Certain services of the US Army showed themselves rather sceptical at the time as far as the possibility of creating such a special vehicle was concerned. The NDRC worked in very close collaboration with a New York firm specialising in naval construction: Sparkman and Stephens Inc., and Yellow Truck, the subsidiary of General Motors. The NDRC did not take long in getting the desired vehicle made, whose prototype, designed on the basis of an AFKWX 353, gave such satisfaction during trials that several hundred were rapidly ordered. The DUKW 353 was declared 'Standard' *matériel* in October 1942.

On the operational side, the first successful intervention of the Duck occurred in March 1943 during the landing of American forces in New Caledonia. A few months later the Sicilian landing by General Patton's Fifth Army provided the Duck with a new opportunity to distinguish itself. General Eisenhower did not hesitate to describe as 'inestimable' the Duck's contribution to the success of the operations of World War Two. For the Anzio landing operations on January 22nd, 1444, three hundred Ducks were used. The DUKW participated in all the big amphibious operations not only in the Pacific, but also in Europe, in the landings of June and August 1944, crossing of the Rhine by the Allied armies in March 1945, etc.

In November 1943, the War Production Board, conscious of the importance of this vehicle, notified General Motors that the production of the Duck was of the utmost urgency in the war programmes, although, for some of its sea equipment the increased rate of production seriously interfered with that envisaged for landing craft.

From a total of 4,053 in 1943, production attained 11,316 units in 1944, or an average of more than 950 vehicles a month. In total, 21,147 DUKW 353s was built for the US Army and US Marines. Never did

any amphibious vehicle attain such quantity production; Britain received some also. The 519th Régiment du Train (baggage train regiment) specialising in transhipment operations stationed at La Pallice-La Rochelle only parted from its Ducks for LARC-XVs in 1980. Therefore, with the Mexican navy which replaced its Ducks with Pegaso amphibians, it was one of the two last military users of the DUKW. The price of a Duck was 6,000 dollars. It was still classified 'Standard' in 1953.

Experimental fitting of an 105 mm gun on a DUKW 353. This type of mounting was used to support the assault troops during the last phases of a landing.

One Duck out of five of the landing companies of the US Marines had a hoist at the rear. This one is photographed during manoeuvres in Corsica, shortly before the GMC amphibian was deleted from the American army lists in 1958.

DUKW	
Length (metres)	9.45
Width (metres)	2.511
Height (metres)	2.692
Wheelbase (metres)	4.66
Weight Empty (kg)	6,425—6,780*
Useful Load	
Land (kg)	2,760
Water (kg)	5,520
Weight, Fully Laden, Land (kg)	9,450
Climbing Gradient (%)	55
Angle of Approach (°)	38
Angle of Departure (°)	25
Speed	
Land (km/hr)	80
Water (knots)	6
Fuel Consumption on road (litres/100 kilometres)	39
Fuel Consumption on water (litres/hour)	67
Range on road (kilometres)	390
Engine Make and Type	GMC Type 270
Capacity (cc)	—
Cylinders	6
Fuel	petrol
* Depends upon Series	

DUKW 353s of the Belgian army, equipped with a ring mounting for a 12.7 mm machine-gun.

Predecessor of the M29, this tracked cargo vehicle was designed by Studebaker (T15) and built in small series under the designation M28.

The Weasel

The threat of a Japanese invasion of the Aleutians prompted the design and preparation of manufacture of a light transport vehicle with low ground pressure, permitting travel on soft snow. The vehicle was the brain child of an Englishman, Geoffrey Nathaniel Pyke—an unrecognised genius, then supported by Lord Mountbatten—who was thinking of operations in the northern terrain of Europe. The project was sketched out in May 1942, by Roy E Cole, chief engineer of Studebaker. The company accepted the job of creating this vehicle although a few preliminary specifications had been fixed.

The first prototype was ready to start its tests on June 24th, 1942. For these, two expeditions were organised in the snowfields of the Columbia glacier. The first experimental vehicle was designed to travel either on snow or on water: propulsion on water was ensured by a propeller in the stern and driven by a transmission mechanism integral with the engine. The engine was more or less in the middle of the vehicle.

Manoeuvring and steering proved very difficult by reason of the great length of caterpillar track on the ground (2.260 m) in relation to the track width (1.150 m). The maximum speed was shown to be less than that envisaged owing to rolling resistance and low engine power in relation to the weight of the vehicle (3,175 kg). Changes were therefore made to remedy these deficiencies.

The second model (T15, ten prototypes), whose construction was pursued in parallel with the work carried out on the first one, was accepted and series production launched. This model was designated M28. The production of M28s reached six hundred. It was declared 'Limited Standard' in September 1943.

In the production model, propulsion by propeller on water had been abandoned, the length reduced in order to save weight and the engine placed at the rear. The length of caterpillar track in contact with the ground had been reduced to 1,580 metres. This arrangement made it possible to overcome the steering difficulties encountered on the first model. At the same time, the width of the caterpillar tracks had been increased from 38 to 46 centimetres, which gave a uniform pressure of 0.14 kg per cm².

As tests, improvements and use of the model progressed, design shortcomings were nevertheless found which were impossible to remedy because of the urgency of maintaining production. For example, the

A fine launch, nice and flat, for this M29 C, amphibious version of the Weasel.

vehicle suffered from a chronic detracking problem. A certain number of improvements appeared necessary: reduction of the rolling resistance, decrease in ground pressure, improvement of the suspension and increase in the load capacity. All these improvements were incorporated in a third model (T24) which was to give rise to the M29.

On the Weasel M29, the 6-cylinder Studebaker inline engine Model 6-170 was installed at the front on the right, almost in a central position, and occupying a good part of the compartment and the useful capacity. Steering was effected by levers each controlling one caterpillar track. This model had caterpillars 50.8 cm wide, whose applied length of 2 m gave a unit pressure of 0.135 kg per cm², or narrow caterpillars. The M29 was standardised in November 1943. An amphibious version, designated M29C, was also built from July 1943 onwards. For this last version, two watertight flotation chambers were simply added at the front and rear. Steering in the water was effected by two rudders controlled by cables and forward propulsion was achieved by rotation of the caterpillar tracks.

Although needing quite a lot of maintenance, the Weasels were considered to be good vehicles.

The Americans tried out a mine clearing vehicle based on an armoured M29 pushing a set of three antimine rollers in reverse. Similar tests were carried out, without any more success, by the British 79th Armoured Division.

Through NATO, Norway received a large number of Weasels for its northern brigades.

A total of 15,124 was Weasels built up to August 1945. The needs were so great that building them at Ford was also envisaged. The M29 and M29C were 'Standard' in 1953, while this same edition of *TM 9-2800* indicates the presence in the inventory of the Carriage, Motor, 105 mm Rifle, T 106 as *matériel* on test with the US armed forces. This was a version of the M29, truncated at the rear to permit installation on a rotating platform of an M27 105 mm recoilless gun and for ammunition. This gun was also mounted on unconverted Weasels. Both versions were used for a short time in the units specialising in Arctic warfare.

On the road from Duren to Cologne, medical orderlies of the 78th Infantry Division evacuate the wounded with a Weasel M29, during February 1945.

The Weasel continued its career after the war in the units of the US Army which had to move about in snow-covered zones. This vehicle here is equipped with a 105 mm recoilless gun which rapidly gave way to the 106 mm recoilless gun (IRON HORSE manoeuvres, Colorado, 1954).

Testing the mounting of a 75 mm recoilless gun on the Weasel at Aberdeen, in 1944.

Studebaker M29 and M29C Weasel		
	M29	M29c
Length (metres)	3.194	4.880
Width (metres)	1.676	1.703
Height (metres)	1.803	1.803
Weight (kg)	2,060	2,710
Climbing Gradient	Limited by Grip Only	Limited by Grip Only
Angle of Approach (°)	60	47
Angle of Departure (°)	60	36
Speed (km/hr)	58	58
Range (kilometres)	265	280
Engine Make	Studebaker	Studebaker
Model	6 170 Champion	6 170 Champion
Capacity (cc)	2,780	2,780
Cylinders	6, in-line	6, in-line
Output (horsepower/rpm)	65/3,600	65/3,600
Fuel	petrol	petrol
Engine heater	some models	some models
Ignition	12-Volt battery	12-Volt battery
Caterpillar Track Type	Flexible	Flexible
Width (cm/inches)	37.5/15 or 50.8/20	37.5/15 or 50.8/20
Gearbox	6 forward 1 reverse	6 forward 1 reverse

M29C of the Norwegian army towing a group of ski scouts. Norway only sold its last twenty-four Weasels in 1983-84. They were painted white and green.

Prototype (T13) of armoured Weasel pushing a mine clearance system.

For the 1950 campaign the Weasels were fitted with an oval plywood casing.

The Weasel and the Expéditions Polaires Françaises

In 1947, Paul-Emile Victor was looking for a light caterpillar vehicle suitable for travel on snow-covered terrain for the expedition which he was planning to Greenland. After numerous fruitless attempts, he was directed to the military stock then kept in the Forest of Fontainbleau where efforts were being made to put the *matériel* left by the different armies on French soil into some semblance of order. In one of these camps, on the Orleans road, in a clearing where the training circuit for motorcyclists of the National Gendarmerie would later be set up, Paul-Émile Victor was at last able to find and have assigned to him a vehicle which suited him: the Weasel.

The first vehicles, painted army green without having undergone any alteration, make the 1948 winter campaign in Greenland. The following year they were painted white and *'EXPÉDITIONS POLAIRES FRANÇAISES',* was painted on their sides. From the 1950/51 campaign, the dozen vehicles were modified, some receiving a plywood cabin of semi-oval or trapezoidal shape. The material was painted orange so as to be more visible against the snow.

The Weasel adapted very well to the task of forays over the ice where it was capable of pulling heavy loads on sledges and where its amphibious capabilities, during the northern summer, allowed it to move about in spite of the numerous wet fissures in the terrain.

On their return to France, the vehicles were reconditioned at the Établissement Régional de Matériel d'Avon (Regional Vehicle Establishment) then from 1963 directly by the Expéditions Polaires in their basement installation in the Boulevard Foyolle in Paris. Military personnel were, also, seconded to maintain the Weasels. Some vehicles were now white again.

In 1955, the vehicles, whether they were assigned to the North or to Adelie Land, were fitted with aluminium bodies simply placed on the coachwork. Cabins made of polyester laminate material made their appearance in 1958, while light alloy was kept for the South. The bodywork and structure of the Weasel was then transformed: the sealed separating bulkhead between the boot and the passenger compartment was eliminated to enlarge the interior space and a half-moon shaped 'passenger' position was installed by taking up spacefrom the front sealed compartment and moving the batteries situated between the engine, which

Another model of bodywork, with a circular opening closed by a canvas panel with a sliding lace-up. These vehicles are painted 'Dayglo Red' (1950).

Progression of two Weasels in Adelie Land. The front has been given a negative slope to give the driver better vision. The interior compartment has been redesigned to increase its volume. The superstructure is of aluminium. All these modifications were carried out by the workshops of the Polaires Expéditions. This photograph makes it possible to appreciate the difficulties of movement and progress (1959).

was itself almost in a central position, and the hull. The front was remodelled, rounded and lowered to increase its volume and provide better visibility for the driver.

Weasels participated in the International Glaciological Year. To supplement the number of vehicles in service and replace those which were too old in spite of the reconstructions, and the attentions of the mechanics, new Weasels were sought which, this time, with the shortage in supply, were M29 land versions. In general, and in spite of the existence of companies specialising in spares of this type, maintenance of the Weasel became more and more problematical. Bodies had to be built in France by SACAM. That is why other solutions were sought, notably from Hotchkiss who proposed a caterpillar vehicle designed by Victor Bouffort, the HB 40, of which several are still in service with Expéditions Polaires Françaises.

Despite this, and in spite of the difficulties due to its age, the attempts at replacement, the lack of spares, its small size, its fairly small useful load capacity and the fragility of its caterpillar tracks, the Weasel is still

First test of conversion of a M29 to a 'cargo' type with an aluminium half-cabin. The caterpillar trailer is based on Weasel components. The photograph was taken in the Avenue du Marechal Fayolle in Paris, where the workshops and offices of Expéditions Polaires Françaises are installed.

Embarkation on board the icebreaker Edisto, at Boston, United States, of the Weasels of the US Navy which are going to participate in Operation DEEP FREEZE in the Antarctic during 1955.

used and renders signal services. The Petrels Island base in Adelie Land has more than a dozen of them, including three foray types (vehicles with a hard top, radio, interior layout), four workshop vehicles (declassified former foray amphibians, whose rear has been converted into a tipper with a tailgate to ensure transport missions on the sea of ice) and five 'land versions'.

The Weasel was also employed by the US Navy and Argentina for their polar campaigns.

TANK TRANSPORTERS

As far as tank transporters are concerned, America started the war with nothing, which was also the case for other equipment.

Whereas between the wars, the USA had been content with a few 6 x 4 8 Ton trucks, and only light tanks in small numbers, the situation changed dramatically with America's entry into the war. Nevertheless, it was the French and the British, following the example given by the Spanish Republicans, who placed the first orders in 1939-40 for tank transporter platforms on 6 x 4 chassis (White 920, White Ruxtall, Mack NR 1 or EXBX), then the British alone for the Diamond-T 980. This vehicle was designed as a 6 x 4 ballasted tractor towing a tank-transporter trailer, following a concept which was very widespread in Britain, and not as a tractor for a semi-trailer.

Similarly, the Federal 604 tractor (1,433 vehicles built), whose production was also assured by Reo (Type 28X5) with a Trailmobile 20 Ton semi-trailer, was principally intended for the British and Canadians. A not inconsiderable number was kept by the USA and figured as standard *matériel* in *TM 9-2800* (1943 and 1947 editions). On the other hand its fairly modest capacities, led to it being mainly used as a vehicle carrier by the engineers, although it was designed as a tank transporter.

These vehicles, besides the fact they were both 6 x 4s, which was not very usual with American vehicles, also had Cummins (Federal) or Hercules (Diamond-T) diesel engines.

Facing the problem of transporting heavier and heavier tanks, like the M26 Pershing, the US Army launched into a research programme which led to the construction of prototypes designed by the Ordnance, Cook Brothers, Le Tourneau and Mack. All these vehicles were characterised by a central tank-transporting platform, suspended between the front and rear axles, both driving ones, which was meant

Top: Diamond-T 980, 6 x 4, 12 Ton, M20, carrying a Churchill. Designed initially at the request of the British who employed them in North Africa, 5,811 of this 20 Ton tractor was built.

The Diamond-T 980 and 981 were fitted with a ballast body permitting the loading of the tandem rear driving wheels with the aim of increasing the grip and therefore the tractive power. The "Mickey Mouse" style of camouflage is typical of British vehicles of the period.

Diamond-T 981 of the Belgian army with open cab, towing a recovered Sherman brought up on to the 45-ton M9 trailer.

Toiling up a slope, two Diamond-T 980 tractors of the US Army had to be harnessed in tandem to pull each M9 transporting an M10 Tank Destroyer, the whole representing a weight of some 40 tons.

to confer good cross-country capabilities on the combination. To load a tank, one or two of the driving wheel units was uncoupled and the vehicle was brought up flat on to the platform which had been lowered to the ground or else, for Le Tourneau's T4, simply—if one can describe it that way—winched on to the platform sideways after being brought parallel to the latter. On the surface, it did seem simple. In reality, things were quite different and the complex mechanisms which had to be put into operation to make the whole function, not to speak of the weight (42.75 tons empty for the Mack T8) and problems of engine power, made this attempt to produce a tank transporter fail.

It was ultimately the Diamond-T 980 and the Dragon Wagon—so named because, with all openings armoured and closed, it was reminiscent of a 'prehistoric monster'—which became the definitive US Army tank transporters. They were also used for transporting the bulky and heavy loads like heavy artillery ammunition boxes, landing vehicles, etc, when circumstances and the logistic crisis compelled the US Army to pull out all the stops, notably in the winter of 1944-45.

Diamond-T 980 and 981, M20, tank transporters

The US Army had immediate need for a vehicle capable of transporting its M3 and M4 medium tanks, and had to make up its mind to ask for the allocation of two hundred M20 tractors built by Diamond-T for the British Army. They were classified 'Substitute Standard' in September 1942 and 'Limited Standard' in 1943, when the M25 went into production, then became 'Substitute Standard' again from 1947. This 6 x 4 tractor had been ordered initially in 1940 by the British Purchasing Commission (the body responsible for orders for military *matériel* in the USA). The British used this vehicle operationally for the first time in North Africa, during winter 1940-41 where, coupled to a Rogers 45 Ton twelve-wheel trailer designated M9, it alone was able to transport M3, Valentine, and Crusader tanks, then in service with the Eight Army. The rear compartment could transport spares or carry ballast to increase the grip.

The M20 tractor and M9 trailer combination formed the M19 tank transporter system. In spite of its qualities, it was unstable in the tractor and trailer connection on bad roads. The small wheels of the

A Diamond-T converted into tractor for semi-trailer for a Centurion tank by the Australian army after the Second World War Semi Trailer Tank-transport, 60-Ton, 20 Wheeled Australian No 1 MK.

trailer very easily became stuck in the sand or mud.

The M20 tractor was powered by a Hercules DFXE Diesel engine, of 14.7 litres cylinder capacity, developing 185 hp at 1,600 rpm. The vehicle was built in sheet-metal and canvas-roofed cab versions. The 18 Ton winch forward was used on the Model 981 in the nomenclature peculiar to Diamond-T but not on the Model 980). Total production, between 1941 and 1945, was 5,871 vehicles. One of them was armoured for a comparative test with the M26.

Some were converted by the British into tractors for semi-trailers, which were easier to manoeuvre (Transporter 30 Ton, Shelvoke, and Drewry semi-trailer), and its rear tandem driving wheels could be fitted with flexible caterpillar tracks.

The M19 combination was very widely used after the war and even recently by Italy. Although less powerful than the M25, it was also very much appreciated by special transport firms, notably because of its diesel engine. Unlike the M25, its cab was not much altered by the 'civilians', being much more convenient for use and not overloaded with armour.

Tests of a Federal tractor, Model 604, with Trailmobile 20-ton semi-trailer, transporting a Chaffee tank. The vehicle was fitted with a 6-cylinder Cummins HD 600 diesel engine developing 150 hp.

The Dart Truck company, of Kansas City in Missouri, built this T13 tractor which, coupled to an M15 trailer, constituted the 40-ton T3 combination. The vehicle was powered by a 6-cylinder Waukesha engine, developing 250 hp. It is at Aberdeen Proving Ground, in April 1942.

The Double Ended, 8 x 8, 45 Ton, T8 tank transporter built by Mack, had an empty weight of 42,750 kg, and consisted of a pusher rear and a tractor front 4 x 4 drive train, each having its own 240 hp Hall Scott engine. The photograph shows the driver beside the rear section whose swan neck could be detached from the platform which was lowered or raised by the rear winch. The front section was in theory integral with the platform but was detachable also. The T8 could be driven from either of the cabs, according to circumstances. This vehicle was also fitted with a 500 hp Ford GAA V8 engine, identical to that of some Shermans, and was then termed T8 E1. In 1950, this prototype was put back into service again for the mobility tests of the 280 mm atomic gun.

An M25 tank-transporter combination, consisting of a Pacific Car and Foundry M26 tractor and an M15 trailer, transports two M8 howitzers.

M20 Prime Mover	
Length (metres)	7.112
Width (metres)	2.534
Height, metal cab (metres)	2.540
Weight Empty (kg)	20,140
Climbing Gradient (%)	25
Angle of Approach (°)	40.5
Angle of Departure (°)	51
Speed (km/hr)	35
at Regulation rpm	1,600
Fuel Consumption on road	
(litres/100 kilometres)	100
Engine Make and Type	Hercules DFXE
Capacity (cc)	14,700
Output (horsepower/rpm)	185/1,600
Cylinders	V-8
Fuel	diesel
Ignition	four 6-Volt batteries
Tyres	12.00 x 20, twinned rear
Brakes	Pneumatic

6 x 4, 20 Ton, Federal 604 Semi-Trailer Prime Mover	
Length (metres)	6.731
Width (metres)	2.419
Height (metres)	2.464
Wheelbase (metres)	4.242
Weight Empty (kg)	9,070
Climbing Gradient (%)	26
Angle of Approach (°)	45
Angle of Departure (°)	45
Speed (km/hr)	44
Engine Make and Model	Cummins Model HB 600
Capacity (cc)	11,014
Cylinders	6, in-line
Output (horsepower/rpm)	131/2,000
Fuel	diesel

Numerous tool chests were installed, even on the armoured shutters of this M26 towing a Fruehauf M15 A1 trailer carrying an M10 A1 tank destroyer of a total weight of 29 tons in Germany, in July 1945.

On several occasions, for example, Crusader tanks, which suffered from severe cooling system and lubrication troubles, had to be abandoned even though they had not been damaged in combat.

The armoured vehicle transports at the time were either trucks of American origin of 6 x 4 type, therefore with limited off road capabilities, of 13 to 18 tons useful load, Models Mack NR 1, 2, 3 or 4, or EXBX and White Rustall 922; or vehicles of British design like the Scammel 20-and 30-ton 6 x 4 tractors. A higher performance vehicle, the Diamond-T 980 tractor, came to reinforce the fleet of these tank transporters, but this did nothing to alleviate the painful shortfall of resources in this area.

In July 1941, the Ordnance Corps, on analysis of these reports, expressed its intention of ordering a means of recovery and transport for light and medium tanks which would if necessary be used for various vehicles of similar size and weight such as bulldozers or artillery caterpillar tractors. In September 1941, the technical characteristics were defined jointly with representatives of the armed forces. The desired vehicle was to consist of a tractor and semi-trailer combination capable of transporting light and medium tanks at a road speed of 35 miles per hour (53 km/h).

In addition, a 21.5 ton winch, rams, a system of anchoring and means which permitted loading of tanks which were incapable of moving on their own were prerequisites. Armour for the protection of personnel and an armament (12.7 mm machine-gun) were further requirements.

On these bases, the motor industry firms were invited to submit their proposals to Washington. The project presented by the Fruehauf Company of Detroit seemed to comply best with the specification. The Ordnance Corps therefore recommended in January 1942 that the project should be developed without further delay. The tractor was an adaptation of a civil model, the 300 AWD.

The two vehicles were in fact built by the firm of Dart Motor Co., under a sub-contracting agreement signed with Fruehauf.

The combination and each of its components in conformity with the system of identification in use in the US Army, were given individual designations. The combination was given the designation Heavy

With all armoured shutters in the closed position, Pacific Car and Foundry tractors of the Austrian army.

The M25 "Dragon Wagon" tank transporter

In 1941, the reports compiled by the American observers who were following operations in Egypt and Cyrenaica by the British Western Desert Forces highlighted the interest in having more numerous and adequate resources available for recovery and transport of armoured vehicles which had been damaged or had broken down. Indeed, these reports emphasised the heavy losses due solely to the inability of the British units to organise the rapid recovery of tanks which were out of action in combat zones.

M26 A1 photographed in October 1956 at the large American base of Kaiserslautern in Germany.

The crew of an M26 A1 belonging to the 486th Evacuation Company of the Ordnance Corps tops up its fuel supplies in 1945.

Wrecker T3. On their own, the tractor was designated Tractor Truck, T13 and the Trailer T28.

In February 1942, the acquisition by the US Army of several prototypes was administratively approved by the Ordnance Corps. Two prototypes were built. In April 1942, they were sent for testing to Aberdeen Proving Ground, the vehicle testing ground of the US Army, situated in Maryland (it also includes a large museum of vehicles). Squabbling between the Ordnance Corps and the Quartermaster Corps, concerning their respective competences in the matter of recovery vehicles, delayed the programme. The conflict was finally resolved by the General Staff which confirmed the Ordnance as responsible for following up Project T3.

During the tests, several deficiencies were found. The Dart tractor did not have the desired manoeuvrability, its clearance was insufficient and its front axle was overloaded.

At this juncture, the firm of Knuckey Truck Co., California, which had specialised in the design and construction of very large specialised trucks for open cast mines and quarries, proposed a new model whose performance and technical qualities appeared to comply better with the needs of the US Army. In June 1942, the order for a prototype of this vehicle was signed. The tractor was designated T25. The combination, that is to say the tractor and its semi-trailer, was designated Tank Recovery Unit, T3, E1. The designation of the Dart tractor and its semi-trailer had been modified at the same time. The combination originally christened Heavy Wrecker T3 had become Tank Recovery Unit T3. This terminological evolution, apparently harmless, was in fact part of the rivalries between the different departments of the US Army. The Ordnance had the job of looking after tanks and allied vehicles, the QMC intervened in the sphere of motor vehicles. All these problems were finally universally settled in August 1942, and the Ordnance obtained exclusive competence for all vehicles, armoured or not.

The tests of the Dart tractor (T13), including a model with armoured cab and bonnet, continued for some time in parallel with those of the T25. The latter, however, in spite of major deficiencies (an overloaded front axle would long remain the black mark of the vehicle) nevertheless proved to be superior overall.

In July 1942, the US Ordnance, after deciding on a new designation for the tank transporter combination which had become Truck Trailer, 40 Ton, Tank Recovery T21, recommended the acquisition of three hundred in a first batch, an objective of five hundred in total being finally envisaged. This recommendation was endorsed and the supply contract approved on August 25th, 1942.

The firm of Fruehauf, still in charge of the programme, preferred to sub-contract with a company

117

of larger production capacities than Knuckey. The firm of Pacific Car and Foundry of Renton (State of Washington) was retained. The firm was already participating in the American war effort by producing M4 "Sherman" medium tanks, and its production in this sphere attained 926 units. The semi-trailer continued to be produced by Fruehauf.

In June 1943, the armoured tractor and its semi-trailer were declared 'Standard' *matériel*. In consequence, the final regulation designations became Truck, Tractor, M26, Trailer, Semi, M15 and Truck, Trailer, 40 Ton, Tank Recovery M25 for the tractor alone, the semi-trailer alone and the combination respectively.

Series production had begun in May 1943 with the delivery to the US Ordnance of the first seven vehicles. The engine had been from the beginning an enormous 6-cylinder Hall-Scott of 240 hp SAE. The components of a hoist which could be mounted at the rear were fixed along the chassis. As with many American heavy vehicles of the time, the transmission to the rear wheels was effected by chains. Knuckey also ensured the manufacture of this transmission.

Although officially adopted by the US Army, the M26 tractor continued to be subjected to tests during which abnormal wear of the front set of tyres was observed. This premature wear was imputable to front axle overload. Then came the idea of lightening the weight of the vehicle by eliminating the armour of the driver's cab. Tests were carried out in December 1943 with a tractor stripped of its armour. In May 1944, a prototype equipped with a new cab entirely roofed in mild steel, but retaining an M49 ring mounting for 12.7 mm machine-gun, was built. Series production of the new model was launched and the Pacific tractor (TR1 in the firm's own nomenclature) was designated Truck, Tractor, M26A1. The uncladding operation saved 1.5 tons and considerably lengthened the life of the tyres. It also improved the range of the vehicle, increasing it (with the standard 450-litre fuel tank) from 400 to 435 kilometres but the consumption still remained astronomical and exceeded a litre per kilometre on a good road. The M26A1 tractor was declared 'Standard' *matériel* in October 1944.

Production of the M26 tractor and of the M15 semi-trailer was stopped in August 1945. In total 1,272 tractors had been produced, including 753 M26s and 519 M26A1s and M26A2s, the latter with 24-volt electrics. The M15 semi-trailer became the M26A1 through the addition of an extra ramp in front of the rear wheels to make it easier for recovered vehicles to pass over the tyres and its widened version became the M15A2. These two sub-versions also had a bigger useful load of 4,500 kg.

On the operational side, an original use of M25s in March 1945 should be noted. Indeed, to permit the seven Allied armies engaged on the western front to cross the Rhine, 124 medium landing craft (LCM) of the US Navy were taken from the Channel coasts to the Rhine by road on M25 tank transporters. The LCMs were used alongside 370 GMC DUKW amphibians and many thousands of small boats.

The M25 combination was still classified 'Standard' in 1953, although the M26 was 'Limited Standard'.

Among the principal countries which used M25 tank transporters besides the USA which retained them in service in reserve units until the beginning of the 1960s, Belgium, Austria, Italy (until recently), France, Spain and Turkey should be mentioned. Great Britain, which had received M25s under Lend-Lease, converted a Pacific tractor in its Fighting Vehicle Proving Establishment (FVPE), fitting it with large-dimension tyres mounted singly at the rear and replacing the tow attachment saddle by a ballast.

In the civil sector, the lack of vehicles of the power of the M26 on the market in the years which followed the war caused the Pacific tractor to be appreciated by companies specialising in exceptional transport jobs. Transformers, boiler parts and nuclear power station components were frequently transported on trailers towed by Pacific M26s, most often stripped of their armour and extensively converted.

M26 and M26 A1 Prime Movers		
	M26	M26 A1
Length (metres)	7.722	7.798
Width (metres)	3.321	3.315
Height (metres)	3.150	3.251
Wheelbase (metres)	4.369	4.369
Weight Empty (kg)	21,970	20,412
All Up Weight (kg)	46,859	46,712
Range (kilometres)	400	435
Ground Clearance (cm)	62	62
Climbing Gradient (%)	30	30
Angle of Approach (°)	35	32
Common Data: M26 and M26 A1		
Speed (km/hr) at Regulation rpm	42 2,100	
Fuel Consumption on road (litres/100 kilometres)	200	
Engine Make and Model	Hall-Scott Type 440	
Capacity (cc)	17,865	
Cylinders	6	
Output (horsepower/rpm)	230	
Coolant	water	
Fuel	petrol	
Gearbox	four forward	
Transfer Box	two-speed	
Ignition	12-Volt; two 6-Volt batteries	
Tyres	14,400 x 24 twinner	
Brakes	Pneumatic	
Front Winch	16,000-kg	
Rear Winch	54,000-kg	
Hoist	Manual, behind cab for handling operations including spare wheel	

Artillery Caterpillar Tractors

Three types of caterpillar vehicles were employed by the American artillery units: tractors of commercial type; 'High Speed' tractors with a body carrying the gun crew and the ammunition; and vehicles improvised from tanks with the turret removed.

Commercial caterpillar tractors

Following the experience gained in the First World War, and although more cumbersome and slower than wheeled vehicles, caterpillar tractors of commercial type, all with diesel engines and frequently with a starter device on a petrol cycle with magneto (International), were used to tow 105 mm, 155 mm, 8-inch and 240 mm guns. Indeed, these vehicles offered better performance (grip, traction) in difficult terrain than heavy trucks, even if the latter were equipped with suitable axles.

Tractors		
Category	Designation	Vehicle
Heavy	M1	International TD9
		Caterpillar
Medium	M1	Allis Chalmers MD7 W
		International TD 14
		Caterpillar RD6
Light	M1	Allis Chalmers MD 10W
		International TD 18

Tractors of commercial type, in spite of the presence of a three-seater bench seat and side luggage compartments, had the inconvenience of being able to transport neither gun crew nor ammunition, consequently imposing the need to use a large number of accompanying vehicles.

The mechanised manoeuvres of 1941, and especially the war operations, highlighted the limitations of this type of vehicle: low speed of movement per hour, weight, maintenance and the necessity of transport on trailers for long journeys. The vehicle was reallocated to other tasks.

High Speed tractors

In order to remedy this state of affairs, more specialised vehicles, sometimes designed using mechanical components of tanks and provided with roomy bodies for personnel and ammunition, were designed. The vehicles produced to this concept were the M4, M5 and M6 which all had their engines at the rear.

The M4 tractor, built by the Allis Chalmers Manufacturing Co., was designed to tow artillery guns of 8 to 13 tons, and had a crew of eleven men. The ammunition transport capacity varied in function of the calibre: 90 mm anti-aircraft, fifty-four rounds, 155 mm, thirty rounds, 203 mm, twenty rounds and 240 mm, twelve rounds. The M4 tractor was powered by a Waukesha engine (Type 145 GZ 6-cylinder in-line, developing 210 hp at 2,100 rpm). The M4 C and M4 A1 C had ammunition stored in the personnel transport compartment. The driver was seated in a central position with two entrance doors, one on either side.

The M5 tractor produced by International Harvester was powered by a Continental R 6572 6-cylinder in-line engine, developing 215 hp at 2,900 rpm and was more particularly intended for towing artillery guns of a weight of 7 tons 105 mm M2

Artillery Caterpillar Tractors Principal Data							
Model	T19	D4	HD7 W	TD14	RD6	MD 10 W	TD18
Length (metres)	3,213	3,353	3,683	4,219	3,860	4,410	4,911
Width (metres)	1,930	2,032	2,057	2,750	2,032	2,515	2,387
Height (metres)	2,003	2,310	2,184	2,570	1,830	2,540	2,384
All Up Weight (kg)	5,057	5,897	7,394	9,640	8,188	11,567	13,732
Max. Speed (km/hr)	8.5	9	13	14	9	18	15
Climbing Gradient (%)	47	75	45	36	60	45	45
Range (kilometres)	82	200	480	290	145	480	300

Allis Chalmer's medium artillery tractor, Model HD 7W. Throughout the war, Russia continued to use Soviet or American heavy and medium M1 tractors to tow its artillery.

High Speed Tractor, 13 Ton, Model M5 A3.

M1 heavy tractor, International Model TD 18. All these diesel tractors originally had petrol engines (5.7-litre tank incorporated).

High Speed Tractor, 13 Ton, International M5, of the Belgian army. The ring mounting for the 12.7 mm Browning machine-gun forms an integral part of the tubular structure supporting the canvas hood. Entry to the vehicle is by the doors situated in front, on either side of the driver's compartment.

and 155 mm M1 howitzers. The M5 A1 had a new body recalling that of the M4, all steel; it transported eleven men as against nine for the M5. The M5 tractor used certain mechanical elements, rolling gear and suspension of the M3 light tank. Its development, with a new rolling gear and a new suspension, continued after the war (M5 A3 and A4).

Studies for a heavy tractor intended to pull 240 mm M1 and 203 mm M1 guns began in February 1942. Two prototypes (T22 and T23) were proposed by Allis Chalmers.

The T22, which was equipped with a tow attachment saddle, was set aside in favour of the T23, which was in any case mechanically identical but equipped with a body which could accommodate eleven men and transport twenty rounds of 240 mm or twenty-four rounds of 203 mm ammunition. This vehicle was declared 'Standard' in June 1943 under the designation High Speed Tractor M6. The M6 was powered by two Waukesha 145 GZ 6-cylinder in-line engines, each developing 193 hp at 2,100 rpm.

Nearly 21,000 caterpillar tractors of all types were built. After the war, only the M5, M5 A3 and M6 were classified 'Standard'. Although successful, fast on the road and with a good performance off road, these tractors were never numerous enough to replace their equivalents on wheels. Their very specialised bodies prevented from being used for other missions. The design of new models was, for a time, continued after the war. Finally, the standardisation of tracked self-propelled artillery in the US Army put everyone in agreement, until the Vietnam war. Several

An M5 tractor towing a 155 mm gun belonging to the US Ninth Army crosses the River Ruh on a pontoon bridge built by the US Engineers in March 1945.

High Speed Tractors			
Model	M4	M5	M6
Length (metres)	5.16	4.7	6.45
Width (metres)	2.46	2.5	3.01
Height (metres)	2.52	2.7	2.60
Weight (kg)	14,130	12,723	34,200
Crew	11	9	11
Fuel Consumption			
(litres/100 kilometres)	50	100	50
Engine			
Make	Waukesha	Continental	Waukesha
Model	145 GZ	R 6572	145 GZ
Cylinders	6, in-line	6, in-line	6, in-line
Output (horsepower/rpm)	190/2,100	207/2,900	190/2,100
Fuel	petrol	petrol	petrol
Ignition	12-Volt	12-Volt	12-Volt
Gearbox			
Forward Gears	3	4	2
Reverse Gears	1	1	1
Transfer Box	two-speed	two-speed	two-speed
Brakes			
Tractor	Mechanical	Mechanical	Mechanical
Secondary for gun	Electrical	Electrical	Electrical

'Full Track, Prime Mover' M33, M34 and M35 improvised artillery tractors

To relieve the shortage of M6 caterpillar tractors, makeshift solutions were adopted through the use of tanks which had the turrets removed and were slightly modified by fitting hooks for towing 203 mm and 240 mm guns. Three types of improvised vehicles were designed in this way. The M33 tractor was derived from the M31 recovery tank (M3 chassis) on which the turret and the lifting arm had been removed. The M34 was derived from the M32 B1 Sherman recovery tank. Finally, the M35 was an adaptation of the M10 A1 tank destroyer.

countries, which were allies of the United States received some, including Japan, Belgium, Spain and Austria. In 1960, Brazil dieselised thirty of the M4s which it had received during the war with 260 hp 6-cylinder Scania engines.

A High Speed Tractor, 18 Ton, Model M4, from Allis Chalmers, positions an 8-inch howitzer in its battery position at Colmar in 1944.

To overcome the scarcity of powerful caterpillar tractors, the US Army was forced to use tank chassis with the turrets removed. Christened M35, this former Tank Destroyer M10 A1 is towing a 240 mm gun, the heaviest in the American arsenal, which had to be transported in two sections.

Below **High Speed Tractor, 38 Ton, Model M6,** *from Allis Chalmers of the US Third Army, seen in 1945.*

Full Track Prime Movers			
Model	M33	M34	M35
Weight (kg)	27,216	28,577	24,950
Speed (km/hr)	40	40	50
Range (kilometres)	240	190	260
Crew	6	6	6

White M3 A1 Scout Car seen during manoeuvres in the United States in 1940.

Scout Cars

The M3 A1 Scout Car was developed from a series of wheeled, lightly armoured reconnaissance vehicles, designed and produced in the 1930s and designated M1, M2 and M3.

Their predecessor was a vehicle designed by White in 1933 on the basis of an Indiana (subsidiary of White) 4 x 4 van chassis. This prototype, T7, had an armoured body with an opening on top, which could carry four men. Its armament comprised: two 12.7 mm Browning heavy machine-guns and two 7.62 mm machine-guns, model 1919 A4, also produced by Browning. The armour was 12.7 mm thick on the front and 6.35 mm on the sides. This vehicle, standardised under the designation M1, was built by Indiana Motors Division, production totalling seventy-six. Two units stationed at Fort Knox, the 1st and 13th Mechanized Cavalry Regiments, were equipped with it.

Two years later, in 1935, a new Scout Car made its appearance, designed by Corbitt (T9). It was standardised under the designation M2. A little bigger and more powerful than the White, twenty of this vehicle was built. Its crew was five to seven men according to the mission.

The M3 was against built by White. A total of sixty four was delivered to the US Army in 1938. Marmon-Herrington also worked on this type of vehicle, notably for Persia.

Finally, the M3 A1 made its appearance in June 1939. It equipped the 7th Mechanised Cavalry Regiment. The body, which accommodated eight persons, had 6.35 mm to 12.7 mm armour. The M3 A1 was powered by a 6-cylinder Hercules engine, Model JXD, developing 110 hp at 2,600 rpm. The four wheels were permanently driven. The M3 A1 E1 received a Buda-Lanova or Hercules DJXD (TM9-1705C) engine and was built in small numbers, not exceeding a hundred units. The armament consisted of one 12.7 mm machine gun and one 7.62 mm. A rail enclosed the combat compartment to permit weapons to be fitted all round its perimeter. In front, the M3 A1 had

Drive past at Algiers on July 14th, 1943, of an M3 A1 Scout Car recently delivered to the French Forces.

received a roller which enabled it to tackle obstacles better. The body of the Scout Car greatly inspired that of the Half-Track.

In total, 20,856 Scout Cars M3 A1 was built, a figure which is all in all fairly modest. Production was stopped early, since the S.N.L. (Spares Nomenclature) G67 of March 1943 indicates that 19,263 vehicles had been built. The contract W303-ORD-1260 for ten thousand Scout Cars was the biggest of all.

Until the appearance of the M8 armoured car, the Scout Car was the only American wheeled combat vehicle. During the war, it was supplied to Great Britain, the Soviet Union, the Free French forces, Canada, the Belgians, among others.

Underpowered, with little armour, and a combat compartment which was a veritable grenade trap, it was a mediocre war vehicle and did not come up to expectations. The British were soon using it as an armoured service vehicle for the engineer, medical, repair and other services. In Tunisia, General Patton used it as a command vehicle after fitting protective shields above the combat compartment.

No derivative version was built for the US Army. Some received 37 mm anti-tank guns in Italy, this mounting having been tried out also at the Aberdeen Testing Centre (M3 A1 E1). Others were lengthened and converted into fire engines or coaches by US Army workshops!

The M3 A1 E2 was also an experimental model, fitted with a superstructure fitted with a fixed armoured roof and lifting side panels. The USSR received the entire production of M3 A1 E1s with the Buda-Lanova diesel engine, and 3,340 Scout Cars in total.

Half-Tracks

Parade in Place de la Concorde, Paris, on August 29th, 1944, of an anti-tank unit equipped with M3 A1 Half-Tracks towing M9 3-inch guns.

In 1925, the US Ordnance bought from Citroën two caterpillar-tracked cars which were sent to Aberdeen Proving Grounds for tests. In May 1931, a third caterpillar-tracked car model, P17, identical to the one in service at the time in the French Army, was acquired. The good results of the P17 encouraged the American authorities to study half-track vehicles. The firm of James Cunningham, of Rochester, acquired the Kegresse licence and made a vehicle christened Car Half-Track T1, which the Rock Island arsenal modified to produce Model T1 E2 and T1 E3.

At the same time, General Motors developed on the basis of a 2.5-ton truck and the rolling gear of the T12 E2, the Truck, Half-Track T1. Subsequently, other half-tracks, with Chevrolet and Ford chassis as a basis, were also built. Marmon-Herrington, taking a Ford commercial chassis as a basis, built Models T9 and T9 E1 which, after a few modifications, produced the M2 half-track truck ordered by the US Army in small numbers.

In 1938, the General Staff showed interest in the half-track formula and, in February 1939, White, in conjunction with the Rock Island arsenal, built its prototype, the T7, which used elements of the M2 truck developed in 1937 by Marmon-Herrington. The tests carried out with the T7 were judged satisfactory and continuation of the development of this vehicle was decided in December 1939. The new studies were carried out by Diamond-T and resulted in an improved version of the T7 which was designated Half-Track, Scout Car M4. It is this vehicle which gave rise to two specific vehicles, one intended for

General Patton's troops prepared to liberate Concarneau in August 1944.

M9 A1 Half-Track. This version, built by International, is easily identified by the flat shape of its mudguards.

towing artillery guns of up to 155 mm calibre (at the time the Schneider 155 Model 17 on wheels, received by the USA during the First World War), the other for transporting troops.

The first of these, designated M2, had a shortened body without a rear door. It was standardised in September 1940. The second, which received the designation M3, had a 22 cm longer body and could transport thirteen men seated (ten infantrymen, or a section, one driver, a gunner and a commander).

These vehicles were built by White, Autocar and Diamond-T with the aim of increasing production, notably to respond to the needs of Lend-Lease. The firm of International Harvester Co. joined the group of the three other manufacturers, but the models built by IHC (M5 and M2) had their own engine, the 6-cylinder Red Diamond 450B, developing 143 hp at 2,700 rpm.

When production ceased in 1944, a total of 41,170 Half-Tracks had been built in about seventy different versions, including the variants and numerous experimental versions. Starting with the M2 and especially the M3 troop transports, many specialised

Prototype of the M16 anti-aircraft vehicle. The vehicle, T28 E1, appeared in 1942. It was armed with a 37 mm gun twinned with two 12.7 mm Browning machine-guns.

versions of half-track were built: 75 mm and 105 mm self-propelled guns, 81 mm mortar carrier, anti-aircraft protection vehicles or even medical vehicles.

The engine that powered the half-tracks built by White, Diamond-T and Autocar was the same, whatever the model; it was a 6-cylinder overhead valve in-line engine, built by White (Model 160 AX) whose principal characteristics were as follows:

Bore:	101.6 mm
Stroke:	130.2 mm
Capacity:	6.3 litres
Output:	153 hp at 3,000 rpm

The body design and the arrangement of seats and internal storage varied according to use, but all (with the exception of the M15 anti-aircraft vehicle, armed with a 37 mm cannon and two 12.7 mm machine-guns) were fully armoured in front, on the sides and at the rear. The thickness of the armour varied from 12.7 mm at the front to 6.35 mm on the body sides and bonnet.

Some vehicles were equipped with a roller mounted on the front bumpers. This equipment helped the vehicle to get over obstacles such as embankments, ditches etc. The roller was fitted with a compression spring on each side, which absorbed the shocks when it struck an embankment or raised obstacle.

When the vehicle was equipped with a Tulsa Model 18G winch, it was mounted between the chassis beams at the front. The winch was driven by a transmission shaft from a power take-off mounted on the rear gearbox. Control was by a worm and pinion. A universal joint, fitted with a shear spindle for safety purposes, connected the transmission shaft to the worm. A safety brake acted on the worm shaft and held the load in any position when power was no longer transmitted to the winch. The maximum pulling capacity of the winch was 4,540 kg.

M3 motor gun-carriage with a 75mm gun.

An M16 anti-aircraft half-track equipped with four .50-cal. machine-guns on a Maxson mounting.

US Army Half-Tracks

M2, M2 A1	Intended as artillery tractor, used mainly as troop transport. No rear door.	**T19 105 mm Howitzer Motor Carriage**	105 mm field gun. 324 built. Towed 1 Ton trailer.
M3, M3 A1, M5, M5 A1	Designed as troop transport, but some artillery units received some, such as the Tank Destroyer Command for towing 3-inch Gun M5 heavy anti-tank guns.	**T48 57 mm Gun Motor carriage**	Anti-tank vehicle. Anglo-American design with 57 mm gun (6-pounder). Used by British and Russians with 57 mm calibre long gun.
M9 A1	International Harvester Co. version of the M2 A1 for towing light artillery guns. Rear door.	**M13 Multiple Gun Motor Carriage**	Anti-aircraft vehicle. Two Maxson 12.7 mm machine-guns in twin turret on M3 chassis. 535 built by White.
M4, M4 A1	81 mm mortar firing along the axis to the rear. No rear door.	**M14**	Identical to M5 chassis. 1,905 built by International Harvester Co.
M21	81 mm mortar firing 30° forwards on either side of the axis	**M15, M15 A1**	Anti-aircraft. A mounting carrying a 37 mm cannon with two co-axial 12.7 mm machine-guns above (M15) or below (M15 A1) cannon. 680 M15s produced. Some converted in Pacific and Korea to carry 40 mm Bofors.
M3, M3 A1 75mm Gun Motor Carriage	75 mm gun model 1897 (French or US model). Used by Tank Destroyer Command. Autocar chassis.		
T30 75 mm Howitzer Motor Carriage	Short 75 mm gun (Pack Howitzer M1). 500 vehicles. Replaced by M8 tank.	**M16, M16 A1**	Anti-aircraft. Electrically operated Maxson 12.7 mm quadruple turret, body sides folded down to allow ammunition magazines through. 500 vehicles from White.
		M17	Identical to M16, but on International Harvester Co. M5. 1,000 vehicles. Used by the USSR.

Jeeps of the headquarters company of the 1st Infantry Division, the famous 'Big Red One', embark on board LSTs. On these vehicles, the white stars are set in a circle of ochre paint which by changing colour, gave warning of the presence of combat gas (Paint liquid vesicant detector M5).

River crossing exercise by a Jeep of an anti-tank company (AT25) with the aid of a makeshift raft.

The omnipresent Jeep here serves as transport for a B-17G crew of the 97th Bombardment Group based at Armendola in Italy. The baseball caps which the gunners wore helped protect them from the sun.

Dodge 4 x 4, ¾ Ton, Model WC 51, of a medical unit crossing the Siegfried Line. Like a large proportion of the auxiliary vehicles of the Medical Corps, it bears the Red Cross symbol painted on the radiator grille, the bonnet and the tarpaulin, although strictly these marks were reserved for ambulances only.

Dodge WC 54 ambulance with its regulation Red Cross markings seen in England in 1944.

Embarking in LST 134, *a GMC CCKW 353 christened* Lil' Nellie, *equipped with a fording kit and transporting a radio shelter. One can observe the US flag affixed to the windscreen and bonnet and the US star painted on a background of gas detector paint.*

A column of CCKW 353s equipped with the M37 ring mounting for a .5-cal. Browning machine-gun photographed on an Italian road in 1943.

A column of CCKW 352s of 'C' Company of the 32nd Field Artillery Battalion of the US 1st Infantry Division towing 105 mm M2 howitzers waits to embark. The names painted on the shields of the howitzers recall the theatres of operations of the unit— North Africa and Sicily.

GMCs embarking in LSTs in Great Britain prior to D-Day, June 1944.

This Studebaker advertisement reminds one of the diversity of the military programmes in which the motor industry was involved.

The last Chevrolet K44 of the French army, from the transmission school, photographed on the day of its arrival at the Saumur Armoured Vehicle Museum.

Ford 19 C, 4 x 2, ½ Ton chassis, modified as a mobile anti-aircraft gun emplacement by Marmon-Herrington, for the Dutch troops stationed in Dutch Guiana.

An LVT 4 of the Amphibious Training Centre seen at Lorient in 1969.

Ford M8 armoured car of the armoured squadron of the Ivory Coast army, equipped with a ring mounting above the turret.

Truck Shovel-Crane 6 x 6, 6 Ton, given by the French army to the Gabonese army.

Wrecker M1 A1 recovering an accident-damaged P45 of a driving school (marines, Senegal, 1960).

Studebaker publicity drawing of the Weasel which appeared in the American magazines in 1944.

Mack 6 x 6, 6 Ton tractor of a French anti-aircraft unit equipped with 90 mm guns photographed in 1962.

This Chevrolet Class 325 fire tender without undergoing any alteration, remained more than twenty-five years in service at the Sartrouville emergency centre, in the Paris region.

Airport fire tender Class 155 on a Kenworth 572 chassis, photographed in 1981 in the United States on Hondo airfield. The International in the foreground transports additional emulsifiant.

Diamond-T-969 of the French army photographed in 1981.c21

Regulation camouflage for snow-covered terrain according to Manual Fm-5-20B *of the US Army.*

International 1 Ton, M-2-4, converted into a fire tender with a high pressure pump for Hawaii airport, photographed in 1975.

One of the Weasels used on the French polar expeditions.

Dodge Carryall of the Air Rescue Service of the US Air Force photographed in 1949.

Dodge WC 56 Command Car crossing a military bridge during a demonstration at Saumur.

The interior of an LVT troop transport photographed in the Musée des Blindés, Saumur.

A DUKW undergoing maintenance at the cavalry armour school at Saumur during 1977.

Armoured Cars

Unlike the other principal belligerent nations, the United States did not particularly develop the concept of armoured cars. Only one model, the M8 along with its derivative, the M20, was produced in series for the US Army in relatively high numbers, 15,648, and used operationally by the US Army.

In the 1930s the American military authorities had practically lost interest in the subject of armoured cars. The war in Europe and North Africa, theatres of operations where the British, Italians and Germans lined up numerous and varied models of armoured cars, awoke some interest in the vehicles in the US authority concerned.

At the end of 1940, the US Ordnance Corps ordered a vehicle, termed T13, from the firm of Trackless Tank Co. This vehicle of 8 x 6 type, armed with a 37 mm cannon in a turret, was tested at Aberdeen Proving Ground in January 1941. The US Ordnance Corps assessed this vehicle unfavourably, but the Armored Force nevertheless wanted to place an order for one thousand vehicles which was reduced, in March 1942, to five hundred before finally being abandoned in 1943. Reo had ensured the manufacture of a better armed model (76.2 mm).

Another vehicle designed on the basis of needs manifested by Great Britain was designated from July 1941 by Ford (T17) and Chevrolet (T17 E1). A first order for 2,260 vehicles was placed with Ford in January 1943. It was followed by a second for 1,500 vehicles, the vehicle then being standardised under the name of M5. This vehicle was rejected by the US Army which preferred light tanks, and the order was finally reduced to 250 units which the USA then proposed sending to Great Britain within the framework of Lend Lease. The latter, not having any use for them, declined the offer. Finally, the 250 T17s were disarmed and entrusted to the Military Police for strictly domestic tasks.

Top: The T13 Trackless during its tests. The armament and turret are not fitted. The chassis is an 8 x 6.

Middle: T18 E2 Boarhound designed by the Yellow Coach division of General Motors. This vehicle was very advanced 57 mm gun, hydraulic motor for the turret, eight driving wheels. The desert war had ended before production could begin. It weighed 27 tons, had two 150 hp engines, and could reach over 60 mph (100 km/hr).

Left: Ford T17 armoured car. A total of 240 was finally built.

Staghound T17 E1 of the Belgian army, photographed during an exhibition of military matériel in 1966. The Italian police was using some at the time, painted red, with a modified turret fitted with two machine-guns instead of the 37 mm gun mounting.

Chevrolet's Staghound T17 E2, with Frazer-Nash twin .50-cal anti-aircraft turret. Although carrying the registration 'USA 6024358', this vehicle was intended for the British. It went into service after the war in the Belgian gendarmerie. The turret was open topped.

One of the prototypes tested during the war, the Tucker 'Tiger' Tank, which in spite of its false appearance of an armoured Jeep, had no connection with the latter.

The vehicle designed by Chevrolet (T17 E1) had a better career, since, after a few vicissitudes concerning the level of orders, 2,687 were finally produced and sent to Britain where they were christened Staghound. The production of the T17 E1 and E2, which was never adopted by the US Army, was interrupted in December 1943. Its engine was a Model 270, the same as that of the $2\frac{1}{2}$ Ton CCKW/AFKWX/DUKW trucks. It was used after the war by Italy, Belgium, Israel, Nicaragua and others.

Other vehicles—T18 (8 x 8, built by General Motors), T18 E1 (6 x 6), T18 E2 (8 x 8, armed with a 57 mm gun) and T19—never passed the prototype stage.

Within the framework of a specification drawn up by Tank Destroyer Command in July 1941, for a fast, very mobile vehicle with six-wheel drive and armed with a 37 mm gun in a partially open rotating turret, giving priority to observation over protection, three other versions (anti-aircraft, 81 mm mortar carrier and ammunition transport) were also envisaged when the cavalry again took up the development of the design, which no longer interested the Tank Destroyer Command, the latter having meanwhile found something better armed and better protected. Ford benefited from a contract for the building of a prototype (T22) which, after comparative tests with the models proposed by Chrysler (T23) and as a private venture by Studebaker (T21, then T43), was adopted, after a few minor modifications (T22 E2), and standardised on May 19th, 1942, under the designation M8.

A first order for 6,000 M8s was placed with Ford, rapidly followed in July 1942 by a second order for 5,070 extra vehicles. Series production, however, only began in March 1943. On April 30th, 1945, the production of the M8 (Ford Gak) was terminated after 11,667 had been produced by the Ford factories of Chicago and Twin Cities. However, the Ford statistics indicate a slightly higher production figure, 12,314. The M8 armoured car was also supplied to Great Britain which christened it Greyhound and, after the war, to most of the NATO countries and allies of the USA.

These were the first vehicles that the German frontier guards received when the former enemies undertook to re-arm Germany. In carrying out the conditions decreed by the Allies and which the latter still applied under pressure from the Russians, 'the

An M8 with a ring mounted for a .50-cal. machine-gun, a relatively common conversion by the field workshops, in front of the Arc de Triomphe, on August 25th, 1944.

Opposite page bottom: The open turret of the M8s was certainly practical in a reconnaissance mission, but was also, notably in street fighting, a very fine 'grenade trap'. To protect themselves from grenades these crews of the French 5th Armoured Division entering Colmar made a protective grille.

The Ford T22, prototype of the M8.

heavy armament', that is to say the poor old 37 mm, was removed and replaced by an MG 34 or 42 machine-gun, after conversion of the shield, or even by a mock gun made of sheet metal. The M8 was very much appreciated throughout the world, as a police vehicle or colonial vehicle when it was no longer usable on European territory. Many of its users replaced the turret of the M8 or the open top of the M20 with closing shutters. The M8 was omnipresent in the French colonial wars and for many years equipped the national gendarmerie.

The M8 armoured car gave rise to an anti-aircraft version armed with four Browning .50-cal machine-guns, designated T69. This vehicle, having proved inferior to the M16 anti-aircraft half-track, was in consequence not adopted. On the other hand, a thinly armoured personnel transport version (T26) was accepted by the US Army as standard *materiel* in April 1943 under the designation Armored Utility Car M10, then M20 to avoid any confusion with the M10 tank destroyer. This vehicle was essentially used as a command and reconnaissance vehicle—for its whole armament it had a single .50-cal M2 on an M49 ring mounting. A total of 3,791 was produced.

Mechanically, the M8 and M20 were identical. They were powered by a Hercules JXD engine mounted at the rear, the same as that of the Scout Car, with a Timken-Detroit axle at the front and a Ford engine-axle group at the rear. The gearbox was of four-speed type, with two-speed transfer box.

The M8 had shown itself to be a good fighting vehicle, although weakly armed and protected, but the troops in the field wondered what benefits the M20

An M8 of the US Army passes through a village in the north of France in 1944.

would offer over and above more inside space for radio sets and crew, in comparison with the M8.

The first months of the Korean War sounded the death knell of the M8/M20, which was no longer up to the mark and was relegated to guarding prisoner of war camps, escorting convoys or protecting bases in the hands of military or air police. From 1947, the M8 was 'Limited Standard', while the M20, benefiting from the fact of being the only one in its category, was still 'Standard'.

Two modernisation programmes were attempted, besides the Dieselisations, one by France on an M20 which was fitted with a complete Hispano-CNP 90 mm turret (from AML Panhard) and the other in the United States by NAPCO who sold twenty-four units of a conversion kit to Colombia in 1983. This kit comprised an automatic gearbox, a Detroit diesel engine

Two AM M8s of the mobile gendarmerie *at Algiers, with conical armour with two trap doors to close the turret.*

This interior view of the turret of the M8 demonstrates why, in order to equip the reconnaissance platoons with extra radio resources, it had been necessary to create the M10. In general, the M8 is a vehicle in which the crew operate in cramped conditions.

M8 and M20 Armoured Cars		
Model	M8	M20
Length (metres)	5.004	5.004
Width (metres)	2.540	2.540
Height (metres)	2.248	2.311
Wheelbase (metres)	2.642	2.642
Weight (kg)	7,802	7,099
Climbing Gradient (%)	60	60
Angle of Approach (°)	60	60
Angle of Departure (°)	45	45
Range (kilometres)	480	480
Engine		
Make	Hercules	Hercules
Model	JXD	JXD
Capacity (cc)	5,245	5,245
Cylinders	6, in-line	6, in-line
Output (horsepower/rpm)	110/2,700	110/2,700
Fuel	Petrol	Petrol

Armament: M8	
Main	
Elevation	37 mm cannon in turret
Performance	-10/+20
Rounds	46 mm armour at 1,000 metres
	80
Secondary	.30-Cal machine-gun co-axial; 1,500 rounds
	.50-Cal machine-gun on turret; 400 rounds

Rear view of an M8 of the 2nd Armored Division. The custom of removing the rear fairings was fairly widespread. The rear section of this M8 with a Hercules engine can be compared with the diesel-engined one in service in Guatemala.

Left **A curious improvisation during the operations in the Congo, the turret has been turned to the rear, equipped with an armoured well, a shield and a .5-cal machine-gun with large movement in elevation. The Renault trucks are from the Belgian army.**

Above **A Guatemalan M8. Notice the new rear cowling and the position of the spare wheel because of the retrospective installation by the American specialist Napco of a Detroit Allison diesel.**

An M8 of the Bundesgrenzschutze on manoeuvres. The turrets were either fitted with mock guns made of sheet metal or an MG42 machine-gun. The frontier police was the first paramilitary organisation set up in postwar Germany (1954).

and a TOW anti-tank missile launcher installation in its turret. The 37 mm gun, which was of no use whatsoever and which would not fit in the turret with the tripod mounting of the TOW, was replaced by a .50 cal machine-gun. Several other projects were undertaken, notably by the Brazilian army which fitted its fleet of M8s with 150 hp Perkins and 120 hp Mercedes diesels in the 1970s.

Launching production of the M8/M20 did not stop research in the USA, which had few illusions and considered the recently adopted material as a stop-gap. General Motors, Chevrolet Division, carried out studies on a chassis, the T28, which was far in advance of its time, notably in the suspension and the location of the three driving axles, which were mounted equidistantly. In view of the work schedule of Chevrolet, the job of building this vehicle was passed to Ford, the T28 having been standardised in December 1944 under the designation M38.

The end of war operations forestalled the setting up of the production line. It was, until the arrival of the Cadillac Gage Commando in Vietnam, the end of wheeled fighting vehicles for the US Army.

The M20 in its standard configuration. A vehicle which was pleasant to drive, manoeuvrable, fast, and finally with enough room inside, but whose utility in combat was very debatable.

An AM M20 in Tonkin during 1953, with a .30-cal. machine-gun behind the shield mounted in front besides the .50-cal. machine-gun on the ring mounting.

Above middle: An AM M20 (AM automitrailleuse, (literally) machine-gun car armoured car) equipped with an armoured cowling system to close the combat compartment in Tunis in 1954. Notice the motorcyclists in British dress on Harley-Davidsons.

Proposal for renovation of the M20 by the DTAT with a 90 mm turret of the model mounted on the AML (AML automitrailleuse légere light armoured car) Panhard (Satory, 1971).

The Chevrolet T19, the most developed of the American armoured cars as far as the transmission and the suspension are concerned. On this test vehicle, the armament is still the 37 mm anti-rank, ineffective at this stage of the war. The vehicle could be given guns of calibres up to 75 mm (Chaffee turret).

ROAD VEHICLES

The US Army has often been reproached for having neglected road vehicles for its transports and having preferred off road tactical vehicles which, for the same deadweight, carry less and consume much more fuel. This impression was doubtless true for a European seeing the convoys of the White, Green or Red Ball express pass by, but certainly needed to be tempered if it were related to the global fleet available to the armed forces of the United States.

The logistic services of the US Army had estimated, and the Italian campaign had certainly not made them change their opinion, that the state of the road network in the external theatres of operations would have to be considered as mediocre or as frankly bad the closer one got to Germany. This view took account of the destruction and overload which war imposed on roads which for a long time had been no longer or poorly maintained.

In these conditions, using road trucks, which were certainly more economical per ton/mile, would at least mean a breaking up of the load on approaching the front, still hoping that the lines of the road network assigned to supply had been re-established and permanently maintained by the engineers, which was not achieved.

All this created a set of problems which had to be solved by the establishment of large and diversified depots specialising in transport units, carrying thousands of catalogued spare parts. The circumstances were further complicated by production delays which made it necessary to find alternatives. Transporting landing craft or cases of ammunition on the tank transporters or petrol jerrycans on tactical vehicles

The three models of body employed by the US Army for its light utility vehicles Top Chevrolet ½ Ton, model BK Carryall; Centre Chevrolet 1½ Ton van 'Canopy Express', fitted with a 6-cylinder engine developing 85 hp; Bottom Chevrolet 1½ Ton 'Panel Delivery' which still possesses the chrome fittings of the civil models. The body was to be taken up again on the model G 7015 with two driving axles. Its mounting is twinned at the rear.

GMC AFX 312 fitted with a Proctor Keefe body. Eighteen of these vehicles were supplied to the Quartermaster Corps in 1940 to serve as mobile recruiting offices. The frame on the van is used for putting up posters.

Ford 4 x 2, 1½ Ton, of the Series 11T80 built from 1940 to 1941, fitted with an 85 hp V8 engine.

Mack EE equipped with a water tank. This vehicle, which was also ordered in a tipper version by the US Army in 1940, was a purely commercial vehicle which was built by Mack from 1938 to 1950, totalling 9,719, essentially for its civil clientele.

Ford 2 G8T 4 x 2, 1½ Ton (1942 model). Most of these vehicle had a 6-cylinder petrol driven engine, while the civil sector used them with a V8.

Ford 4 x 2, 1½ Ton, Model G8T, equipped for tests of a canvas-topped cab and a cargo body identical to that mounted on the Ford 'Low Silhouette' GTBs.

Tractor 4 x 2, 2½ Ton, GMC with 6-cylinder 308 engine.

International 6 x 4, 2½—5 Ton, Model M5 6 x 4. A total of three thousand was supplied, predominantly for countries benefiting from Lend-Lease.

International 6 x 4 equipped by the Soviet Red Army with the famous Stalin Organ rocket launchers. Identical mountings were fitted to GMC and Studebaker chassis. This photograph is the first published showing an International in the Red Army and thus removes any ambiguity about its use by that country.

because of the scarcity of tankers, are examples of this realistic, pragmatic approach to logistics under the pressure of events. Tactical vehicles which were found to be able to fulfil dual roles were given priority in Europe. In the Pacific where operations often took place on small islands, the needs were not so great.

On the other hand, in the United States, on the Alcan route and the multifarious large war construction projects, on the Burma road, on the long and terrible crossing to Australia and in India, in short, wherever it was a question of travelling and trans-

International 6 x 4, 2½—5 Ton, Model US 6 x 4 U7.

Studebaker tractor for semi-trailer, Model US 6 x 4 U6.

porting supplies along a network over which one had control, out of reach of the enemy, it was the Fords, International Ks, Federals, Mack EHs, Chevrolets and others which ruled the road in their thousands, all the more so since these trucks, very simple to assemble and identical to the civil models (year models 1940, 1941, 1942), could also be delivered partly knocked down or completely knocked down (PKD or CKD) to the allies of the United States, or built by the Canadian and Australian subsidiaries of the American manufacturers to build vehicles like the Mapleleaf, Dodge T110, Chevrolet 1543 and International K5. Although built outside the United States, these remained undeniably 'American'.

Of course, the maintenance of thousands of bases, depots, camps, training grounds and the support and supply of the units based in the United States also demanded thousands of trucks, most often of the 1½/2½ Ton class. Sometimes they were used either by the armed forces or by their auxiliary corps and the Conservation Corps (civilian workers under military law with the job of maintenance and reafforestation of the camps).

The bodies ranged from Panel Delivery to Pick-Up through the Carryall and the Express Delivery (a van body with fold-up tarpaulin sides), the Stake and the

A convoy of Studebaker 6 x 4s of the US Army halted in China. The sixth vehicle and those of the end of the column have sheet-metal cabs with a circular opening for the 12.7 mm machine-gun, a version unknown till now. (See close-up, opposite)

The GMC CCW 353 6 x 4, 2½—5 Ton was equipped with a Budd cargo body. A total of 23,649 was built.

The semi-trailer tractor version of the Mack EH, which was powered by a Mack EN356 110 hp straight-six engine.

Great Britain received 2,400 Mack EH 4 x 3, 5 Ton Trucks.

An Autocar 4 x 2, 5 Ton, Model C50, here equipped as a dump truck of which seven were supplied to the Quartermaster Corps.

Platform (a flat-bed with lattice-work rails), water tankers to supply isolated outposts, and the inevitable all-purpose dump trucks. This range of tasks formed the administrative transport, as opposed to logistic transport (carrying consumables, fuels, munitions and equipment from military depots to combat zones) and to tactical transport (transporting from the rear area to the combat zone all general *materiél*, supplies and equipment necessary for maintaining in the field and re-equipping combat units and for the accomplishment of operational tasks.

The tables at the end of this chapter list the production and the models of the road-going 4 x 2 vehicles built by Ford, GMC, Dodge and International for the US Army and the US Government.

The White 6 x 4, 10 Ton, Model 1064, was fitted with a 150 hp Cummins diesel engine. The box on the cab was intended for stowing the tarpaulin.

Mack NR6 towing a 240 mm gun, Model M1.

The T48, an International H542-9 converted into a 10 Ton 6 x 4 cargo. These vehicles, if construction of them had been undertaken, were principally intended for the Burma road.

Mack NR 14. Models NR 14, NR 15 and NR 16 were the last of the NR series. NR 15 was characterised by a cargo body of steel. They did not have spare wheels behind the cab, unlike the preceding models.

This poor photograph, taken from a post-war car magazine on surplus stocks, does seem to show the carrier version of the tractor M425/426 which was seen in Holland by Bart H. Vanderveen at the end of the war.

A reconditioned Mack NR 8 seen at Marseille.

Corbitt model 40 SD6, 6 x 4, 8 Ton, powered by a Continental 22R engine of 133 hp.

The Mack EH 4 x 2, 5 Ton

This chassis in itself is unusual for, even though it had mechanical similarities to the civil model Mack EH, it not only received a military platform, but also a cab, a radiator grille and mudguards which were specifically military, only retaining the bonnet parts from the original. Furthermore, along with the International KR11 and a few Federal 55Ls and GMCs or Diamond-Ts and others, it was one of the rare heavy road carriers (5 Ton and over) to have been acquired by the US Army. The Mack EH was also used with a short wheelbase (3.65 m) as for a semi-trailer.

The EHs were to have been built mainly for the US Army, and production totalled 4,564, but were principally used by the British who received 2,400 of them. They were still classified 'Standard' in 1947 by the US Army. The civilian cab version was also used by the US Army, notably as a tipper and water tanker, and supplied to the British, including the EHT semi-trailer tractor, EHU version of the chassis with semi-forward cab, and the EH with civilian cab, totalling 510.

Dynamometer vehicle, used by the Aberdeen Proving Ground, made by Mack on a FKSW chassis. Delivered in September 1940, this truck, of an all-up weight of 22.7 tons, was powered by a Mack EY engine of 11.6 litres cylinder capacity.

A 6 x 4 tractor employed with 77-foot trailers in the United States for transporting B-24 bomber parts. The name of its manufacturer—EL Transport—was for a long time a puzzle, only solved in 1986 by Bart H. Vanderveen.

Mack EH 4 x 2, 5 Ton	
Length (metres)	6.75
Width (metres)	2.40
Height (metres)	2.825
Wheelbase (metres)	4.25
Weight Empty (kg)	4,725
Useful Load (kg)	9,225
Climbing Gradient (%)	35
Angle of Approach (°)	35
Angle of Departure (°)	23
Engine Make	Mack
Model	EH354
Cylinders	6, in-line
Output (horsepower/rpm)	110/2,620
Fuel	petrol
Tyres	9.00 x 20, twinned rear
Brakes	Pneumatic

A Russian ZIS or ZIL—150, was an exact copy of the International K.

The end of the evolution the Chinese Jay-Fong.

The International K

Launched in 1940, the Series K 2 x 4 completely revitalised the International Harvester range, this company being at that time the third manufacturer of American heavy vehicles, building 86,000 units that year. Three models of cab were used according to the weight class of the vehicle, those intended for $\frac{1}{2}$ Ton to 3 Ton vehicles (K1 to K5) being more streamlined with the headlights in the wings, a narrower radiator grille and other features.

The US Army, either for its own use or for its Allies, acquired fairly large quantities of them, a total of 11,999 vehicles—excluding the coaches. Primarily the K7, K8 and K11 models representing the heaviest tonnages (5 to 8 Ton) of the range.

It was principally Britain, China, Russia and Australia that received these vehicles under Lend-Lease. Of course, the US Navy, Marines and Coast Guard, International's most faithful customers, also bought some, some of which remained in service until the 1960s, notably on Naval airfields.

The K swiftly acquired a reputation for being a very strong truck. Although it only had a single driven axle, the rear, it was capable of good performance over bad terrain, partly due to the double reduction gearing of the live rear axle (an option).

In Britain, where they were delivered in cases and reassembled on the spot (PKD), they were allocated to priority civil firms participating in the war effort, and to the Petrol Pool, and Royal Air Force and Royal Navy.

Australia used them especially on the Australian North-South Road and the East-West Road, two roads crossing the continent and making it possible, thanks to a pool of trucks, to transport supplies from one coast to the other. Such a heat reigned there that the bodies, manufactured for the most part of wood, were reduced to their strictest minimum; no door, no hood, and sometimes no mudguards. Frequently a bunk was provided to permit rotation of drivers, the transport of greater quantities, faster, without stopping.

After the war, International resumed production of the K range, which became the KB from 1946 to 1950 until it was replaced by a new series, the L. But the already eventful history of the K did not stop there.

The ZIS factory *(Zavod Imieni Stalina)* of Moscow was instructed to copy the K in order to equip Russia with a modern truck, and the copy was practically exact. Thus was born the ZIS-150, which became the ZIL-150 when, under de-Stalinisation, the factory was renamed after its former director, Likhachev. Production began in 1949 and only stopped in 1957, when the ZIL-150 was replaced by a slightly more powerful lorry (100 instead of 90 hp), air brakes and not hydraulic, etc), the ZIL-164, itself a very close copy of the model 150.

The Russians, not content with having built tens of thousands of them, chose this type of vehicle, considered as excellent, particularly robust and very simple, to fulfil the demand of Communist China which wanted to develop a new heavy truck industry. Factory No 1 of Kirin in Manchuria, equipped with some of the machine tools rendered surplus to requirements by the forthcoming stoppage of production at ZIL,

International Harvester supplied 7,498 K7 chassis to the US Army. Among these, nine were fitted with this typically American body known as stake and platform, designed by the firm of Watson.

Among the 2,231 International KR 11, 4 x 2, 5 Tonners, 482 were built with a Galion tipper body which could be converted into a troop transport with a tarpaulin. This use was quite widespread in the US Army, notably on the Chevrolet 1½ Ton and GMC 2½ Ton vehicles.

In total, 282 KR 11 tractors, 4 x 2, 5 Ton, were put into service. The bumpers are still civilian type, but small headlights and a black-out light have been installed (above).

General Clayton L. Bisset, commanding the US Tenth Air Force, supervises the unloading of a C-47 in China. A thousand KB and a thousand KBR, 4 x 2, 3½ Ton lorries were delivered under Lend-Lease.

began production in November 1956. Christened CA-10 Jay-Fong ('Liberation'), this vehicle, still basically a copy of the International K, was destined to become **the** Chinese truck.

For two years, production hovered around ten thousand. After the Cultural Revolution, whose upheavals practically stopped all industrial activity, production was resumed on a national scale in several factories. Many versions were produced including short chassis, tipper, trolleybus, fire engine and 6 x 6 versions. A new 110 hp 6-cylinder side-valve engine was offered; then a diesel version.

The CA-10 is still the standard truck of the Chinese army—and of all China. More than one million have been built.

The K is truly an exceptional chapter in the history of the truck!

Identification of GMC Truck Chassis

Contract Number	Model	Load Class — Wheelbase (Feet/Inches) Cab Type — Body Type — Supplier	Engine Type	GMC Model	US Army registration Number
		Chassis 4 x 2			
W-398-QM-7322	1940	1½ ton - 193¾" W.B. 984 Cab - Heil/Cargo	228	AC-305	313467 thru 313494
W-398-QM-7520	1940	1½ Ton - 144" W.B. 984 Cab - Budd/Cargo	228	ACX-353	317800 thru 317807
W-398-QM-7533	1940	1½ Ton - 123½" W.B. 1544 Cowl - Proctor Keef/Van	228	AFX-312	317781 thru 317798
W-398-QM-7571	1940	5 Ton - 160" W.B. 1500 Cab - Perfection/Tipper	426	AC-723	5876 thru 5881
W-398-QM-7571	1940	5 Ton - 196" W.B. 1500 Cab - Perfection/Stage	426	AC-725	5882 thru 5887
W-398-QM-7571	1940	2½ Ton - 145¼" W.B. 984 Cab - Perfection/Tipper	228	ACX-353	412952 thru 412966
W-398-QM-7571	1940	2½ Ton - 193¾" W.B. 984 Cab - Perfection/Stake	228	AC-355	412967 thru 412980
W-398-QM-7808	1940	2½ Ton - 145¼" W.B. 984 Cab - Perfection/Tipper	228	ACX-353	413461 thru 413476
W-398-QM-7810	1940	1½ ton - 107⅞" W.B. 1544 Cowl - Luce/Van	248	AF-361	601379 thru 601423
W-398-QM-7857	1940	2½ ton - 145¼" W.B. 984 Cab - Perfection/Tipper	256	ACX-453	413477 thru 413516
W-398-QM-7857	1940	2½ ton - 157¼" W.B. 984 Cab - perfection/Stake	256	AC-453	413517 thru 413524
W-398-QM-7982	1940	½ ton - 113½" W.B. 993 Break	228	AC-101	206472 thru 206485
W-398-QM-8010	1940	Tractor 110" W.B. 1506 Forward Cab	361	AFX-622	413694 thru 413700
W-398-QM-8010	1940	2½ ton - 160" W.B. Gerstenslager/Forward Cab Van	278	AF-503	413701 thru 413714
W-398-QM-8011	1940	5 ton - 160" W.B. 1500 Cab - Heil/Tipper	426	AC-803	5997 thru 5999, 51000 thru 51002
W-398-QM-8927	1941	2½ ton - 147¼" W.B. 1574 Cab - Perfection/Tipper	270	CCX-453	428339 thru 428357
W-398-QM-8927	1941	2½ ton - 159¼" W.B. 1574 Cab - Heil/Cargo	270	CC-453	428358 thru 428366
Q-398-QM-8927	1941	2½ ton - 171¼" W.B. 1574 Cab - Perfection/Stake	270	CC-454	428367 thru 428370
W-398-QM-8927	1941	2½ ton - 159¼" W.B. 1574 Cab - Square Deal/Pick-up	270	CC-453	428371
W-398-QM-9078	1941	1½ ton - 109½" W.B. 1585 Cowl - Hicks/Radio Van	248	CF-351	607386 thru 607640
W-398-QM-10313	1941	1½ ton - 109½" W.B. 1585 Cowl - Hicks/Radio Van	248	CF-351	343561 thru 343563
W-398-QM-11014	1942	2½ ton - 159¼" W.B. 1574 Cab - Perfection/Stake	270	CC-453	487174 thru 487191
**W-398-QM-11610	1942	1½ ton - 109½" W.B. 1585 Cowl - Hicks/Radio Van	248	CF-351	6010711 thru 6010819
W-398-QM-11990	1942	1½ ton - 160" W.B. 1578 Cowl - W.S. Darley & Co/Fire Fighting Truck	248	CC-303	501589 thru 501608
W-398-QM-11992	1942	2½ ton - 178" W.B. 1502 Cowl - General Detroit/Fire Fighting Truck	426	AC-724	501664 thru 501678
W-398-QM-12453	1942	1½ ton - 160" W.B. 1574 Cab - Central Fire/Fire Fighting Truck	228	CC-303	501816 thru 501841
W-398-QM-13058	1942	1½ ton - 134½" W.B. 1574 Cab - Budd/Cargo	228	CC-302	3109490 thru 3109497
W-398-QM-13058	1942	1½ ton - 134½" W.B. 1574 Cab - Heil/Tipper	228	CC-302	3109498 thru 3109500

Chassis 6 x 4						
W-398-QM-8162	1940	2½ ton - 167" W.B.	1571 C.O.E. - Hercules/Cargo	256	AFWX-354	605305 thru 605404 605407 thru 605455
W-374-ORD-2597 (W-398-QM-11595)	1942	5 ton - 164" W.B.	1608 Cab - Cargo - Steel Body	270	CCW-353	4300459 thru 4315158 (Chass. Ser. No 11441, 11701 thru 11703, 11705 thru 19246, 19248 thru 19266, 19268 thru 19285)
W-374-ORD-2597 (W-398-QM-11595)	1942	5 ton - 164" W.B.	1608 Cab-Cargo - Wood Body (antiparasite treated)	270	CCW-353	4300459 thru 4315158 (Chass. Ser. No 19247, 19267 and 19286 thru 21200)
W-374-ORD-2597 (W-398-QM-11595)	1942	5 ton - 164" W.B.	1608 Cab - Cargo - Wood body (anti-parasite treated)	270	CCW-353	4300459 thru 4315158 (Chass. Ser. No 21201 thru 26400)
DA-W-398-QM-62	1941	5 ton - 164" W.B.	1608 Cab - Budd/Cargo	270	CCW-353	(Chass. Ser. No 2003 thru 3987)
DA-W-398-QM-62	1941	5 ton - 164" W.B.	1608 Cab - Prefection/Platform	270	CCW-353	(Chass. Ser. No 3988 thru 4002)
DA-W-398-QM-78	1941	5 ton - 164" W.B.	1608 Cab - Budd/Cargo	270	CCW-353	(Chass. Ser. No 4003 thru 6102)
DA-W-398-QM-203	1942	5 ton - 164" W.B.	1608 Cab - Budd/Cargo	270	CCW-353	(Chass Ser. No 7001 thru 11440, 11442 thru 11700 and 11704).

Identification of Ford Trucks Supplied to the US Army

	Model	Wheel base (inches)	Engine Cylinders	H.P.	Year	Contract Number	Technical Manual Number	US Army Registration Number
½ Ton 4 x 2 Pick-up	2GC	114"	6	90	1942	W-398-QM-11623	TM-10-1436	254793 thru 258292
½ Ton 4 x 2 Pick-up	21C	114"	8	90	1942	W-374-ORD-3013	TM-10-1436	254793 thru 258292
1½ Ton 4 x 2 Panel Delivery	2GT	134"	6	90	1942	W-398-QM-11210	—	W-364188 thru 364197
1½ Ton 4 x 2 Tipper	2GU	134"	6	90	1942	W-374-ORD-2735 W-398-QM-10857	TM-10-1328	356673-356691
1½ Ton 4 x 2 Stake	2GT	134"	6	90	1942	W-374-ORD-2730 W-398-QM-10857	TM-10-1328	35348-356672
1½ Ton 4 x 2 Tractor for Semi-Trailer	Special	134"	6	90	1942	W-374-ORD-2730 W-398-QM-10887	TM-10-1256	364714 thru 365013
1½ Ton 4 x 2 Tractor	Special	134"	6	90	1942	W-398-QM-11621 W-374-ORD-2757	TM-10-1432	368869 thru 369368
1½ Ton 4 x 2 Cargo	19T	134"	8	100	1941	W-398-QM-CIV-23	—	
1½ Ton 4 x 2 Chassis	11T	134"	8	90	1941	DA-W-398-QM-23	—	
1½ Ton 4 x 2 Tipper	19U	134"	8	100	1941	W-398-QM-10612	TM-10-1138	345420 thru 345478
1½ Ton 4 x 2 Platform	29T	134"	8	100	1942	W-398-QM-11506	—	
1½ Ton 4 x 2 Stake	19T	134"	8	100	1941	W-374-ORD-3009 W-398-QM-10612	TM-10-1138	343911 thru 345419
1½ Ton 4 x 2 Cargo	2G8T	158"	6	90	1942	W-398-QM-11621 W-374-ORD-2757	TM-10-1432	
1½ Ton 4 x 2 Cargo	2G8T	158"	6	90	1942	W-2021-QM-4	—	and Lend-Lease
1½ Ton 4 x 2 Cargo	2G8T	158"	6	90	1942	W-2021-QM-8	—	
1½ Ton 4 x 2 Cargo	2C8T	158"	6	90	1942	DAW-398-QM-187 W-374-ORD-2806		
1½ Ton 4 x 2 Cargo	2G8T	158"	6	90	1942	DA-W-398-QM-378 W-374-ORD-2824	TM-10-1432	Lend-Lease
1½ Ton 4 x 2 Cargo	2G8T	158"	6	90	1942	W-398-QM-12874	TM-10-1538	None
1½ Ton 4 x 2 Cargo	G8T	158"	6	90	1943	W-374-ORD-2780 W-2425-QM-283	TM-10-1346	3130134 thru 3144038
1½ Ton 4 x 2 cargo	G8T	158"	6	90	1943	W-374-ORD-2856 W-2425-QM-655	TM-10-1346	3260774 thru 3279876
1½ Ton 4 x 2 Stake	2G8T	158"	6	90	1942	W-374-ORD-2865 W-398-QM-11621 W-374-ORD-2757	TM-10-1432	366369 thru 368868
1½ Ton 4 x 2 Stake	2G8T	158"	6	90	1942	W-2021-QM-4	—	
1½ Ton 4 x 2 Stake	2G8T	158"	6	90	1942	DA-W-398-QM-187 W-374-ORD-2806	—	
1½ Ton 4 x 2 Stake	2G8T	158"	6	90	1942	DA-W-398-QM-378 W-374-ORD-2824	TM-10-1432	Lend-Lease
1½ Ton 4 x 2 Stake	2G8T	158"	6	90	1942	DA-W-398-QM-420	—	
1½ Ton 4 x 2 Stake	G8T	158"	6	90	1943	W-2425-QM-261	TM-10-1346	3144039 thru 3146423
1½ Ton 4 x 2 Stake	G8T	158"	6	90	1943	W-374-ORD-2553 W-2425-QM-655	TM-10-1346	3279877 thru 3283885
1½ Ton 4 x 2 Cab-Over-Engine Chassis	198W	158"	8	100	1941	W-374-ORD-2865 DA-W-398-QM-23	—	
1½ Ton 4 x 2 Chassis	198T	158"	8	100	1941	DA-W-398-QM-23	—	
1½ Ton 4 x 2 Chassis with Open Driveaway Front End (RHD)	Special	158"	8	90	1942	DA-W-398-QM-70	—	
1½ Ton 4 x 2	118T	158"	8	90	1941	DA-W-398-QM-23	—	Lend-Lease
1½ Ton 4 x 2 Stake Body (RHD)	218TF	158"	8	90	1942	W-398-QM-12875	TM-10-1540	Lend-Lease
1½ Ton 4 x 2 Cargo	2GT	134"	6	90	1942	W-374-ORD-2781 DA-W-398-QM-522	TM-10-1432	3121032 thru 3121091
1½ Ton 4 x 2 Chassis	G8T	158"	6	90	1943	W-374-ORD-2781 W-398-QM-13441 W-374-ORD-2796	TM-10-1346	3147737 thru 3148928

Notes
All these types were supplied with commercial metal cabs, except the 4 x 2, 1½ Ton Special (open 'Driveway Front End') which was supplied as a bare chassis/canopy.

Chassis without US Army Registration Numbers were for Lend-Lease distribution to Allies.

'Platform': a flat-bed
Cab Over Engine': chassis with forward cab
RHD: right hand drive

Ford produced 93,217 trucks in total during the war, a very modest number for such a giant.

Identification of International K Series

VEHICLE DESIGNATION

Trucks per Contract	IHC Model	Type of Body (Supplier)	Tonnage Drive	Wheel base (Inches)	IHC Model Type and Series No	TM No of Spares with Truck	US Government Contract No	US Army Registration Number
176	KR-11	Tipper with canvas top (Gallon)	5 - 4 x 2	179	KR-11-800 thru 867, 869, 871 884, 886 thru 893, 895 thru 922, 924 thru 930, 932 thru 935, 937, 956 thru 1000	TM-10-1144	W-398-QM-10745	W-53284 thru 53484
25	KR-11	Compartmented Tipper (GarWood)	5 - 4 x 2	161	KR-11-868, 870, 885, 894, 923, 931, 936, 938 thru 955	TM-10-1144	W-398-QM-10745	W-53284 thru 53484
29	KR-11	Tipper with canvas top (Gallon)	5 - 4 x 2	161	KR-11-1001 thru 1029	TM-10-1144	W-398-QM-10881	W-53494 thru 53522
30	KR-11	Tipper with cab (GarWood)	5 - 4 x 2	161	KR-11-1046 thru 1075	TM-10-1336	W-398-QM-10973	W-53696 thru 53750
25	KR-11	Tipper with canvas top (Gallon)	5 - 4 x 2	161	KR-11-1076 thru 1100	TM-10-1336	W-398-QM-10973	
200	KR-11	Tipper with canvas top (Gallon)	5 - 4 x 2	161	KR-11-1151 thru 1400	TM-10-1382	W-398-QM-11401	W-54910 thru 55159
50	KR-11	Hi-lift tipper (Galion)	5 - 4 x 2	161		TM-10-1382	W-398-QM-11401	
100	KR-11	Tipper (Daybrook)	5 - 4 x 2	161	KR-11-1501 thru 1600	TM-10-1508	W-398-QM-11750	W-55351 thru 55450
32	KR-11	Tipper with cab (Daybrook)	5 - 4 x 2	161	KR-11-1601 thru 1632	TM-10-1554	W-398-QM-12930	W-57405 thru 57436
1190	KR-11	Tipper (Gallon)	5 - 4 x 2	161	KR-11-1701 thru 2890	TM-10-1682	W-271-ORD-2831 W-2425-QM-633 W-271- ORD-3970	W-542304 thru 543493 W-546535 thru 546786
30	KR-11	Semi-trailer tractor	5 - 4 x 2	161	KR-11-2926 thru 2955	TM-10-1686		
252					KR-11-3026 thru 3277			
1	K-7	Derrick (GarWood)	2½ - 4 x 2	176	K-7-6542	TM- 10-1114	W-398-QM-10615	W-463280
789	K-7	Tipper (GarWood)	2½ - 4 x 2	146	K-7-6804 thru 7592	TM-10-1172	W-398-QM-10788	W-483912 thru 484701
1	K-7		2½ - 4 x 2	146	K-7-7593	TM-10-1172	W-398-QM-10788	
5	K-7	Tipper with cab (GarWod)	2½ - 4 x 2	146	K-7- 760 thru 7605	TM-10-1172	W-398-QM-10797	W-482654 thru 482658
16	K-7	Stake (Hercules)	2½ - 4 x 2	192	K-7-7901 thru 7915	TM-10-1172 Change N° 1	W-398-QM-10973	W-487117 thru 487132
457	K-7	Tipper (GarWood)	2½ - 4 x 2	146		TM-10- 1344	W-398-QM-11201	
150	K-7	Hi-lift Tipper (GarWood)	2½ - 4 x 2	158		TM- 10-1344	W-398-QM-11201	W-487366 thru 487823
50	K-7	Cargo (Anthony)	2½ - 4 x 2	158	K-8-8401 thru K-7-9058	TM-10-1344	W-398-QM-11201	W-492532 thru 492731
1	K-7		2½ - 4 x 2	176		TM-10-1344	W-398-QM-11201	
2000	K-7	Tipper (Galion)	2½ - 4 x 2	146	K-7-10001 thru 12000	TM-10-1510	W-398-QM-11750	W-4108584 thru 4110583
2505	K-7	Tipper (St Paul)	2½ - 4 x 2	146	K-7-15350 thru 17854	TM 10 1684	W 271 ORD 2830 W-2425-QM-647	W-4452135 thru 4454639
1000	K-8		3½ - 4 x 2	179			W-298-QM-10064	
500	KR-8		3½ - 4 x 2	137			W-298-QM-10064	
500	KR-8		3½ - 4 x 2	161			W-298-QM-10064	
220	KR-8R	Semi-trailer tractor with winch	2½ - 4 x 2	149	KR-8R-2101 thru 2320	TM-10-1560	DA-W-398-QM-510	
100	K-7		2½ - 4 x 2	146			W-298-QM-10064	
7	K-7	Tipper (GarWood)	2½ - 4 x 2	146	K-7-5856, 5857, 5862, 5866, 5867, 5874, 5881		DA-W-398-QM-150	
601	K-7	Tipper (Anthony)	2½ - 4 x 2	146	K-7-2101 thru 2591 K-7-3501 thru 3610	TM-10-1140	W-398-QM-9268	W-459022 thru 459512 W-460037 thru 460146
4	K-7	Cargo (Anthony)	2½ - 4 x 2	158	K-7-2592 thru 2595	TM-10-1140	W-298-QM-9268	W-459513 thru 459516
6	K-7	Stake (Watson)	2½ - 4 x 2	158	K-7-2596 thru 2601	TM-10-1140	W-398-QM-9268	W-459517 thru 459522
1	K-7	Stake (Watson)	2½ - 4 x 2	192	K-7-2602	TM-10-1140	W-398-Qm-9268	W-459523
2	K-7	Tipper (Dempster-Dumpster)	2½ - 4 x 2	146	K-7-3649 and 3650 K-7-6019 and 6020 K-7-6041 thru 6141	TM-10-1140	W-398-QM-9268	W-460147, W-460148
761	K-7	Tipper (GarWood)	2½ - 4 x 2	146	K-7-6143 thru 6212 K-7-6214 thru 6541 K-7-6544 thru 6803	TM-10-1114	W-398-QM-10615	W-462779 thru 463279 W-463282 thru 463541
20	K-7	Tipper (GarWood)	2½ - 4 x 2	146	K-7-6001 thru 6018 K-7-6142, 6213	TM-10-1114	DA-W-398-QM-26	
19	K-7	Cargo (GarWood)	2½ - 4 x 2	158	K-7-6021 thru 6039	TM-10-1114	W-398-QM-10615	W-462759 thru 462777
2	K-7	Stake (Watson)	2½ - 4 x 2	192	K-7-6044 thru 6543	TM-10-1114	W-398-QM-10615	W-462778 thru 463281
50	KR-10	Cargo (Galion)	4 - 4 x 2	197			DA-W-398-QM- 25	
50	KR-11	Cargo (Galion)	5 - 4 x 2	197			DA-W-398-QM25	
2	KR-11	Cargo (Galion)	5 - 4 x 2	179	KR-11-758 and 759	TM-10-1144	W-398-QM-10745	W-53242, 53243
40	KR-11	Compartmented tipper (Galion)	5 - 4 x 2	161	KR-11-760 thru 799	TM-10-1144	W-398-QM-10745	W-53244 thru 53283

Notes
Vehicles without US Army Registration Numbers were ordered by the US Government and supplied to Great Britain under Lend-Lease.

Type of Body
Stake: Platform with large-dimension wooden-spar body with gaps between slats.
High Lift: Tipper Body mounted on scissor-type elevator for unloading coal.
Dump with Batch Gates: Compartmented Tipper for transport and dumping of different kinds of material without mixing.

In the mud of one of the US Ordnance Corps depots at Monteburg, an M425, identified by the fuel tank filler near the cab, and a GMC Model AFKWX 353, awaiting repairs during January 1945.

M425/426

In contrast, the majority of the production of tractors for semi-trailers was devoted to manufacturing the 5 Ton Truck Tractor, 4 x 2, M425 and M426, at least as far as vehicles assigned to general transport were concerned. It was the only vehicle of this category specially designed for military use.

The tractor for semi-trailer of 4 x 2, 5 Ton type was built in two versions by International. It was, the company said at the time, the consolation prize for the cancellation of the orders for the M7 light tank. This would explain why the US Army turned to a manufacturer which was not familiar to it, but which had unused potential available. The sudden halt in production of the M7 cost ten million dollars!

The first version was M542 9 in its manufacturer's nomenclature, but M425 according to the designation given by the US Army. A total of 4,640 was built. The M425 tractor was powered by a Red Diamond 450D 7.4 litre engine, developing 143 hp at 4,600 rpm. This model was replaced on the production lines by the M426 (or M 542 11) which was almost identical externally. The size of the tyres, the wheelbase, but above all the positioning of the petrol tank filler, in front of the M425 but in the centre on the M426, make it possible to distinguish the two vehicles, as well as the slightly more prominent radiator grille on the M425. The M426 permitted the towing of 10 Ton semi-trailers

International M426 tractors towing refrigerated 10 Ton semi-trailers capable of transporting meat at temperatures between 0° and -12°, photographed in the east of France in the winter of 1945.

An M426 tractor being loaded on to a pontoon. The number plate above the radiator grille ('T-65912') is typical of the US vehicles stationed in Europe after the war. The petrol filler is in the middle of the tank.

and the M425 that of 5 Tonners. Originally, they were built with a canvas-roofed cab.

Marmon-Herrington and Kenworth joined International in producing the M426 of which a total of 10,978 was ordered and allocated, 6,678 to International, 3,200 to Marmon-Herrington and 1,100 to Kenworth. Marmon-Herrington and Kenworth did not build the M426, but only carried out fitting and assembly work (PKD: partly knocked down) from complete sub-assemblies.

This vehicle, although for use on roads, was envisaged for tactical use and was therefore widely employed by forward formations. Thereby, it constitutes an exception among American 4 x 2 vehicles. Both models could be fitted with a ring mounting for a 12.7 mm machine gun. The M425/426 quickly earned an excellent reputation. It was much sought after by the civil sector after the war. The M425 was classified 'Limited Standard', and the M426 'Standard', in 1953.

Bart H. Vanderveen mentions, in *Wheels and Tracks* No 13, a long chassis cargo version of the 4 x 2 developed from the tractor version, of which he had seen an example in his native Holland at the end of the war. This vehicle, of course, had nothing to do with the civil modifications which would soon be on the production line.

M426s with Highway Trailer Co. 10 Ton semi-trailers unload Douglas C-54s which are supplying Berlin during the Soviet blockade of 1949.

165

4 x 2, 5 Ton M425 and M426 Trucks		
	M425	M426
Length (metres)	5.080	5.080
Width (metres)	2.403	2.476
Height (metres)	2.603	2.660
Wheelbase (metres)	2.970	3.050
Weight Empty (kg)	5,170	5,490
Useful Load (kg)	3,680	5,895
All Up Weight (kg)	8,850	11,385
Climbing Gradient (%)	41	25
Speed (km/hr)	56	61
Range (kilometres)	515	515
Tyres	9.00 x 20 twinned	11.00 x 20 twinned

Dodge Trucks Ordered by the US Government						
Model	Useful Load	Constructor's Type N°	Constructor's Series N°	Number Built	Year of Production	End-User
WF-31	1½	T98 E-163	8782501 thru 8782715	215	1940	US Army
WF-31	1½ Ton	T118 E-135	81304900 thru 81305015	116	1941	US Army
			81334245 thru 81334444	200	1942	US Army
T234	3 Ton	T234-170	83000001 thru 83015000	15,000	1944-45	Nationalist China

Note
Dodge also produced 1,542 ½ Ton vans for the US Army in 1941–42. Out of a total of 16,216 1½ Ton trucks, only 531 were finally allocated to the US Army.

Ford G8 TA (model 42), G.M.C., Chevrolet MR, Dodge 1½ Ton, Mack EH and International road tractors (4 x 2) for semi-trailers were also to be found in use for purely administrative transport.

6 x 4 chassis

As for the 6 x 4s, this category of vehicles had seemed rather a hybrid form to the Americans who had never really been interested in it, except for a large order for searchlight carriers in 1939 from GMC, Mack and Federal. It was largely due to the orders placed by the French, British and Dutch that the USA was led into their production, and put some into service, but even then at a rather gingerly pace. But, except for the Mack NR's (total production 16,548) which were sent in large numbers to Europe and the Middle East, the other models, largely the 6 x 6s with their front driving axle and transfer box removed, hardly left the United States. These were essentially GMC and Studebaker 2½–5 Tonners, used mostly in Alaska, and White 1064s of which 2,500 were bought.

In contrast, the majority of Studebaker US 6 x 4s and all the 3,000 International M65 6 x 4s (sheet-metal cab) were sent to Russia, either by sea or by convoys using the Iranian corridor. The Studebaker, particularly suitable for the wide open spaces, was also currently employed in China.

The GMC 6 x 4 (CCW 353) only existed in the long wheelbase cargo form and only received special equipment after the war (5,100 litre Heil or Garwood petrol tank, or rubbish tipper, Heil work site water sprayer). A total of 23,500 was built. On the other hand, as shown below, the Studebaker was built in several versions.

The 6 x 4, 2½ Tonners passed into the 5 Ton class when they were used on the road. The biggest semi-trailer which could be harnessed officially to a 2½–5 Ton tractor was Fruehauf's 12½ Ton Payload, 4 Wheels, Tandem Van.

It was, on the other hand, in this truck category that the greatest number of vehicles equipped with diesels was to be found, whether the Mack Lanova Eds for the NR or even, an extreme case, the Cummins HB 600s fitted to the White 1064s, that is to say the 6 x 4, 10 Ton version, derived from the 666, 6 x 6, 6 Tonner, which had a petrol-driven Hercules HX.

Studebaker 6 x 4 Trucks			
Type	Year	Wheelbase (metres)	Use
US 6 x 4-U6	1942-44	3.759	Semi-Trailer Tractor without winch; metal cab
US 6 x 4-U7	1941-44	4.115	Cargo without winch; metal or canvas-roof cab
US 6 x 4-U8	1942-44	4.115	Cargo with winch; metal or canvas-roof cab

The Diamond-T 980 6 x 4 tank transporters were powered by a Hercules DFXE diesel engine because they had originally been built for the British who were much more favourably disposed to this type of engine than the Americans. It is quite obvious that to give preference to petrol and therefore only to have one stock fuel, made transport and distribution easier, and greatly simplified logistics.

Long-distance transport across the United States was predominantly by rail. However, for

Table of Specific Vehicles of the US Army Ordnance Department After Redistribution of Responsibilities

Extracted from Technical Manual 9-2800

Designation	Purchase and Maintenance: Service Issuing Order		Storage		
	Chassis	Body	Complete Vehicle	Spare Part Maintenance: Chassis	Spare Part Maintenance: Body
Ordnance Department					
Ambulance, metropolitan	Ord	Ord	Ord	Ord	Ord
Ambulance, 1/2-ton, 4 × 4	Ord	Ord	Ord	Ord	Ord
Ambulance, 3/4 ton, 4 × 4	Ord	Ord	Ord	Ord	Ord
Ambulance, 1 1/2-ton, 4 × 2 field	Ord	Ord	Ord	Ord	Ord
Bus, passenger, 25-passenger	Ord	Ord	Ord	Ord	Ord
Bus, passenger, 40-passenger	Ord	Ord	Ord	Ord	Ord
Bus, passenger, 33-passenger	Ord	Ord	Ord	Ord	Ord
Bus, sedan, converted, 15-passenger	Ord	Ord	Ord	Ord	Ord
Bus, commercial type 20- to 29-passenger	Ord	Ord	Ord	Ord	Ord
Bus, semitrailer, converted, 40- to 45-passenger	Ord	Ord	Ord	Ord	Ord
Cars, armored, all types	Ord	Ord	Ord	Ord	Ord
Cars, scout	Ord	Ord	Ord	Ord	Ord
Cars, 5-passenger light sedan	Ord	Ord	Ord	Ord	Ord
Cars, 5-passenger medium sedan	Ord	Ord	Ord	Ord	Ord
Carriers, half-tracks, all types	Ord	Ord	Ord	Ord	Ord
Carriages, self-propelled, artillery, all types	Ord	Ord	Ord	Ord	Ord
Scooters, all types	Ord	Ord	Ord	Ord	Ord
Truck, 1/4-ton, 4 × 4, cargo	Ord	Ord	Ord	Ord	Ord
Truck, 1/4-ton, 4 × 4, amphibian	Ord	Ord	Ord	Ord	Ord
Truck, 1/2-ton, 4 × 2, ammunition	Ord	Ord	Ord	Ord	Ord
Truck, 1/2-ton, 4 × 2, canopy express	Ord	Ord	Ord	Ord	Ord
Truck, 1/2-ton, 4 × 2, carry-all	Ord	Ord	Ord	Ord	Ord
Truck, 1/2-ton, 4 × 2, C.S. & P.	Ord	Ord	Ord	Ord	Ord
Truck, 1/2-ton, 4 × 2, panel delivery	Ord	Ord	Ord	Ord	Ord
Truck, 1/2-ton, 4 × 2, pick-up	Ord	Ord	Ord	Ord	Ord
Truck, 1/2-ton, 4 × 2, sedan, delivery	Ord	Ord	Ord	Ord	Ord
Truck, 1/2-ton 4 × 4, carry-all	Ord	Ord	Ord	Ord	Ord
Truck, 1/2-ton, 4 × 4, command-reconnaissance w & wo/w	Ord	Ord	Ord	Ord	Ord
Truck, 1/2-ton, 4 × 4, emergency repair	Ord	Ord	Ord	Ord	Ord
Truck, 1/2-ton, 4 × 4, panel delivrery	Ord	Ord	Ord	Ord	Ord
Truck, 1 1/2-3ton, 4 × 4, automotive repairs, M-2	Ord	Ord	Ord	Ord	Ord
Truck, 1/2-ton, 4 × 4, pick-up, w & wo/w	Ord	Ord	Ord	Ord	Ord
Truck, 1/2-ton, 4 × 4, radio	Ord	Ord	Ord	Ord	Ord
Truck, 3/4-ton, 4 × 2, panel delivery	Ord	Ord	Ord	Ord	Ord
Truck, 3/4-ton, 4 × 2, pick-up	Ord	Ord	Ord	Ord	Ord
Truck, 3/4-ton, 4 × 4, carry-all	Ord	Ord	Ord	Ord	Ord
Truck, 3/4-ton, 4 × 4, command, w & wo/w	Ord	Ord	Ord	Ord	Ord
Truck, 3/4-ton, 4 × 4, ermergency repair	Ord	Ord	Ord	Ord	Ord
Truck, 3/4-ton, 4 × 4, weapons carrier, w & wo/w	Ord	Ord	Ord	Ord	Ord
Truck, 1 1/2-ton, 4 × 2, canopy express	Ord	Ord	Ord	Ord	Ord
Truck, 1 1/2-ton, 4 × 2, pick-up	Ord	Ord	Ord	Ord	Ord
Truck, 1 1/2-ton, ammunition body	Ord	Ord	Ord	Ord	Ord
Truck, 1 1/2-ton, 4 × 2, canopy express	Ord	Ord	Ord	Ord	Ord
Truck, 1 1/2-ton, 4 × 2, cargo	Ord	Ord	Ord	Ord	Ord
Truck, 1 1/2-ton, 4 × 2, combination stake and platform	Ord	Ord	Ord	Ord	Ord
Truck, 1 1/2-ton, 4 × 2, dump	Ord	Ord	Ord	Ord	Ord
Truck, 1 1/2-3-ton, 4 × 4, machine shop, M-4	Ord	Ord	Ord	Ord	Ord
Truck, 1 1/2-ton, 4 × 2, explosives	Ord	Ord	Ord	Ord	Ord
Truck, 1 1/2-ton, 4 × 2, panel delivery	Ord	Ord	Ord	Ord	Ord
Truck, 1 1/2-ton, 4 × 2, refuse collector,G-W	Ord	Ord	Ord	Ord	Ord
Truck, 1 1/2-ton, 4 × 2, pick-up	Ord	Ord	Ord	Ord	Ord
Truck, 1 1/2-ton, 4 × 2, recruiting	Ord	Ord	Ord	Ord	Ord
Truck, 1 1/2-ton, 4 × 2, tractor	Ord	Ord	Ord	Ord	Ord
Truck, 1 1/2-ton, 4 × 4, bomb service,M-6	Ord	Ord	Ord	Ord	Ord
Truck, 1 1/2-ton, 4 × 4, cargo w & wo/w	Ord	Ord	Ord	Ord	Ord
Truck, 1 1/2-ton, 4 × 4, C.O.E., S. & P. Body, 15-feet	Ord	Ord	Ord	Ord	Ord
Truck, 1 1/2-ton, 4 × 4, C.S. & P.	Ord	Ord	Ord	Ord	Ord
Truck, 1 1/2-ton, 4 × 4, dump w & wo/w	Ord	Ord	Ord	Ord	Ord
Truck, 1 1/2-ton, 4 × 4, panel delibery	Ord	Ord	Ord	Ord	Ord
Truck, 1 1/2-ton, 4 × 4, tractor	Ord	Ord	Ord	Ord	Ord
Truck, 1 1/2-ton, 6 × 6, cargo and personnel carrier	Ord	Ord	Ord	Ord	Ord
Truck, 1 1/2-3-ton, 4 × 4, artillery, repair, M-2 and M-1	Ord	Ord	Ord	Ord	Ord
Truck, 1 1/2-3-ton, 4 × 4, instrument repair, M-1	Ord	Ord	Ord	Ord	Ord
Truck, 1 1/2-3-ton, 4 × 4, small arms repair, M-1	Ord	Ord	Ord	Ord	Ord
Truck, 1 1/2-3-ton, 4 × 4, spare parts, M-2	Ord	Ord	Ord	Ord	Ord
Truck, 1 1/2-3-ton, 4 × 4, tank maintenance, M-1	Ord	Ord	Ord	Ord	Ord
Truck, 2 1/2-ton, 4 × 2, ammunition	Ord	Ord	Ord	Ord	Ord
Truck, 2 1/2-ton, 4 × 2, canopy express	Ord	Ord	Ord	Ord	Ord
Truck, 2 1/2-ton, 4 × 2, cargo	Ord	Ord	Ord	Ord	Ord
Truck, 2 1/2-ton, 4 × 2, chassis only	Ord	Ord	Ord	Ord	Ord
Truck, 2 1/2-ton, 4 × 2, C.S. & P.	Ord	Ord	Ord	Ord	Ord
Truck, 2 1/2-ton, 4 × 2, dump	Ord	Ord	Ord	Ord	Ord
Truck, 2 1/2-ton, 4 × 2, explosives	Ord	Ord	Ord	Ord	Ord
Truck, 2 1/2-ton, 4 × 2, tank, 1,000-gallon, fuel and oil	Ord	Ord	Ord	Ord	Ord
Truck, 2 1/2-ton 4 × 2, tank, 1,000-gallon, water	Ord	Ord	Ord	Ord	Ord
Truck, 2 1/2-ton, 4 × 2, tractor	Ord	Ord	Ord	Ord	Ord
Truck, 2 1/2-ton, 4 × 2, utility w/hoist and buckets	Ord	Ord	Ord	Ord	Ord
Truck, 2 1/2-ton, 4 × 2, van	Ord	Ord	Ord	Ord	Ord
Truck, 2 1/2-3ton, 4 × 2, load packer	Ord	Ord	Ord	Ord	Ord
Truck, 2 1/2-ton, 4 × 4, tractor	Ord	Ord	Ord	Ord	Ord
Truck, 2 1/2-ton, 6 × 4, tractor	Ord	Ord	Ord	Ord	Ord
Truck, 2 1/2-ton, 6 × 4, cargo w/and wo/w	Ord	Ord	Ord	Ord	Ord
Truck, 2 1/2-ton, 6 × 6, amphibian	Ord	Ord	Ord	Ord	Ord
Truck, 2 1/2-ton, 6 × 6, artillery repair, M-9	Ord	Ord	Ord	Ord	Ord
Truck, 2 1/2-ton, 6 × 6, automotive repair, M-8	Ord	Ord	Ord	Ord	Ord
Truck, 2 1/2-ton, 6 × 6, cargo, LWB w/and wo/w	Ord	Ord	Ord	Ord	Ord
Truck, s 1/2-ton, 6 × 6, cargo, SWB w/and wo/w	Ord	Ord	Ord	Ord	Ord
Truck, 2 1/2-ton, 6 × 6, cargo, C.O.E., 15-foot body wo/w	Ord	Ord	Ord	Ord	Ord
Truck, 2 1/2-ton, 6 × 6, dump, LWB w/and wo/w	Ord	Ord	Ord	Ord	Ord
Truck, 2 1/2-ton, 6 × 6, electrical repair, M-18	Ord	Ord	Ord	Ord	Ord
Truck, 2 1/2-ton, 6 × 6, instrument repair, M-10	Ord	Ord	Ord	Ord	Ord
Truck, 1 1/2-ton, 6 × 6, machine shop, M-16	Ord	Ord	Ord	Ord	Ord
Truck, 2 1/2-ton, 6 × 6, small arms repair, M-7	Ord	Ord	Ord	Ord	Ord
Truck, 2 1/2-ton, 6 × 6, spare parts	Ord	Ord	Ord	Ord	Ord
Truck, 2 1/2-ton, 6 × 6, stock rack	Ord	Ord	Ord	Ord	Ord
Truck, 2 1/2-ton, 6 × 6, tank, gasoline, 750-gallon	Ord	Ord	Ord	Ord	Ord
Truck, 2 1/2-ton, 6 × 6, tank, water, 700-gallon	Ord	Ord	Ord	Ord	Ord
Truck, 2 1/2-ton, 6 × 6, tool and bench, M-13	Ord	Ord	Ord	Ord	Ord
Truck, 2 1/2-ton, 6 × 6, welding, M-12A1	Ord	Ord	Ord	Ord	Ord
Truck, 2 1/2-ton, 6 × 6, instrument bench, M-23	Ord	Ord	Ord	Ord	Ord
Truck, 4-ton, 6 × 6, cargo	Ord	Ord	Ord	Ord	Ord
Truck, 4-ton, 6 × 6, cargo, LWB	Ord	Ord	Ord	Ord	Ord
Truck, 4-ton, 6 × 6, wrecker, w/winch	Ord	Ord	Ord	Ord	Ord
Truck, 4-ton, 6 × 6, dump	Ord	Ord	Ord	Ord	Ord
Truck, 4-5-ton, 4 × 4, tractor	Ord	Ord	Ord	Ord	Ord
Truck, 5-ton, 4 × 2, ammunition	Ord	Ord	Ord	Ord	Ord
Truck, 5-ton, 4 × 2, cargo	Ord	Ord	Ord	Ord	Ord
Truck, 5-ton, 4 × 2, C.S. and P.	Ord	Ord	Ord	Ord	Ord
Truck, 5-ton, 4 × 2, dump	Ord	Ord	Ord	Ord	Ord
Truck, 5-ton, 4 × 2, explosives	Ord	Ord	Ord	Ord	Ord
Truck, 5-ton, 4 × 2, tractor	Ord	Ord	Ord	Ord	Ord
Truck, 5-6-ton, 4 × 4, tractor, w/w	Ord	Ord	Ord	Ord	Ord
Truck, 6-ton, 6 × 6, prime mover, w/w	Ord	Ord	Ord	Ord	Ord
Truck, 7 1/2-ton, 6 × 6, prime mover, w/w	Ord	Ord	Ord	Ord	Ord
Truck, 8-ton, 6 × 4, tractor	Ord	Ord	Ord	Ord	Ord
Truck, 10-ton, 6 × 6, heavy wrecker, M-1	Ord	Ord	Ord	Ord	Ord
Truck and trailer, 40-ton, wheeled, tank recovery, T-21	Ord	Ord	Ord	Ord	Ord
Trailer, 1/4-ton, 2-wheel, cargo, amphibian	Ord	Ord	Ord	Ord	Ord
Trailer, 1/2-ton, 2-wheel, van, public address	Ord	Ord	Ord	Ord	Ord
Trailer, 3/4-ton, 2-wheel, cargo	Ord	Ord	Ord	Ord	Ord
Trailer, 1-ton, 2-wheel, cargo	Ord	Ord	Ord	Ord	Ord
Trailer, 1-ton, 2-wheel, 250-gallon, water	Ord	Ord	Ord	Ord	Ord
Trailer, 1-ton, 2-wheel, 2-horse van	Ord	Ord	Ord	Ord	Ord
Trailer, 1 1/2-ton, 4-wheel, recruiting	Ord	Ord	Ord	Ord	Ord
Trailer, armored, 2-wheel, M-8	Ord	Ord	Ord	Ord	Ord
Trailer, bomb, M-5	Ord	Ord	Ord	Ord	Ord
Trailer, plotting room, M-4	Ord	Ord	Ord	Ord	Ord
Trailer, 6-ton, Athey, track-laying	Ord	Ord	Ord	Ord	Ord
Trailer, 20-ton, Athey, track-laying	Ord	Ord	Ord	Ord	Ord
Semitrailer, 6-ton, gross, 2-wheel, cargo	Ord	Ord	Ord	Ord	Ord
Semitrailer, 6-ton, gross, 2-wheel, dump	Ord	Ord	Ord	Ord	Ord
Semitrailer, 6-ton gross, 2-wheel, stake and platform	Ord	Ord	Ord	Ord	Ord
Semitrailer, 6-ton gross, 2-wheel, van	Ord	Ord	Ord	Ord	Ord
Semitrailer, 2-wheel, combinaison animal and cargo	Ord	Ord	Ord	Ord	Ord
Semitrailer, 7-ton (PL), 10-ton gross, cargo	Ord	Ord	Ord	Ord	Ord
Semitrailer, 10-ton gross, 2-wheel, van	Ord	Ord	Ord	Ord	Ord
Semitrailer, 10-ton gross, 2 wheel mobile record unit	Ord	Ord	Ord	Ord	Ord
Semitrailer, 12-ton gross, 2-wheel low platform	Ord	Ord	Ord	Ord	Ord
Semitrailer, 16-ton gross, 4-wheel tandem, van	Ord	Ord	Ord	Ord	Ord
Tanks, all types	Ord	Ord	Ord	Ord	Ord
Tractor, crane, 1-ton, M-1	Ord	Ord	Ord	Ord	Ord
Tractor, light (track-laying)	Ord	Ord	Ord	Ord	Ord
Tractor, medium (track-laying)	Ord	Ord	Ord	Ord	Ord
Tractor, heavy (track-laying)	Ord	Ord	Ord	Ord	Ord
Motorcycles, solo, chain driven, 45 cubic inches	Ord	Ord	Ord	Ord	Ord
Motorcycles, solo shaft drive	Ord	Ord	Ord	Ord	Ord
Motorcycles, w/side car, chain driven	Ord	Ord	Ord	Ord	Ord

Table of Specific Vehicles Supplied by the Quartermaster Corps after Redistribution of Responsibilities

Designation	Purchase and Maintenance: Service Issuing Order		Storage		
	Chassis	Body	Complete Vehicle	Spare Part Maintenance: Chassis	Spare Part Maintenance: Body
Quartermaster Corps					
Truck, 2 1/2-ton, 6 × 6, sales commissary	Ord	QMC de to Ord	QMC	Ord	Ord
Truck, 5-ton, 4 × 2, refrigerator	Ord	QMC de to Ord	QMC	Ord	Ord
Semitrailer, 10-ton gross, 2-wheel, sterilizer and bath	QMC	QMC	QMC	Ord	Ord
Semitrailer, 10-ton gross, 2-wheel, clothing repair	QMC	QMC	QMC	Ord	Ord
Semitrailer, 10-ton gross, 2-wheel, laundry	QMC	QMC	QMC	Ord	Ord
Semitrailer, 10-ton gross, 2-wheel, shoe repair	QMC	QMC	QMC	Ord	Ord
Semitrailer, 10-ton gross, 2-wheel, textile repair	QMC	QMC	QMC	Ord	Ord
Semitrailer, 10-ton gross, 2-wheel, refrigerator	QMC	QMC	QMC	Ord	Ord
Semitrailer, 15-ton gross, 2-wheel, refrigerator	QMC	QMC	QMC	Ord	Ord

TransAmerican road transport, the US Army bought from Corbitt some 6 x 4, 40S D 6 tractors (Continental 22R engine). These, although rather austere in appearance, had something very rare at the time—a cab with a bunk. Part of the elements of the cab and transmission came from the 6 Ton 6 x 6.

The transport of parts of consolidated B-24 liberator bombers from one factory to another necessitated the creation of special trailers towed by a curious lorry powered by a petrol-driven twin Ford V8 Mercury. This practice, although not common, was nevertheless fairly frequent at the time in order to make up for the lack of powerful engines for lorries among some manufacturers. These very handsome forward-cab 6 x 4s, whose history was for a long time an enigma, had been specially built by Ellenstein and Lawson Transport Co., a company specialising in transport for Ford. Thornton, a specialist in conversions, also participated in the design. A hundred tractors were built, including ninety-six for the US Army.

In May 1945, Logistics Command, responsible for transport on the Burma road along which the supplies for China passed, was looking for a long-chassis 6 x 4 (20-foot body). The Command thought it could thus replace two $2\frac{1}{2}$ Ton trucks with a single vehicle, and thereby make significant savings in fuel and personnel and in immobilisation of vehicles through breakdowns, and so on. A first vehicle was built on the spot using as a basis an M425 with a lengthened chassis and a Diamond-T rear axle-engine combination.

The concept looked promising. International took up the design again in the USA in order to industrialise the concept. The vehicle did its trials under the designation of Truck, 10 Ton, 6 x 4, Cargo, T48. A metal semi-van body was intended to protect the load from the damp. However the approach of the end of hostilities did not allow the project to be pursued any further.

Buses

Buses, which were in very widespread use in American territory, corresponded to vehicles usually supplied by specialised coachbuilders like Wayne and Superior to civil firms and they were not renowned for their comfort. For the most part, they were simple truck chassis, given a new body of the 'School bus' type with an accordion-type folding door at the front.

Besides their normal role of personnel transport, buses were frequently used by the Medical Service for the transport of patients and wounded.

Ford $\frac{1}{2}$ Ton 2 GC or 2 1C Pick-up with V6 or V8 engine.

Truck, Cargo, 6 x 4, 10 Ton Mack NR	
Climbing Gradient (%)	32
Angle of Approach (°)	36
Angle of Departure (°)	38
Speed (km/hr)	60
Engine Make	Mack
Model	Ed Lanova
Cylinders	6, in-line
Fuel	diesel
Ignition	6-Volt battery
Tyres	
Front	11.00 x 24
Rear	14.00 x 20
	single/twinned

A twenty-five seat bus on an Available Truck Co. chassis, fitted with a 4.3 litre Waukesha engine.

A bus of commercial type for twenty-nine passengers on a Ford 1½ Ton chassis (1941 model).

An International K7 twenty-nine seat bus.

An available bus for forty passengers, with a 6-cylinder 5.3 litre Waukesha 6 BZ engine.

After the war, to make up for the shortage of personnel transport vehicles and to ensure the starting up again of German industry, the US Army had numerous GMCs given a new body or modified, like this one converted by Magirus who was an accredited supplier of the American armies.

Diamond-T 972 of the French army in Algeria in 1956.

Side tipper on Studebaker US 6, 2½ Ton chassis.

GMC CCKW 382 rebuilt and converted with an open-cab by Holden, the Australian subsidiary of General Motors.

Engineering Vehicles

The US Engineering Corps, given its role as a technical branch, was provided with a large number of special vehicles. Thus, from the end of 1943, the engineers possessed thirty thousand trucks and yet it was a close shave, its mechanisation having been one of the most difficult and controversial, all the more so as before the war its credits were for a long time restricted.

Bridging vehicles

Military bridges have always demanded a large, heavy vehicle for transporting them. In order to facilitate their transportation, the American engineers turned to the semi-trailer hitched to an off road tractor with two driving axles. This vehicle was for the heavy pontoon bridges (US 1940, 10 Ton and 25/40 Ton), and there was a specialised version with positioning gantry for bridges US/DB M1 or M2 Treadway, and a two-wheel sling trailer with extending towbar for infantry footbridges (Bridge M2) or transport of boats, abutment material, planks, trestles, etc.

Units for heavy bridges US 1940, 10 Ton and 25/40 Ton

The flat semi-trailers were either of 25 Ton Pontoon (Electric Wheel, Dart, Frueharf, Trailer Co. of America) or 10 Ton Pontoon (Frueharf) type with single axle and carried flat bottomed boats or bridge-building elements. They were hitched to Mack NJU 1 or Autocar U 8144 T tractors of the 5-6 ton class. They were both equipped behind the cab with a compartment with folding-down metal spar sides making transportation possible of the tackle, cordage and equipment material used for assembling the bridge.

Right: American troops entered Manila on February 4th, 1945. The town was only completely liberated following nineteen days of bitter fighting. The engineers, using bulldozers, shovel cranes and tipper lorries, clear the city. The vehicle in the foreground is a Diamond-T model 972, fitted with a ring mounting for a 12.7 mm machine gun. The shovel is a Bucyrus-Erie.

The US Engineers clear the ruins of the town of Saarlauten in Germany, conquered by the troops of the Third Army. The tipper lorry is a GMC CCKW 353.

Above: For big projects like the Alaska highway or the work of equipment of the Panama Canal, the engineers acquired in large numbers civil vehicles like this Ford, 1½ Ton, 1942 model, converted into four-wheel drive by Marmon-Herrington. These vehicles were used both by military units and by civil companies working under contract for the Ministry of Defence or the Civilian Conservation Corps, a civilian formation under military administration with the job of maintenance and reafforestation of the US Army's vast training camps and all its real estate property.

Couse workshop lorry on Ford 29 W of the French army, photographed in 1950.

Workshop lorry on Ford 4 x 2 chassis, Model 29 W, with Couse equipment, in service with the aviation engineers battalion.

Engineers' workshop lorry on GMC, 6 x 6, 2½ Ton chassis.

Engineers' workshop lorry on Studebaker, 6 x 6, 2½ Ton chassis.

A Sullivan air compressor on Ford 09W, 1½ Ton chassis, with Marmon-Herrington conversion.

The US Army received 537 GMC AFK 353s equipped with a LeRoi compressor.

Totals of 2,711 Autocars, of which 1,431 were delivered on February 1st, 1943, and 700 Macks were purchased. Only the Autocar was retained after the war. It was 'Standard' in 1953.

The tractors were also built without the load compartment behind the cab (Mack NJU 2 and Autocar U 7144 T) for towing tanker or transport semi-trailers. They then moved into the 4-5 Ton class. In practice, especially after going into the field repair parks, a certain mixing of these vehicles, whose performance in towing was identical, existed. This led to the engineers receiving 4-5 Ton tractors and other branches of the army or services receiving 5-6 Tonners.

4 x 4, 5-6 Ton Bridging Tractor		
Model	Autocar U 8144 T	Mack NJU 1
Length (metres)	6.27	6.10
Width (metres)	2.47	2.48
Height with cab (metres)	2.80	2.87
with canvas top (metres)	2.91	–
Wheelbase (metres)	4.15	3.76
Weight Empty (kg)	7,530	7,525
Ground Clearance (cm)	27	23
Fording (cm)	61	55
Climbing Gradient with trailer (%)	30	25
Angle of Approach (°)	32.5	33
Angle of Departure (°)	54	50 +
Speed (km/hr)	80	74
at Regulation rpm	2,400	2,400
Fuel Consumption on road (litres/100 kilometres)	90.5	78.5
Engine Make	Hercules	Mack
Model	RXC	En 532
Capacity (cc)	8,700	8,700
Cylinders	6, in-line	6, in-line
Fuel	petrol	petrol
Ignition	6-Volt battery	6-Volt battery
Tyres	12.00 x 20 rear twinned	12.00 x 20 rear twinned
Brakes	Pneumatic	Pneumatic
Winch	9,000-kg	6,800-kg

An elementary US 1940 25/40 Ton bridge unit was composed of twelve 25 Ton Pontoon semi-trailers, two of trestles and two of abutment loads, all towed by 4 x 4, 5-6 Tonners, a Quickway crane for manhandling boats and two Caterpillar D7 or R7 dozer-blade caterpillar tractors for work on the banks.

A 10 Ton bridge in the same condition necessitated six 10 Ton Pontoon semi-trailers with their 4 x 4, 5-6 Ton tractors, and four Diamond-T (long chassis, metal body) 6 x 6, 4 Tonners towing trailers for the abutment

Air compressor on Studebaker, 6 x 6, 2½ Ton chassis. This drawing figures in the 1952 edition of the Manual of engineers' vehicles of the Angers school, although there is no knowledge of a LeRoi compressor actually being mounted on a Studebaker.

Companion of the 'Asphalt Distributor', the water tanker with motor pump and folding bars at the rear, permitted the spraying of roads under construction. This vehicle was also used as a supply vehicle by the fire services of the US Air Forces, notably in Korea.

elements and the trestles.

Although designed for the transport of field bridge elements (Pontoon Truck), the Diamond-T 970 or 970A was in general use and put into service in other branches of the US Army. Its metal body was very resistant.

On June 30th, 1945, the engineers included 15 Heavy Pontoon Battalions and 44 Light Pontoon Companies.

Truck 6 x 6, 6 Ton — bridge erection

The bridge building lorries were derivatives of those of the 6 x 6, 6 Ton class and were used by the engineers for the handling, loading, unloading and assembly of bridge elements USDB M1 or Treadway M2 for armoured divisions. They were fitted with a lifting device comprising a double-jib hydraulic gantry fixed to the rear of the body. This gantry, capable of lifting 3,600 kg, was operated by hydraulic rams actuated from the power take-off on the gearbox, moving in an arc of a circle of about 150° in the vertical plane. Operation was controlled from a platform situated on the left-hand side at the back of the driver's cab. The body, which was all steel, was designed for carrying pneumatic floats and metal spans. A double drum winch, made by Heil or Gar Wood, with a capacity of 11,340 kg, was mounted at the front of the vehicle. This winch was also used for Quickway crane chassis and some fuel tankers.

In addition, each truck was fitted with a 700 litres/minute auxiliary air compressor and tubing for inflating the floats. The gearbox and transfer box used the same ratios as those adopted by Corbitt, whose reduction ratio was higher than on the Whites. The tyres had a larger radius under load and were therefore 12.00 x 20. They were powered by a Hercules type HX engine, the larger capacity D version. The wheelbase was lengthened.

The bridge building lorries were designed and built by Brockway from April 1st 1942 to March 9th 1944

GMC CCKW 353 with 3,000 litres/minute, LeRoi air compressor, characterised by its short chimney.

First model of asphalt distributor with 800-gallon (3,058 litres) tank equipped by Roscoe Manufacturing Co.

Asphalt Distributor an 800-gallon asphalt tanker permitting the spread of the binding agent. These vehicles were among the last Diamond-T 6 x 6, 4 Tonners to remain in service in the USA, since they were still, in 1958, on the inventory of the US Air Force to which they had been allocated after the war.

GMC CCKW 353 equipped with a special cartographic reproduction workshop body.

(Model B 666), totalling 166 units. Identical vehicles were then produced from 1943 by White (1,152), Ward LaFrance (589) and finally FWD (168) who only joined the programme in 1945.

A US Army bridging company had an establishment of thirty-six bridge building lorries, sixteen GMC 2½ Tonners with 1 Ton trailer, four GMCs with LeRoi compressor, one Quickway crane and two GMCs each towing a 19-foot launch.

There followed a 4 x 4 of the 5-6 Ton class built by FWD on a long chassis with forward cab (model YU), which included a winch at the front and a removable hoist at the back, for launching bridge building elements, an operator's station behind the cab on the right and, on some, the possibility, via a gantry, of taking the cable of the front winch to the rear, above the cab.

The FWD developed in summer 1941 proved slow, taking minutes to fit the hoist, and fifteen minutes for the handling of a single element. Following the Carolina manoeuvres in 1941, it was decided to use a twin-beam system capable of lifting the two elements of the bridge at the same time, which reduced the whole operation to one or two minutes.

The Bridge Erection Trucks permitted mechanisation and acceleration of bridge building operations, already greatly facilitated by the 'Meccano' principle of the different elements, and were responsible for spectacular results such as the positioning of a Class 60 road bridge over the Rhine in ninety-six hours. Each bridge building lorry made it possible to build 7.30 m of bridge in forty-five minutes (M2 Treadway).

At the end of June 1945, the US Army had thirty-three Treadway Bridge Companies.

Map reproduction and printing installation on Diamond-T long chassis, Model 970 A.

This drill manufactured by Highway Trailer Co., mounted on a GMC 2½ Ton chassis, was used by the US Army Engineers for putting in posts or drilling work.

4 x 4, 5/6 Ton, Pontoon Tractor, used here for towing semi-trailers carrying vehicles of the US Army engineers (1958).

This convoy is waiting on the banks of the Rhine near Remagen on March 7th, 1945. In ninety-six hours of uninterrupted work, the engineers of the US First Army would build a pontoon bridge. The Autocar tractors are in their classic Engineers-bridge building semi-trailer configuration, characterised by the load compartment with folding spars.

A total of 692 of the Mack 4 x 4, 5/6 Ton tractor, models NJU 1 and NJU 2, was built. This one belonged to the 87th Engineers Battalion.

This FWD 4 x 4, 6 Ton truck, model YU, was used by the US Corps of Engineers in 1941-42 for the transport and installation of bridges. The Jeep is a Ford GP which belongs to the 17th Engineers Battalion.

A Brockway B 666 of the French engineers using the M2-USDB bridge on Treadway pontoons, in the construction of which it has just participated in 1953.

The 6 x 6, 6 Ton truck, Model B 666, intended for transporting Treadway M2 bridge elements, was built by Brockway (1,166 vehicles), White (1,152), Ward LaFrance (589) and FWD (168).

Towards the end of hostilities new models of bridge had come into service. To permit the crossing of Pershing and then Patton tanks, a vehicle of reinforced capacities was built. It was based on the Ward LaFrance B666. Essentially the track of the tandem rear wheels was increased to 2.05 metres from the 1.89 metres of the basic chassis and the suspension and axle load capacity were reinforced. They were distributed to the NATO Allies in 1951-52.

After the war, GMC CCKW 353 chassis were converted to tractors for semi-trailers by Oneida for towing elements of the M4 bridge.

Below left: Brockway B 666 of the 994th Engineers Battalion, First Army.

B666 and Modified B666 6 x 6, 6 Ton Bridge-Laying Truck		
	B666	Modified B666
Length (metres)	9.47	9.55
Width (metres)	2.59	2.90
Height (metres)	2.74	3.22
Wheelbase (metres)	5.60	5.59
Weight Empty (kg)	12,000	13,860
All Up Weight (kg)	17,443	20,000
Ground Clearance (cm)	28	26
Fording (cm)	140	–
Climbing Gradient (%)	37	–
Angle of Approach (°)	28	–
Angle of Departure (°)	40	–
Speed (km/hr)	58	–
at Regulation rpm	2,500	–
Fuel Consumption on road (litres/100 kilometres)	117	–
Engine Make	Hercules	Hercules
Model	HXD-6	HXD-6
Capacity (cc)	14,000	14,000
Cylinders	6, in-line	6, in-line
Fuel	petrol	petrol
Ignition	two 6-Volt batteries	two 6-Volt batteries
Tyres	12.00 x 20	14.00 x 20
Brakes	Air	Air
Bridge	Treadway M2	Widened US Class 60 Treadway M2

Oil Field Body equipment on a Diamond-T chassis. This equipment was a 7-ton winch behind the cab, a cab protector, a removable hoist and a steel platform with loading roll. Note the single mounting of 900 x 20 tyres. The same type of body was also put on a GMC chassis in the 2½ Ton class, called Truck 6 x 6, 2½ Ton, Pipe-Line Equipment.

The US Army Engineers used a number of long wheelbase Diamond-Ts equipped with an Eidel Manufacturing Co. body, to transport pipeline pipes, tree trunks and, as a general rule, long loads. The equipment consisted of a removable hoist, a set of cab protectors, a 7-ton rear winch, a hitching pivot and a sling type trailer or semi-trailer with adjustable towbar.

Construction of a railway bridge over the Rhine in March and April 1945. Railway elements are transported by a Diamond-T tractor with sling trailer.

Left: Caterpillar D4 tractor with Le Tourneau C4 dozer blade. The driver's compartment is partly protected by a makeshift armour.

Armoured Caterpillar D7 tractor. Its use was common in Normandy and in the Pacific. The British developed their own model.

The M1 bulldozer was created by mounting a dozer blade designed by La Plante Choate Manufacturing Co. on the Sherman M4 tank.

Sherman equipped with a minesweeping system (Flail Tank) in the streets of Arnhem, during the fighting to liberate the town, April 14th, 1945.

An ACKWX 353 (registered 'W 60455') fitted with a body for water purification, photographed in 1939. An equipment of the same capacity (Wallace and Tierman) was mounted on the CCKW 353.

Searchlight carriers

Searchlights were classified among priority *matériel* and, although the responsibility of the engineers, were especially employed to find aeroplanes in flight by the coast artillery, which was responsible for the fixed anti-aircraft batteries. Although before the war the firm of Sperry Gyroscope Co. was the only one to build this type of *matériel* and, worse still, there only existed in the whole of the United States the Bart Laboratories which had mastered the technique of metal parabolic mirrors, the US Army engineers managed from 1938, by devoting to it a large part of their small budget, to initiate the production of field searchlights which was very satisfactory in quantity and quality. This fine success, which contrasted with the delays in providing earth-moving vehicles or bridges, was, alas, negated when, from the end of 1942, it was clear that searchlights no longer interested the gunners who, henceforth, believed in nothing but Radar.

In 1939, the US Army purchased a series of searchlight carrying trucks from Federal (Model 75 K 131), GMC (AFWX 354 10-A, 149 in number) and Mack (Model NB 1). All were equipped with a generator to supply their Sperry searchlights. The NB 1 had a 77 hp 6-cylinder Continental engine and a double cab with four doors, while the Federal and the GMC had deepened three-door cabs. Notice the height of the tarpaulin hoops. Derived from the civil type EEU, 368 NB 1s were purchased.

It had always been necessary to use specially-equipped trucks which had an electricity supply unit or generator for the electric current and ramp loading and haulage systems for transporting and putting the searchlights into operation.

In 1939, 149 GMC AFWX 354s, 368 Mack NB 1s and some Federal K131s were ordered. They all had a spar-sided platform with a very high tarpaulin on hoops to accommodate the searchlight which was very bulky on its wheels. They had a double cab with three doors, except the Mack which had four. All the chassis were 6 x 4s with semi-forward cab, scarcely derived from the civil models.

The GMC had also been ordered by France, but with a more powerful engine than the 91 hp unit powering the American model.

Finally, all this *matériel* remained in the United States and hardly participated in operations. The searchlights were sometimes used for lighting up battlefields and were only employed in their primary role in the Philippines and, in the first months of the war, in the Pacific.

GMC AFWX 354 chassis, with Hercules metal body.

The Quickway crane, Model E55, on a Coleman 4 x 4, 4 Ton chassis, Model G55A, was one of the lifting vehicles most widely used by the US engineers. The different elements that could be fitted (bucket, reverse, ram, drag, trenching equipment for cables) were transported in a Timpte trailer, Model QW-18 (Morocco, 1943).

Mobile cranes

Although this type of equipment has been used since the 1920s, it was to a great extent due to the use that America made of them during the war that mobile cranes have come to be in general use today. In view of the mechanisation of the engineers, the enormous amount of supplies to be handled, the work to be undertaken and the unprecedented logistic operations, such vehicles would soon prove to be indispensable.

The most commonly used was a cable type mechanical crane with trellis jib, built by Quickway, either on a Coleman chassis or on a C666 6 x 6, 6 Ton chassis. It was powered by a petrol-driven 4-cylinder 35 hp International engine. Very flexible in employment, the Model E 55 could be fitted with different equipment—grab bucket, prop equipment, dragline bucket, stamping ram, hook—which were all transported on a Timpte QW 18 two-wheeled platform trailer weighing 10,650 kg loaded.

The crane was mounted level with the rear driving axle, with its cab projecting a long way over the chassis. It could lift 5 tons to 3 metres on rams and half of this load to 7.50 m. Its capacity as a shovel and as a grab bucket in soft earth was 30 and 15 cubic metres an hour respectively.

The Coleman G 55 A chassis with two driving axles was powered by a petrol-driven 125 hp Buda and had a five-speed gearbox. The very large front winch had a capacity of 5,400 kg on the first wire. The spare wheel was placed on the right, alongside the bonnet, a 'trade mark' of Coleman. The 6 x 6, 6 Ton chassis was that of the bridge building lorry. The cab was modified in such a way that the crane jib rested on the right half while the left-hand part was occupied by the vehicle's driver's compartment. A certain number of 6 x 6, 6 Tonners received, in the 50s, GS Good 200 5-Ton cable type cranes with trellis jib instead of their Quickways.

The standard class of power over 9/10 Ton was a Thew Showel-Lorain. The engine was a petrol-driven 6-cylinder Hercules HXC of 180 hp with a two-speed transfer box and a chassis with three driving axles and with forward cab specially designed for this use.

The Lorain cable crane was powered by a petrol-driven 70 hp 6-cylinder Waukesha. The vehicle could tow a two-wheeled trailer (Clamshell Trailer MK 16)

The Quickway E55 was also mounted on the Brockway 6 x 6, 6 Ton chassis, Model 666.

The Lorrain MC 6 x 6 M2 mobile crane. The crane was powered by a Waukesha MZR 6-cylinder engine developing 70 hp.

Mobile Crane: Quickway Model E 55 On Coleman Model G55A 4 x 4, 4 Ton Chassis	
Length (metres)	10.363
Width (metres)	2.428
Height (metres)	3.251
Wheelbase (metres)	3.734
All Up Weight (kg)	11,415
Speed (km/hr)	85
Range (kilometres)	400
Engine, Vehicle	
Manufacturer	Buda
Model	LO 525
Cylinders	6, in-line
Capacity (cc)	8,556
Output (horsepower)	125
Engine, Crane	
Manufacturer	International
Model	U 9
Cylinders	4, in-line
Capacity (cc)	5,482
Output (horsepower)	35

specially adapted for the transport of a grab bucket.

This type of crane was also very often used for the positioning and assembly of 240 mm and 8 inch heavy artillery guns transported on two vehicles.

Other models of the same power were built by Bay City and by Michigan (Type TMCR 16), the latter intended for the Air Corps, on a Biedermann P1 chassis, a derivative of the F1 tractor for semi-trailer with single-seat driver's compartment offset to the right.

Finally, a certain number of cranes of this class (Lorain MC 3, Bay City T 50) were mounted on special 6 x 4 chassis.

Compressors

These vehicles were intended to provide the compressed air supply for operating pneumatic tools and for the inflation of inflatable boats. They were mounted either on a trailer or on a motor vehicle chassis.

In 1940, the engineers received 1,500 litres/minute compressors on Ford 09 W/Marmon-Herrington chassis (Sullivan compressor). In 1940-41 they ordered the GMC AFKX 352, 4 x 4 (819 LeRoi compressors and one Ingersoll-Rand for testing). The essential part of the equipment was, however, the LeRoi type 318s (3,000 litres/minute—short gas exhaust chimney) or D71s (6,000 litres/minute—long gas exhaust chimney) mounted on a GMC CCKW 353 chassis (weight 6,485 kg). A total of 4,035 vehicles was delivered in 1944 and 1945. The tool chests permitted the transport of very large *matériel*: pneumatic concrete breaker, drill, shovel-spade, and wood drill, chain and rotary saws, and pneumatic drill.

The output of the D 318's only permitted the supply of the two work stations for the shovel-spade, the wood drill and the pneumatic drill, for the others consumed per unit more than 2000 litres/minute. That is why, at the end of production, the D 71 compressor, supplying double the output, replaced the D 318, thus making it possible to supply two tools at the same time, whatever the type.

A notice about the mechanical appliances of the US Army engineers, published in 1952 by the school of the engineers at Angers, contained a line drawing representing a LeRoi D 318 compressor on a Studebaker US-6 chassis, although this mounting does not seem to have actually been produced.

After the war, only the CCKW 353 chassis was retained, although the Ford-Sullivan was still 'Limited Standard' in the 1947 edition of *TM 9-2800*.

Drills

The first models were acquired on Ford and Marmon-Herrington chassis, makes which the land forces were quite faithful to before the war. The *matériel* adopted by the Signal Corps on a Chevrolet chassis, standardised in 1942, was also adopted by the Engineers under the designation of Earth Auger 4 x 4, 1½ Ton, M1.

Certain heavy drills were mounted on CCKW 353s or Diamond-T 6 x 6, 4 Tonners taken from the stocks of bare chassis to be specially equipped. Regularly included in the purchase contracts, this allowed special demands to be met without having recourse to non-Standard chassis.

At the end of the war, the Continental autonomous motor drill, built by Highway, was standardised (Auger, Earth, Skid Mounted, Gasoline Engine Driven) and mounted, using a supporting frame, without any other modification directly in the cargo body of a CCKW 353. The metal mast of the drill rested in the travelling position on the cowling of the auxiliary motor. The same drill could also be fixed on a Caterpillar D7 tractor and was then powered by the tractor engine. A total of 343 Highway drills for GMCs was supplied in 1944 and 1945.

Dump trucks

The US Army's Engineers were very far from being the only user of them since the Ordnance procured some for nearly all the services or branches of the US Army, because this equipment was widely used for the service of camps, maintenance and the transportation of dung or rubbish. According to American practice, tippers were commonly fitted with a tarpaulin and bench seats for the transportation of troops.

In fact, it was principally the GMC and the Diamond-T which went into service in the Engineer Dump Truck Companies, of which the theoretical composition was forty-four $2\frac{1}{2}$ Ton tippers. A GMC tipper which could be dismantled for transport by air was intended for the Airborne Engineer Aviation Battalions.

Ford Marmon-Herrington and Studebaker 6 x 6s, including some with side tipper bodies, were employed in large numbers on the big wartime construction sites in Alaska and Panama, as well as caterpillar trailers with opening bottom or Mack large capacity tipper lorries.

Earth moving vehicles

In this category, the Americans excelled with varied, numerous and high-quality equipment such as no army had ever dreamed of possessing. It is true that the US Army accorded to the Engineers a much more important place than the other belligerents did. It did not mete out men and *matériels*— at least during the war—so parsimoniously as was the general rule, for example, for the Italians or the Germans—except for fortification works, although they had mainly been carried out by the Todt Organisation with conscripted manpower or civil firms.

Of course, it cannot be said that the US Army invented modern mechanised earth moving nor can it be credited with the 'tactical invention' of the caterpillar tractor with blade or bulldozer, since they were already very widely used in the civil sector and from winter 1939-1940 the French army had placed orders with Caterpillar, but it was able, thanks to its methods and the efficiency of its *matériels*, to take military engineering out of the era of strong arms and pick and shovel into that of the motor. However, that was not done without opposition, with the Engineers only abandoning its traditional team of four mules, which until then had pulled the earth moving equipment, after 1938 following tests of Cleveland bulldozers by the 5th Regiment.

From simple earth moving vehicle or road or runway preparer, the bulldozer was going to become a fighting vehicle, because of its extraordinary flexibility of use. In order to permit it to operate under fire—where its operators formed a priority target so efficient was its action in opening up roads, to attack field fortifications, to fill in obstacles or set up firing positions—they armoured summarily (Pacific, Normany landing) first the driver's compartment (1943—report on the New Georgia operations), then the whole vehicle, with more or less efficiency in the degree of protection offered (driver's injuries due to impact against the cabin metal owing to the blast of a mine explosion, etc.).

The main bulldozers were the Caterpillar D7, D4, D6, and R4 (Company of Aviation Engineers) and International Harvester TD9.

The main Caterpillar tractors for towable scrapers or heavy equipment were the International Harvester TD9 W, the Caterpillar D6, D7, D8 and D4. They were transported on vehicle-carrying trailers towed by 6 x 6, 6 Tonners, as a general rule. A total of 28,785 caterpillar tractors was produced, including a certain number of Cleveland light caterpillar tractors.

The cable type trellis jib cranes or mechanical shovels on caterpillars were predominantly Bucyrus-Eries or Lorrains. The scrapers were from Le Tourneau, a future subsidiary of Westinghouse, controlled by a Frenchman.

Map-making, printing, photography

Specialised vans on semi-trailers or mounted on standard chassis were produced to meet mapping, printing and photographic requirements in the field. Mounted on a GMC 2½ Ton chassis was the Map Reproduction Equipment body by Peter Wendel and Son or McCabe Powers Autobody Co. It weighed 6,530 kg to 8,660 kg loaded, according to the machines transported. Mounted on a Diamond-T, 6 x 6, 4 Tonner was the Reproduction Equipment Press Section body. The truck weighed 12,195 kg loaded. It had the same coachbuilders as the Map Reproduction Equipment.

The photographic reproduction, development or printing vehicles on trailers or semi-trailers were operated by the Signal Corps. The trailers or semi-trailers for reproduction of maps or topographical surveys, being of the 10 Ton class, were hitched to 4 x 4, 4/5 Ton tractors.

Transport and treatment of water

It is surprising to learn that it was the Engineers and not the Chemical Corps which put into service the van with Wallace Tierman purification unit on the CCKW 353 (weight loaded 6,950 kg). This *matériel*, being considered camp material, made it possible to purify and render fit for consumption water in the field, but not to treat chemically affected water which was an operation of a different degree of difficulty and would have been the responsibility of the Chemical Corps, which had the job of combating the toxic substances of warfare.

The transport of the water necessary for work sites (sprinkling of roads and runways, concrete compounds, etc.) was either by trailers or semi-trailers or by tankers on GMCs (Columbian 700 US gallons, 2,646 litres, with one compartment or tankers of the same capacity with two compartments fitted directly at GMC. When these vehicles were used for the transport and distribution of drinking water, they then came under the Ordnance.

Diamond-T produced, on its 6 x 6, 4 Ton chassis, a vehicle specifically designed for the distribution and sprinkling of water on work sites (Distributor, Water Truck Mounted—100 gallons (3,700 litres)—Rosco Manufacturing Co. equipment with Wisconsin motor pump unit and bars which could be unfolded at the rear. It had a loaded weight of 11,925 kg. A total of 476 had been produced in 1944 (234) and 1945 (242).

Pipe laying equipment

It was on the pipeline that the whole logistic concept of fuel transport for the US Army rested, a system imposed by the Engineers with the technical assistance of the Shell Oil Co. against the advice of the Quartermaster Corps which, in this sphere as in so many others, was distinguished by its conservatism but which, however, was responsible for supplies. Three special vehicles were therefore created to support the pipe laying sites, directly inspired by those used commercially after they had tried to convert production GMS 2½ Tonners by repositioning their original winches behind the cab to operate a hoist at the rear.

The Oil Field Body, on a CCKW 353 chassis was designated Truck 6 x 6, 2½ Ton, Pipeline Equipment, and was made by McCabe Powers Auto. It had a loaded weight of 7,560 kg. Mounted on a Diamond-T, the second vehicle was designated Truck, Flat Bed 6 x 6, 4 Ton, 'A' Frame (12,285 kg). These permitted the transport of a heavy load (pumping or welding units, etc.) thanks to a reinforced metal platform and their handling by means of a removable hoist ('A' Frame) operated by a winch situated behind the cab. A heavy section tubular structure protected the cab.

The third vehicle, a sling trailer tractor designated Truck-Tractor 6 x 6, 4 Ton, was also based on a long chassis Diamond-T to which was attached a set of twinned wheels with extending towbar, designated Trailer, 4 Wheels, Special Tandem 7/14 Tons, whose function was to transport pipes. The tractor and trailer bodies were by Eidel Manufacturing Co. This tractor was fitted with a swivelling tow saddle, a tubular cab protector and a front winch, and could put into operation a hoist for handling the pipes. At its maximum permissible weight, the combination could reach 27 tons. This unit was also employed for transporting billets of wood, pre-assembled railway sections, etc. Fifty-nine Petroleum Distribution Companies figured in the inventory at the end of hostilities.

Asphalt spreader

It was again the Diamond-T, decidedly much appreciated by the Engineers, which served as a basis for two models of bitumen tankers which transported and heated (Little Ford Bros Manufacturing Co. equipment, Model 101 L, 2,960 litres) or the transport, heating and spreading, by spreader bars through a line of holes. (E.D. Etnyre equipment, 2,960 litres).

Armoured vehicle

In view of their combat missions, the Engineers had to have specialised armoured vehicles for opening up roads, clearing the battlefield and removing natural or artificial obstacles. To do this they used armoured bulldozers, and Sherman tanks with bulldozer blades or with flail type mine exploding equipment (Flail Tank) (1,398 delivered in 1944 on M4, M4 A1, A2 and A3 hulls).

The Sherman with bulldozer blade was one of the most useful vehicles of the war. Yet its usefulness was disputed when it first appeared, since the budget for its development was cut and the Le Tourneau and La Plante-Choate companies, which designed this adaptation, built the prototypes with their own funds, without being paid, for they at least believed in this vehicle.

The engineering squads in the armoured divisions were transported on Half-Tracks.

Workshop trucks

To maintain in an operational state such a large and diversified fleet which, furthermore, by the very nature of its use was rarely employed in contained units but rather scattered among the workshops, the Engineers had built or used three types of workshop trucks. First of all a Dodge chassis, most of the Emergency Field Repair vans were assigned to them. In total, 383 models M1 were built on a WC 41 or WC 20 $\frac{1}{2}$ Ton and 296 of the model M1 on a $\frac{3}{4}$ Ton WC 60, with American Coach and Body Co. body.

Then, a workshop on a GMC or Studebaker 6 x 6, $2\frac{1}{2}$ Ton chassis was produced. It was extremely well equipped, possessing greater flexibility than its equivalent of the Ordnance, taking account of the complexity and variety of the vehicles with which it had to deal. In addition, regulations also envisaged its use as a general purpose mobile field workshop, in some sort the factory in the field.

The body was a metal platform whose sides could be lowered and raised, closed by an all covering tarpaulin with rather complex lacing and installation. For its transport by sea, its technical manual stipulated that the whole body with tarpaulin should be covered with a planked packaging specially manufactured for the purpose—by the truck's own machines. The fittings were provided by Hicks Body, P.A. Thomas, Superior, Krieger Steel Corporation. Four Special Shop Battalions and twenty-seven Heavy Shop Companies had been formed in June 1945.

Also responsible for the Engineer Aviation Battalion created during the summer of 1940, the US Engineers Corps had workshops made, on Ford 4 x 2, $1\frac{1}{2}$ Ton, 29 W chassis, by an American specialist, Couse Laboratories. Characterised by single-bay side panels which were fully removable, these vehicles transported impressive equipment, even allowing for work on aeroplanes.

Two models, A and B, of Shop, Motorized, Aviation Battalion were built. Each vehicle weighed 8,100 kg loaded. The two models differed in size by their length (type A: 5.55 m; type B: 6.05 m) and height (type A: 2.9 m; type B: 3.2 m) and by their use, the type A possessing a welding installation absent from type B. A fixed crane at the end of a short jib was mounted at the rear. It was difficult to stow more equipment in a vehicle of this size than was contained in a Shop, Engineer, Aviation Battalion, which was really full to the brim. They were still 'Limited Standard' in 1947.

Wallace Tierman water purification unit on a CCKW 353.

Table of Specific Vehicles of the US Army Ordnance Department after Redistribution of Responsibilities
Extracted from Technical Manual 9-2800

Designation	Purchase and Maintenance		Storage		
	Service Issuing Order		Complete Vehicle	Spare Part Maintenance	
	Chassis	Body		Chassis	Body
Corps of Engineers					
Trailer, 2-ton tandem axle searchlight	Engr	Engr	Engr	Engr	Engr
Trailer, full, flat bed 8-ton	Engr	Engr	Engr	Ord	Ord
Trailer, full, flat bed 16-ton	Engr	Engr	Engr	Ord	Ord
Trailer, full, low bed, 20-ton	Engr	Engr	Engr	Ord	Ord
Trailer, 2-wheel, utility, pole type, 2 1/2 ton, types I, II, III, IV and V	Engr	Engr	Engr	Ord	Ord
Trailer, platform, low-bed 60-ton	Engr	Engr	Engr	Ord	Ord
Trailer, fire-pumper, 2-wheel, 500 gpm, class 1000	Ord	Ord	Engr	Ord	Ord
Trailer, fire-crash, 2-wheel, high pressure, class 1000	Ord	Engr	Engr	Ord	Ord
Searchlight, 24-inch, complete with power plant, trailer-mounted	Engr	Engr	Engr	Engr	Engr
Welding equipment, electric arc, 300 amp., trailer-mounted	Engr	Engr	Engr	Engr	Engr
Dolly, 2-wheel, dt, ponton	Engr	Engr	Engr	Ord	Ord
Power plant, trailer-mounted, 5 kw	Engr	Engr	Engr	Engr	Engr
Semitrailer, ponton, 10-ton	Engr	Engr	Engr	Ord	Ord
Semitrailer, ponton, 25-ton	Engr	Engr	Engr	Ord	Ord
Semitrailer, flat bed with dolly, 20-ton	Engr	Engr	Engr	Ord	Ord
Tank, water, semitrailer, mounted, 1,500-gallon	Engr	Engr	Engr	Ord	Ord
Reproduction equipment, camera section, 24 × 30, semitrailer mounted, 10-ton, w/van body	Engr	Engr	Engr	Ord	Ord
Reproduction equipment, combination section A, semitrailer mounted, 10-ton, w/van body	Engr	Engr	Engr	Ord	Ord
Reproduction equipment, combination section B, semitrailer mounted, 10-ton, w/van body	Engr	Engr	Engr	Ord	Ord
Reproduction equipment, camera section, 24 × 24, semitrailer mounted, 10-ton, w/van body	Engr	Engr	Engr	Ord	Ord
Reproduction equipment, photographic section, semitrailer mounted, 10-ton, w/van body	Engr	Engr	Engr	Ord	Ord
Reproduction equipment, plate grainer section, semitrailer mounted, 10-ton, w/van body	Engr	Engr	Engr	Ord	Ord
Reproduction equipment, plate process section, semitrailer mounted, 10-ton, w/van body	Engr	Engr	Engr	Ord	Ord
Reproduction equipment, laboratory section, semitrailer mounted, 10-ton, w/van body	Engr	Engr	Engr	Ord	Ord
Reproduction equipment, press section, 20 × 22 1/2 semitrailer mounted, 10-ton, w/van body	Engr	Engr	Engr	Ord	Ord
Reproduction equipment, press section, 22 × 29, semitrailer mounted, 10-ton, w/van body	Engr	Engr	Engr	Ord	Ord
Reproduction equipment, camera section, 24 × 24, semitrailer mounted, 2 1/2-ton, w/van body	Engr	Engr	Engr	Ord	Ord
Reproduction equipment, press section, 17 × 19, semitrailer mounted, 10-ton, w/van body	Engr	Engr	Engr	Ord	Ord
Crane, gasoline, engine driven, truck-mounted, 3/8-cubic yard bucket (chassis 6-ton, 6 × 6)	Ord	Engr	Engr	Ord	Engr
Truck, powered, fire, crash, class 135	Ord	Engr	Engr	Ord	Engr
Truck, 6-ton, 6 × 6, 4b, bridge, construction Brockway	Ord	Engr	Engr	Ord	Engr
Compressor, air, gasoline engine driven, truck-mounted, 105 CFM, 2 1/2-ton, 6 × 6 G.M.C.	Ord	Engr	Engr	Ord	Engr
Auger, earth, gasoline engine powered, motorized M-2, 1 1/2-ton, 4 × 4 Chevrolet	Ord	Engr	Engr	Ord	Engr
Distributor, bituminous, truck-mounted, 800-gallon, 4-ton, 6 × 6 Diamond-T	Ord	Engr	Engr	Ord	Engr
Shop, motorized, general purpose, 2 1/2-ton, 6 × 6 G.M.C.	Ord	Engr	Engr	Ord	Engr
Shop, motorized, emergency repair, 3/4-ton, 4 × 4 Dodge	Ord	Engr	Engr	Ord	Ord
Shop, motorized, electrical repair, 2 1/2-ton, 6 × 6 G.M.C.	Ord	Engr	Engr	Ord	Engr
Shop, motorized, machine shop, light, 2 1/2-ton, 6 × 6 G.M.C.	Ord	Engr	Engr	Ord	Engr
Shop, motorized, machine shop, heavy, 2 1/2-ton, 6 × 6 G.M.C.	Ord	Engr	Engr	Ord	Engr
Shop, motorized, small tool repair, 2 1/2-ton, 6 × 6 G.M.C.	Ord	Engr	Engr	Ord	Engr
Shop, motorized, tool and bench, 2 1/2-ton, 6 × 6 G.M.C.	Ord	Engr	Engr	Ord	Engr
Distributor, water, truck, mounted, 1,000 GM 4-ton, 6 × 6 Diamond	Ord	Engr	Engr	Ord	Engr
Tank, bituminous supply steel, truck-mounted, 800-gallon, 4-ton, 6 × 6 Diamond-T	Ord	Engr	Engr	Ord	Engr
Water purification unit, mobile, 2 1/2-ton, 6 × 6 G.M.C.	Ord	Engr	Engr	Ord	Engr
Reproduction equipment camera section, 24 × 24, 4-ton, 6 × 6, standard truck chassis w/van body G.M.C.	Ord	Engr	Engr	Ord	Engr
Reproduction equipment laboratory section, motorized, 2 1/2-ton, 6 × 6, standard truck chassis, w/van body G.M.C.	Ord	Engr	Engr	Ord	Engr
Reproduction equipment map lay-out section, motorized, 2 1/2-ton, 6 × 6, standard truck chassis w/van body G.M.C.	Ord	Engr	Engr	Ord	Engr
Reproduction equipment photographic section, motorized, 2 1/2-ton, 6 × 6, standard truck chassis w/van body G.M.C.	Ord	Engr	Engr	Ord	Engr
Reproduction equipment, plate grainer section, motorized, 2 1/2-ton, 6 × 6, standard truck chassis, w/van body G.M.C.	Ord	Engr	Engr	Ord	Engr
Reproduction equipment, plate process section, motorized, 2 1/2-ton, 6 × 6, standard truck chassis, w/van body G.M.C.	Ord	Engr	Engr	Ord	Engr
Reproduction equipment, press section, 20 × 22 1/2, motorized, 4-ton, 6 × 6, standard truck chassis, w/van body G.M.C.	Ord	Engr	Engr	Ord	Engr
Reproduction equipment, press section, 20 × 29, motorized, 4-ton, 6 × 6, standard truck chassis, w/van body G.M.C.	Ord	Engr	Engr	Ord	Engr
Reproduction equipment, camera section, 24 × 24, motorized, 2 1/2-ton, 6 × 6, standard truck chassis, w/van body G.M.C.	Ord	Engr	Engr	Ord	Engr
Reproduction equipment, press section, 20 × 22 1/2, motorized, 2 1/2-ton, 6 × 6, standard truck chassis, w/van body G.M.C.	Ord	Engr	Engr	Ord	Engr
Truck, powered, fire pumper, class 500 (500 gpm)	Ord	Engr	Engr	Ord	Engr
Truck, powered, fire pumper, class 525 (500 gpm)	Ord	Engr	Engr	Ord	Engr
Truck, powered, fire pumper, type A, oversea, class 325 G.M.C.	Ord	Engr	Engr	Ord	Engr
Truck, powered, fire, brush, class 300 (300 gpm)	Ord	Engr	Engr	Ord	Engr
Truck, powered, fire, crash, class 110 (Co. 2)	Ord	Engr	Engr	Ord	Engr
Truck, powered, fire, crash, class 125	Ord	Engr	Engr	Ord	Engr
Compressor, air, motorized, chassis 1 1/2-ton to 3-ton, 4 × 4	Ord	Engr	Engr	Ord	Engr
Truck, 2 1/2-ton, 6 × 6 earth auger G.M.C.	Ord	Engr	Engr	Ord	Engr
Truck, 5-6-ton, 4 × 4 tractor ponton	Ord	Engr	Engr	Ord	Ord
Truck, 5-6-ton, 4 × 4 tractor, topographical	Ord	Engr	Engr	Ord	Ord
Truck, powered, fire, class 155, 5-ton, 6 × 6	Ord	Engr	Engr	Ord	Engr
Truck, powered, fire crash, 7 1/2-ton, 6 × 6	Engr	Engr	Engr	Ord	Engr

FIRE FIGHTING VEHICLES

The Americans have always shown themselves very sensitive to problems of fire fighting. That is why, with the Germans, they were the only belligerents to have their armies followed on campaign by large resources assembled within independent formations of firemen coming under the Engineers (cf. *The Dodge, Five Generations of Off-Road Vehicles*). Ninety-two Fire Fighting Platoons existed in June 1945. The Quartermaster also had at his disposal vehicles for the protection of stocks and depots.

The US Army Air Forces, the US Navy, the US marines, the US Coast Guard and in a general manner the many services of the Federal administration had their own resources, either by making available vehicles acquired by the Engineers for the first of these, or by direct purchase for the others. Furthermore, numerous vehicles were supplied to the Allies of the United States, either for their municipal fire brigades, which had the job of protecting the harbours, docks or the entry zones where the Americans unloaded war *matériel* in Australia and Canada, for example, or to equip their military formations (Royal Air Force, French First Army and Air Force, etc.). The different vehicles were identified by the indication of the 'Class' to which they belonged and by the indication of their function.

A large number of vehicles was therefore made, especially when compared with the very low production capacities of the specialised manufacturers. Mack, one of the largest traditional suppliers along with American LaFrance, Maxim, Seagrave and Ward LaFrance, had on its own supplied 854 units of different models according to an inventory of December 31st, 1944, and still had 203 on order.

Engineers vehicles

The Engineers, under the war programme, operated Class 300, 325, 500, 525 and 750 vehicles. The **Class 750** were the most powerful vehicles built by the traditional suppliers of the civil fire brigades. The chassis, in accordance with American custom, were specially designed and manufactured for this use by the equippers: the hydraulic equipment came either from companies specialising in the manufacture of pumps (Hale, Waterhouse, etc.), or were of a model peculiar to the equipper.

They were, but for the paint and the absence of chrome, identical to those in service for the protection of large towns in the United States. Their use

Truck Fire, Class 150, Low Pressure Carbon Dioxide Cardox 9508, on Reo 29 FF chassis, for the US Army Air Forces. The front diffuser and the one mounted above the cab on a turret made it possible to attack an aircraft fire with CO_2 simultaneously at the base of the flames and from above, getting over the obstacles. Two manual hoses, mounted on large reels behind the cab, completed the equipment. These vehicles were the largest CO_2 vehicles made, but their efficiency was rather poor (range limited, rather poor performance of the extinguisher product in the open air on a fuel fire in a pool). Some were also mounted on Reo 27XFS and Mack Nos.

The hundred first Trucks, Fire Crash, Class 155, were mounted on Kenworth chassis identical to that of the M1 recovery vehicle. The equipment came from American LaFrance or Mack. This one is in Morocco in 1947.

by the Engineer units was reserved for the protection of camps and sensitive installations having plentiful water supplies available. Their pump had a nominal delivery of 2,840 litres/minute. The capacity of the tank was 560 litres.

Built on Dodge or Ford road chassis or on Chevrolet 4 x 4s the **Class 525** had the same performance as the Class 500, but a simplified body. They can be considered as 'war fire engines', which were less costly and were easy to build, usable both in the theatres of operations and on installations in the rear areas. The pump was at the front.

Built of a Ford chassis. the **Class 500** fire engine was also quite comparable to civil vehicles. It had the job of protecting installations whose size or water supply did not justify the use of a Class 750. Very robust, built in large numbers, these vehicles remained in service for a very long time. The pump had a delivery of 1,892 litres/minute and the tank a capacity of 560 litres.

Intended to be used where water supply was poor, the **Class 325** vehicles were equipped with a 1,135 litres/minute front pump and a 1,120-litre tank, double the capacity of the other fire engines of the Engineers. The chassis were either Ford, Chevrolet or Dodge road vehicles, or Chevrolet 4 x 4s. Some were used as first intervention vehicles by the US Army Air Corps.

The **Class 300** category of vehicles was specifically for fighting brushwood and forest fires, and was designated Brush Fire Truck. They were built on Chevrolet road or off-road chassis, with a 1,135 litres/minute pump at the front. Working principally at high pressure, their water capacity could be main-

The next series of Fire Crash, Class 155, intended for the protection of airfields, was equipped either by American LaFrance on Ward LaFrance B 666 chassis or by Mack on Brockway C 666. Although identical in appearance, there were quite substantial differences between the Mack equipment (6-cylinder Continental R 602 motor for the pump) pictured above and that of American LaFrance (V-12 motor of its own construction), which equipped the Kenworth of the B 666. In addition, the Mack models carried in front a structure fitted with a ring which was used, in theory, to move parts of a crashed aeroplane during the rescue.

tained at 950 litres, taking account of the efficiency of this procedure which conserves water while increasing its extinguishing power. They received stirrup pumps and 10-litre buckets in large quantity, stowed on the steps, for tackling fires in places unreachable in a vehicle, or for such problems as undergrowth, etc.

To these fire engines must be added the towed motor pump Class 1000 and the fixed motor pump Class 1100 on a frame, both with a delivery of 1,892 litres/minute. The latter was used for fixed installations or for the conversion of platform lorries into fire engines. The towing of the motor pumps (one per section, three sections and a motor pump forming a company) was ensured either by Dodge ¾ Ton or by 1½ Ton lorries.

Overseas fire engine

These vehicles were designed, unlike the preceding ones, to work outside the United States. They had larger-volume water tanks than those of the other Classes, the Americans expecting to operate in countries without hydraulic fire systems and which, in addition, had different systems of hose joints.

The 530, built on a CCKW 353 chassis, was fitted with a large-volume elliptical tank (1,800 litres), under the hose compartment, a very rare case for an American vehicle, equipped more often with a fairly low capacity L-shaped or T-shaped tank.

Comparatively few motor pumps were built, which led the Engineer companies to have GMCs converted by vehicle fleets or to use motor pumps Class 300, 325 and 525 on external theatres of operations.

Auxiliary Vehicles

The decontamination vehicles of the Chemical Warfare Service on GMC chassis could be used, thanks to their 1,200 (M4) or 1,500 (M3 A1) water tanks and their high pressure pumps (120 litres/minute at 28 bars pressure), as auxiliary fire fighting vehicles, even according to the terms of their particular regulations.

Some vehicles were improvised from platform lorries by the addition of a tank and a Class 1100 Skid Mounted Motor Pump, either because specific equipment was not available or when conditions of use or

Another giant tested for aircraft fires was this semi-trailer unit with American LaFrance 500 tractor. The tank is an F2 fuel tank, converted to transport water and emulsifier. The foam was spread by the water cannon mounted in front of the bonnet and another at the top of the mast. The tractor, with its big V-12 engine, was generally used for towing ladder semi-trailers of the civil fire brigades.

Sterling DDS-235 chassis, with Cardox 9506 CO_2 equipment. The engine was a 210 hp Waukesha. Notice, in front and on the pivoting arm, the two CO_2 diffusers. The US Navy was a faithful customer of Cardox and Sterling.

the resources of the theatre of operations imposed the use of chassis which were not intended to be equipped as fire engines.

Besides the Engineers, vehicles were also acquired by the Ordnance and the Quartermaster Corps.

The US Army Air Forces

The protection of airfields was ensured by specialised vehicles acquired and maintained by the Engineers. The organisation was similar to that of the companies of the Engineers, while still coming under the Air Service Command which was responsible for support of the air bases.

As an extinguishing agent most of the vehicles used water under very high pressure as a mist, with the possibility of a wetting or foaming product being added to it. Light and heavy CO_2 vehicles were also built. The light models were equipped with six to eight 50-kg bottles and two grenade launchers and were used to complement the Class 125 and 135s.

The **Class 125** was a high pressure motor pump, with a piston type pump mounted in the middle of the vehicle (227 litres/minute at 40 bars pressure), on a road chassis. It had a 1,135-litre water tank. In spite of its efficiency, this vehicle was limited by its inability to move over difficult terrain and by its poor extinguishing agent capacity.

The **Class 135** was a high pressure motor pump with centrifugal pump (227 litres/minute or 378 litres/minute according to the types) mounted in front. It too had a 1,135-litre tank. Very widely used, in its version on a Chevrolet 4 x 4 chassis, as a first aid vehicle or as a Crash Fire Truck in fighter and reconnaissance groups.

Faced with a new generation of aeroplanes of high load capacity and long range—B-17, B-29, C-54, etc.—the Army/Air Forces had to have a new generation of powerful vehicles developed, because the vehicles which it had available proved very inadequate. One of the first to be built was the work of American LaFrance which used a Series 500 tractor of its own manufacture with a V12 engine, intended for towing ladder-carrying semi-trailers, hitching to it an F2 tanker semi-trailer intended originally for transport of fuel, containing for this use 7,500 litres of water and emulsifying products.

The tractor was equipped, in front, with a high-delivery hose, making it possible to attack fuel fires in a pool and protect the vehicle. The tank received at its front end a trellis mast which rotated and elevated, equipped with a water cannon, making it

This motor pump ladder carrier of the US Navy, with its chrome and beautiful flowing lines, conforms in all respects with the vehicles which Seagrave supplied to the American fire brigades.

The Pumper Class 325, on Chevrolet G 7133, with the Barton pump at the front and its high pressure installation, was both intended to fight forest fires (Brush Fire Truck) and aircraft fires on the ground. This one was photographed in 1946 in the US Army Air Forces compound at Orly, France. Other models were made with a pump in a central position and were not, in theory, usable on airfields. Notice Popeye's head painted on the door.

possible to attack the fire from above.

The Classes 150, 155, 1010 and 1020 vehicles, built in series, although of much reduced capacity, were, for the time, the best that was made.

The **Class 150** was built by Cardox (type 9503) on a Mack NM3 chassis (type 0-1, March 1942), then in series on a Reo 29FF or 27XFS, 6 x 6, $7\frac{1}{2}$ Ton. It was characterised by the exclusive use of CO_2, more commonly called carbon snow, as extinguishing agent (22,700-litre tank of products in the gaseous phase). The vehicle did not have a pump, the expulsion of the product being effected by release of the CO_2 stored under pressure in the tank. It comprised two manual hoses on large-dimension reels, because of the diameter of the pipes, behind the cab, a high-delivery diffuser swivelling through 180° at the front, in front of the radiator, and another at the end of a swivelling perch mounted on a turret above the cab.

Although this vehicle was technically quite a success, it was tricky to use and of more or less average efficiency, the action of the CO_2 used by the Cardox procedure being limited by its physico-chemical characteristics and its short range obliged the vehicle to attack from near and even from far too near when the damaged aeroplane still had ammunition on board.

The first hundred **Class 155** were built on a Kenworth 572 chassis, the same as that of the Wrecker,

The first model of a vehicle for fighting aircraft fires on the ground, on a Chevrolet chassis, was designed and built directly by the Quartermaster's technical services and therefore does not rate any mention in TM 9-2800 of make of specialised equipment. It bore along the bonnet a plate 'Quartermaster 110'. Its performance was equivalent to that of the Pumper 325 which succeeded it.

Motor pump Class 125 Crash Truck, on International K5.

then on a Brockway or Ward LaFrance 6 x 6, 6 Ton chassis, identical to that of the bridge laying vehicle. The equipment was made, with no distinction between them, by American LaFrance (American LaFrance V12 pump motor) and Mack (Continental pump motor).

The tank contained 3,600 litres of water and 400 litres of foam. Two water cannon were mounted on the tank. The chassis were without winches, although the mounting, behind the bumper, remained. The model equipped by Mack had a steel quadripod fitted with a ring, fixed on the longerons and bumper in front of the radiator, to permit the lifting and towing of aircraft debris.

They were the first vehicles with high-delivery foam to be entered in the inventory of the US Army Air Forces. Very successful, these excellent vehicles remained in US service for more than fifteen years. The first powerful modern vehicles to have been built in series in the world, they had a great influence after the war in France, when the regulations for the protection of airports were being considered.

The **Class 1010 and 1020** two-wheel crash trailers were towed normally, by a Dodge 4 x 4, ¾ Tonner, and were intended for attacking aircraft fires on the ground. The pump was a high pressure piston model on the 1010 (130 litres/minute) or a centrifugal type on the 1020 (300 litres/minute) and the water tank contained 570 litres. Two 30 metre hoses long with high pressure nozzle permitted attacking the fire from both sides.

Very limited in their actions, Crash Trailers were only used for a short time and served rather as fixed equipment for protection of the depots or tented villages on the airfields.

The US Navy and the Marines

The US Navy possessed vast installations which included, unlike the land forces camps where the famous single-storey, wooden dormitories predominated, numerous very high buildings (dirigible hangars, dry docks, hull tracing buildings, etc.). It had

Motor pumps Class 500 on Ford 1942 chassis await delivery to the US Army in front of the porch of the Maxim factory, (1,700 litres/minute Hale centrifugal pump mounted in a central position). On this same chassis there existed, in a short wheelbase version, a Pumper Class 325 with an American Marsch Baryton centrifugal pump mounted in front.

Mack 75 fire engine which although stripped down in the extreme, is basically similar to the vehicles supplied to the civil fire brigades. The Class 750 represented the most powerful vehicles in service with the US Engineers.

acquired vehicles similar to those of the civil fire brigades, since, all in all, it had the same risks and therefore employed ladders, fire tenders, first aid vans (ventilation—respiratory aid, etc.). It continued, during hostilities, to acquire the same type of vehicles, often painted 'battleship grey' and without chrome, bought from the manufacturers with the best reputation like Pirsch, Seagrave and American LaFrance.

For the protection of its airfields (NAS: Naval Air Station), the US Navy had in service either motor foam pumps on 6 x 4 chassis (specific chassis coming from the manufacturers of fire fighting vehicles, White, etc.) or, from 1940, vehicles similar in spirit to those of the US Army Air Forces but on different chassis, such as the Chevrolet NX-G-7153, 4 x 4, with forward cab, or on those of accredited suppliers of the US Navy: Sterling 6 x 6 DDS 235, with Cardox equipment (Type 9506) or International, 4 x 4, $1\frac{1}{2}$ Ton, or 6 x 6.

The US Marines protected their training camp with high pressure motor pumps (Triple Combination, High Pressure, Chemical) on International M3 4, $2\frac{1}{2}$ Tonners, with American LaFrance equipment.

After the war airport vehicles were made in small numbers on International 6 x 6, $2\frac{1}{2}$ Ton chassis, equipped with two water cannon on a platform above the cab.

Left: The US Navy, besides International M3 4, $1\frac{1}{2}$ Tonners, also used on its air stations a certain number of Chevrolet 235s with semi-forward cab converted to 4 x 4s (6-cylinder 93 hp SAE engine). This equipment is that of a classic fire engine (300-gallon, 1,240-litre water tank), complemented by a CO_2 installation. The very long wheelbase (4.44 metres) is very unusual for a vehicle which is called upon to move over rough ground, as well as the spare wheel, which was usually omitted from fire engines.

Mack also produced some on ENF 5 10A chassis. In this case, it received a 100-gallon (380 litres) tank and of course a 750-gallon centrifugal pump in a central position (Mack factory, Allentown, 1942). The famous dog, in spite of war restrictions, still adorns the bonnet, but only for a short time. This photograph illustrates well the modest nature of the fire fighting vehicle production installations at Mack's, who were, however one of the principal American suppliers in this field.

Fire and Rescue Vehicles

Class & Output	Use	Chassis	Equipper	Remarks
125 60 gallons [227 litres]/minute 40 bars	Airport	International K5, Dodge, Ford, 1½ Ton	Mack, Seagrave General Pacific John Bean Mfg. Corp., General Detroit Corp., Ward LaFrance	High pressure and foam equipment. Bean or Hardie Piston pump in middle of chassis. 4 x 2 Chassis. Used by USAAFs.
135 60 gallons [227 litres]/minute	Airport	GMC Ford International 1½ Ton 4 x 2	American LaFrance and Foamite Corp., W.S. Darley Co., Central Fire Corp., General Detroit corp.	46 GMC CC 303 and 14 AC-724 supplied in 1942. High pressure and foam equipment. Pump at front or American Marsh centrifugal pump in middle of chassis. 2 lateral reels. 1 rear reel under the hose compartment used by the USAAF
100 100 gallons [378 litres]/minute 30 bars		Chevrolet 1½ Ton 4 x 4	Oren Fire Apparatus Co., American LaFrance and Foamite Corp., Minnesota Fire Equipment Co., W.S.Darley corp.	Centrifugal pump in front, of Darley type H Champion. High pressure and foam equipment Used by USAAF
150	Airport	Reo 27 x FS Reo 29 FF Mack NM3	Cardox - model 9503 Cardox - model 01	No pump. Heavy vehicle for aircraft fires on the ground. CO$_2$ equipment used by USAAFs. Similar equipment on Sterling for US Navy (9506)
155 325 gallons [1,230 litres]/minute	Airport	Brockway C 666 Ward B 666 Kenworth 572	Mack, American LaFrance and Foamite Corp.	Used by the USAAF. High pressure and foam equipment. Hale centrifugal pump (Mack) and American La France centrifugal pump. Continental R602 (Mack) or V12 American LaFrance motor for the pump. Two water cannon on the tank.
300 300 gallons [1,135 litres]/minute	Brush-wood & building fires	Chevrolet 1½ Ton, 4 x 2 Chevrolet 1½ Ton, 4 x 4	W.S. Darley, Central Fire Truck, American Fire Apparatus Co. Central Fire Truck	Road chassis Two large high pressure reels behind cab. Pump in front meant removing part of radiator grille. 3 CO$_2$ extinguishers at side. Few built. Darley pump of the same type in front. No high pressure reels. Stirrup pumps on sides. Side reels under equipment. Few built. First were built directly by Quartermaster Corps in its workshops.
1000 500 gallons [1,892 litres]/minute	Towable motor pump	Chassis, wheels and axle of the standard 1 Ton trailer	Hale Fire Pump Co., Twin John Deere, Wagon Works	Provided with reel box on each side of motor pump, pump identical to 'class 1100 Skid Mounted Pumping Unit' Hale pump with Dodge T118 motor. Besides this model, classified 'Standard' by engineers, motors pumps of various models were bought in small numbers for all Branches and Services
325 Overseas 300 gallons [1,135 litres]/minute	Motor pump	Ford or Chevrolet 1½ Ton	American LaFrance	American LaFrance pump in the middle of the chassis (Ford) or in front. Intended for American military establishments outside USA, pre-1942. Tanks 1135 litres of water
530 Overseas 500 gallons [1,832] litres/minute	Motor pump	GMC CCKW 353	General Detroit Co.	General purpose vehicle, for Engineers, including petroleum product fires, for troops outside USA Contrary to American usage, elliptical tank under hose compartment. Reels behind cab, pump in middle of chassis. Single mounted tyres at rear. 6 men. Few of this model built.
325 300 gallons [1,135 litres]/minute	Motor pump	Ford, Dodge, Chevrolet 1½ Ton, 4 x 2 Chevrolet 1½ Ton, 4 x 4	W.S. Darley, Approved Fire Equipment, Boyer Fire apparatus, Maxim Motors, Hahn Motor Truck Co., American Fire Apparatus W.S.Darley, Maxim Motors, General Detroit Corp.	Road chassis. American Marsh centrifugal pump at front. Body identical to Class 300 Chevrolet 4 x 4 equipped by Central Fire Truck. Equipment by best known makers. Identical but on off-road chassis
500 500 gallons [1,892 litres]/minute	Motor pump	Ford (1941 or 1942) or Chevrolet 1½ Ton.	American LaFrance and Foamite Corp., Seagrave Corp., Peter Pirsch Corp. Maxim Motors Buffalo Fire Appliance, Oren Fire Apparatus Ward LaFrance Corp., General Fire Truck, Howe Fire Apparatus, Boyer Fire Apparatus, Mack Minnesota Fire Equipment, American Fire Apparatus	4 x 2 chassis Most widely used of Engineers' motor pumps. Hale G 55 centrifugal pump in middle of chassis. 2 men in cab, 4 standing at rear on platform. Identical to vehicle in service in civil brigades.
525 500 gallons [1,892 litres]/minute	Motor pump	Dodge, Ford (1942) 1½ Ton 4 x 2 Chevrolet 1½ ton 4 x 4	Boyer Fire Apparatus, Oren Fire Apparatus, Hahn Motor Trucks Corp., W.S. Darley Corp. Oren	4 x 2 chassis. Body simplified in relation to Type 500. American Marsh centrifugal pump at front Same equipment on Chevrolet 4 x 4
750 750 gallons [2,840 litres]/minute	Motor pump built by	Special chassis equippers	Seagrave, Maxim Buffalo Fire Appliance, Peter Pirsch Co., American LaFrance and Foamite Corp.	Road chassis. Most powerful of Engineers' motor pumps. rarely used outside USA. Body and equipment identical to civil models. Hale centrifugal pump mid-chassis or Waterous, American LaFrance, etc. CO$_2$ installation on some models.
750 750 gallons [2,840 litres]/minute	Motor pump power.	Mack EN 510 2½ Ton	Mack	Hale pump mid-chassis. Mack's commercial model. Engine of 5 Ton chassis to give more

195

The Pfischerer brewery of Sickenheim was converted into an aid centre by the 1208th Fire Fighting Platoon of the US Engineers to protect the Continental Advance Section, Communications Zone, Headquarters, which occupied the whole town. The CCKW 353 corresponds, as far as its use is concerned, to the Class 500 GPM Overseas, but is not identical to it. A certain number of GMCs were also converted in the army depots to fire fighting vehicles.

One of the motor pumps bought for the programme of protection of American towns against dangers from air raids, a peril which, although hypothetical, was nevertheless taken very seriously from 1940 to mid-42. This one has its reels under tarpaulins and its own water cannon which can be supplied with water without being taken down (900 gallons/minute). Some parts, like wheels, and mudguards, came from surplus stocks of the civil manufacturers of Chrysler who assembled the vehicle in their factory of Jefferson-Kercheval. Others were mounted on skids. Some thirty-four thousand Chrysler motors were used by different manufacturers of motor fire pumps. Owing to the absence of any danger of bombing, a large proportion of these motor pumps was allocated to different services including the US Coastguard to equip 'makeshift' fire-fighting vessels.

Chrysler also built smoke screen emitters and alarm sirens for the American passive defence programme. The US Navy used some of the sirens which had been issued to it for fog dispersal tests in England (use of high frequencies, 170 decibels, to convert 'water aerosol' into rain).

SIGNAL CORPS VEHICLES

Chevrolet 4 x 2, ½ Ton, light vehicle for installation and maintenance of telephone lines K50.

Diamond-T Model 614, 4 x 2, 2½ Ton, vehicle for laying and maintaining telephone lines. The technical body was built by McCabe Powers Autobody Co. of Saint Louis, Missouri. This vehicle, powered by a 6-cylinder 86 hp Hercules JXD engine, had a weight in running order of 6,897 kg.

Right: GMC CF 351, equipped with a radio body built by Hicks. A total of 364 was produced (registrations W 607386 to 607640 and 6010711 to 6010819).

The Signal Corps was responsible for transmissions in the widest sense of the term, from administrative telephone lines to Radar, from pigeons (PG 45 trailer, 1 Ton, Pigeon Loft) to the battlefield radio network, or even for the mine detectors, the famous 'frying pans' and for the testing and supply of *matériels,* for their transport and implementation, except for ground-air-ground links of the Army Air Forces. In addition, it controlled most of the photographing for the US Army and the processing of films and prints, but received its vehicles in this case from the Engineers or from the US Army Air Forces and only possessed as its own a single specialised trailer (K45, 1½ Ton, Two Wheels, Photographic).

At first equipped with semi-mobile equipment on trailers or semi-trailers, the Signal Corps had to follow the movement, and mechanise. All the specific vehicles received a special nomenclature number preceded by the letter K for the vehicles and the letters DSC (Signal Corps) for transmission *matériel* and Radar. The equipment and vehicles were spread over several uses, the automobile chassis coming from models and types selected and supplied by the Ordnance.

Line laying

This mission was carried out in the field by Chevrolet 1½ Tonners, with either a drill or a line laying van body, which replaced a few Ford E5 4 (Model 39) or 0-18 T (Model 1940) chassis converted to 4 x 4s by Marmon-Herrington. Two types of bodies and layout were used for the K44 drill, either a simple

Dodge Model WC 59, intended for maintenance of telephone lines.

Dodge 4 x 4 ¾ Ton, of the Swiss army, Model SE 408, built on the basis of the Command Car WC 58.

platform with high metal spars, of rectangular form, with the petrol tank placed between the cab and the body (symbol YC), or with rounded metal spars at the rear with the body and cab side by side (symbol NR). The drill was fitted at the head of the boom with a pulley for handling posts for their installation and removal. A hundred 4 x 4 GMC chassis (thirty-two CCK 353 in 1940 and sixty-eight ACK 353 in 1941) with Buda drill had previously been acquired.

Its companion was the K42 Telephone Maintenance workshop lorry, with the job of installing and repairing field telephone lines.

When the body installations enabled it to transport a dismantable metal hoist, it became the K43—Telephone Maintenance and Pole Setter. The hoist was mounted at the rear of the vehicle and actuated by a mechanical winch.

In the transport configuration, it was attached along the body, partially protected by a locker, and projected considerably at the rear. In addition, it prevented the driver from operating his door. Several models of line laying vans existed, distinguished by a symbol.

The Chevrolet 1½ Ton truck, Model G 7105, was used for the transport and putting into operation of SCR 299 radio sets. It is towing a 1 Ton trailer with an electricity generating unit. It is equipped with two extra side lockers for the materiél.

British mobile station of the Army Broadcasting Service, composed of Dodge D60s and a Chevrolet 1½ Tonner (1943).

Predecessor of the Chevrolet drill-carrying vehicles, this Ford Marmon-Herrington went into service with the US Army Signal Corps in 1940.

Chevrolet 1½ Ton, Panel, used by Radiodiffusion Française as a mobile reporting station during the Alsace campaign in 1944.

Signal Corps Designations		
Signal Corps Designation	Symbol	Identification Features
K42	YB	No hoist or winch; body and cab separate; fuel tank between cab and body.
K43	YA	Hoist and mechanical winch; fuel tank between cab and body. Hoist and mechanical winch; fuel tank between cab and body.
K43	NS	Hoist and mechanical winch; fuel tank between cab and body; body close-up on the cab.

A periscope mounted on the cab enabled the driver, whose view to the rear, even with the door open, was masked by the body, to position the vehicle. This device was, however, not systematically fitted, in particular for the K44 drills, symbol YC, and for some K43s.

The K42, K43 and K44 all had bracing struts at the rear.

Quick repairs of the telephone network were entrusted either to the Dodge ½ Ton WC 43, Telephone Repair (374 produced), or to the ¾ Ton WC 59/K50 (Highway Trailer body, 549 made) recognisable at first glance for its ladder diagonally fixed to the outside of the body, or to the WC 61/K50 B (American Coach body, fifty-eight built in number).

The same functions were carried out for the administrative lines in the training camps or installations in the United States by Chevrolet vans or Diamond-T 614 or Federal 3G road lorries, similar in all respects to those used by the big American private telephone companies and combining the operations of installing the poles (drill) and line pulling and laying.

A total of thirty-two drills on GMC 4 x 4, 1½ Ton chassis, Model CCK 353, were ordered in 1941. In the previous year sixty-eight ACK 353s had been ordered from the firm of Buda.

The first version of the drilling vehicle—Telephone Earth Borer—was fitted with a rectangular-shaped body (symbol YC).

The most widely built version was this one, designated Earth Borer and Pole Setter, type K44, by the Signal Corps and Earth Auger M1 by the Engineers. The basic chassis is that of the Chevrolet NR G 7163. The periscope on the cab roof is used by the driver to position his vehicle correctly and follow the drilling operations.

Radio vehicles

The bulkiness of the majority of radio telephone sets at that time meant that a specially equipped vehicle was needed for any unit at battalion level. This role was at first entrusted to the Command Car (½ Ton VC2; ½ Ton WC8; ¾ Ton WC58) which received a console for the sets behind the front bench seat. This installation was very small and only protected the *matériel* very imperfectly. They did not receive a nomenclature number from the Signal Corps.

The sheet-metal clad vans ½ Ton Dodge WC42 and Chevrolet 1½ Ton (G 7107) were also used, their bodywork being meant basically to offer more volume, better comfort and sufficient protection against the weather. Further, that made it possible to use a chassis without any real use elsewhere, since the Chevrolet was supposed originally to be allocated to the cavalry and the Army Air Forces. The WC42s were all handed over to the British. The Chevrolets received the special designation of the Signal Corps K51 or K70, some being used by the British forces.

The K51/70 towed a 1 Ton Trailer K52/53 equipped with an electric generating unit and could be fitted on its sides with removable lockers or coils of co-axial units. (A K51 modified as a cinema vehicle by a fairground operator was to earn a place in history, since it served as a bait to make the Sicilian bandit Giuliano fall into the trap which cost him his life.)

Putting into service radio communications sets of the new generation, which were less cumbersome, and the improvement in performance made it possible to dispense with this category of vehicle and to provide for almost all these needs using the Jeep.

The higher category (regimental level and above) necessitated the use of much bigger vehicles, either on GMC chassis or on 6 x 6, 6 Ton chassis. The GMC CCKW 353s were fitted with either K60 York Hoover or Hackney Bros bodies (SCR 545 A sets) for artillery observations, or K53 bodies (SC 53 set) for the Army Air Forces. The models K57, 59 and 61 were externally identical, but differed in internal installations. A total of 1,801 had been delivered by the end of 1942.

The 6 x 6, 6 Ton (equipment K56) was fitted with a Superior or P. A. Thomas sheet-metal clad van body containing the SCR 545 A set, the most powerful one of the US Army Air Forces. For the US Army Air Forces, a large-volume metal body, whose four

Chevrolet YB Telephone Maintenance without hoist which can be dismounted.

Chevrolet YA Pole Setter, second version, with fuel tank between the body and the cab, without periscope.

Telephone Maintenance and Pole Setter (NS) without periscope on the cab. Compare in the photograph of the same vehicle, the differences in the lockers along the sides of the body.

Chevrolet G 1707 K51/70 Radio Van 4 x 4. 1½ Ton	
Length (metres)	5.62
Width (metres)	2.20
Height (metres)	2.31
Interior of Body	
Length (metres)	2.86
Width (metres)	1.42
Wheelbase (metres)	3.68
Weight Empty (kg)	3,066
All Up Weight (kg)	4,426
Ground Clearance (cm)	25
Climbing Gradient (%)	65
Angle of Approach (°)	45
Angle of Departure (°)	30
Speed (km/hr)	77
at Regulation rpm	3,100
Fuel Consumption on road with 1 Ton Generator Unit Trailer (litres/100 kilometres)	36
Engine Make	Chevrolet
Model	BV-1001 Up
Capacity (cc)	3,850
Cylinders	6, in-line
Fuel	petrol
Tyres	7.50 x 20 rear twinned
Body	Van; may have two side lockers

side panels could be opened and folded down, was designed by York. It was first fitted in 1941-42 on a GMC forward cab AFKX 804 (4 x 4, 4 Ton, 316 built), then from 1942 to 1944 on an Autocar U 8144 chassis (4 x 4, 5 Ton, 607 produced) derived from the tractor for semi-trailer U 8144 T. These two vehicles, having the same equipment and the same use, were both designated K30/31. The Autocar, taking account of the change in the internal equipment, was designated K62. Some Autocars were used as general transport vans.

Of course, building and fitting out sheet-steel bodies specific to each type of sets was long, costly and demanded a lot of raw materials. Furthermore, the communications equipment was bound to the chassis, while its function led it to remain for a long time in one place which was bad for the chassis, tyres and suspension, and entailed problems of chocking, etc. Therefore the Signal Corps, for its SCR 299 or 399 sets, decided to create movable bodies—shelters—which could be set down made of 'non strategic' materials, which made it possible to convert any 2½ Tonner with a spar-sided platform into a radio truck. This equipment was termed Shelter HQ 17A.

The Signal Corps also used numerous models of trailers or semi-trailers (tractor 4 x 4, 4-5 Ton, K32 or M 425/426), whose transmission or Radar equipment were easily usable in semi-permanent positions.

Transmitters of the US Ninth Army unload a telephone cable reel to be laid under the Rhine from a Duck, in early 1945. The K43 Telephone Construction and Maintenance vehicle had a body adjacent to the cab, while on the K42 the fuel tank was positioned between the two. The body, built by American Coach and Body Co., was arranged as a workshop. The roof panels slid to disengage the position of the dismantlable hoist actuated by a winch mounted in a mid position between the chassis members.

The Chevrolet YX G 7123 and NN G 7123, of which only 598 were built, were used by the Signal Corps under the designations K54 and K33. This one is loaded with its antennae.

6 x 6, 6 Ton Radio Truck Type K56 White 666	
Length (metres)	7.25
Width (metres)	2.44
Height (metres)	3.12
Wheelbase (metres)	4.70
Weight Empty (kg)	10,387
All Up Weight (kg)	15,830
Ground Clearance (cm)	27
Climbing Gradient (%)	55
Angle of Approach (°)	59
Angle of Departure (°)	47
Speed (km/hr)	56
Fuel Consumption on road (litres/100 kilometres)	79
Range (kilometres)	400
Engine Make	Hercules
Model	HXC
Capacity (cc)	12,800
Cylinders	6, in-line
Fuel	petrol
Ignition	two 6-Volt batteries
Tyres	10.00 x 22 rear twinned
Brakes	Air

Right: Transmitters of the 27th Transmissions Construction Company lay a telephone cable in the Mannheim region in April 1945. This CCKW 353 with sheet-metal clad cab is equipped with a ring mounting for a 12.7 mm machine-gun.

Below: GMC CCKW 353 carrying a radio shelter, model HQ 17A, for SCR 999 or 459 sets photographed on the Burma road in February 1945.

4 x 4, 5-6 Ton Truck Technical Van Types K30 and 31/62 Autocar U 8144 with York Hoover Body*		
	K30	K31/62
Length (metres)	7.54	7.60
Width (metres)	2.48	2.50
Height (metres)	3.30	3.29
Wheelbase (metres)	4.15	4.15
Weight Empty (kg)	8,900	8,750
All Up Weight (kg)	12,529	12,379
Ground Clearance (cm)	28	27
Climbing Gradient (%)	65	58
Angle of Approach (°)	56	56
Angle of Departure (°)	18	15
Speed (km/hr)	65	72
at Regulation rpm	2,300	2,300
Fuel Consumption on road (litres/100 kilometres)	94	67
Engine Make	Hercules	Hercules
Model	RXC	RXC
Capacity (cc)	8,700	8,700
Cylinders	6, in-line	6, in-line
Fuel	petrol	petrol
Ignition	two 6-Volt batteries	two 6-Volt batteries
Tyres	12.00 x 20 rear twinned	12.00 x 20 rear twinned
Brakes	Air	Air

Note: Dimensions of body interior vary by model

Special equipment

In this category are vehicles used specifically for power production, for the transport of antennae (semi-trailers K22 and 64, Chevrolet 1½ Ton, forward cab K33, K54), and special units (loud-speaker trailer Streich V 12342 for the Field Chaplain Service, mobile pigeon loft, trailer for cable splicing K38, transport of telegraph poles, cable-unreeling equipment on trailer or 2½ Ton truck Model LC 60, etc).

K60 radio van with York Hoover body. The body was also built by Superior, Wayne, Hackey Brothers and Oneonta Line Corps.

Vehicle with York Hoover body on GMC chassis, 4 x 4, 4 Ton, Model AFKX 804, of which 316 was built in 1941.

Radio van, Type K53, transporting the SC53 set.

Fitted with a body built by York Hoover, this radio vehicle, on an Autocar U 8144 chassis, transported radio equipment of the Army Air Forces; it replaced the GMC AFKX 804. In all, 607 vehicles of this kind was built from 1942 to 1944 with sheet-metal clad cab then canvas roofed one.

Radio vehicle of the US Army Air Forces with a body built by Superior Coach Body for the SCR 545A set. An identical vehicle with P. A. Thomas Car Works body was also built.

Table of Specific Vehicles of the US Army Signal Corps
Extracted from Technical Manual 9-2800

Designation	Purchase and Maintenance Service Issuing Order		Complete Vehicle	Storage Spare Part Maintenance	
	Chassis	Body		Chassis	Body
Signal Corps					
Truck, 1/2-ton, 4 × 2, telephone maintenance	Ord	Sc de to Ord	SC	Ord	Ord
Truck, 1/2-ton, 4 × 4, light maintenance and installation K-50 Dodge	Ord	Sc de to Ord	SC	Ord	Ord
Truck, 3/4-ton, 4 × 4, light maintenance and installation K-50 Dodge	Ord	SC de to Ord	SC	Ord	Ord
Truck, 1 1/2-ton, 4 × 4, K-18	Ord	Sc de to Ord	SC	Ord	Ord
Truck, 1 1/2-ton, 4 × 2, telephone maintenance and construction w/w	Ord	Sc de to Ord	SC	Ord	Ord
Truck, 1 1/2-ton, 4 × 4, combination stake and platform, K-33 Chevrolet	Ord	Ord	SC	Ord	Ord
Truck, 1 1/2-ton, 4 × 4, combination stake and platform, K-54 Chevrolet	Ord	Ord	SC	Ord	Ord
Truck, 1 1/2-ton, 4 × 4, earth borer and pole setter, K-44	Ord	Sc de to Ord	SC	Ord	Ord
Truck, 1 1/2-ton, 4 × 4, panel delivery, K-51 Chevrolet	Ord	Ord	SC	Ord	Ord
Truck, 1 1/2-ton, 4 × 4, panel delivery, K-70 Chevrolet	Ord	Ord	SC	Ord	Ord
Truck, 1 1/2-ton, 4 × 4, telephone construction and maintenance wo/w, K-42 Chevrolet	Ord	SC de to Ord	SC	Ord	Ord
Truck, 1 1/2-ton, 4 × 4, telephone construction and maintenance w/w, K-3 Chevrolet	Ord	SC de to Ord	SC	Ord	Ord
Truck, 2 1/2-ton, 4 × 2, telephone construction	Ord	SC de to Ord	SC	Ord	Ord
Truck, 2 1/2-ton, 6 × 6, van, K-53 G.M.C.	Ord	SC	SC	Ord	Ord
Truck, 2 1/2-ton, 6 × 6, van, K-57 G.M.C.	Ord	SC	SC	Ord	Ord
Truck, 2 1/2-ton, 6 × 6, van, K-59 G.M.C.	Ord	SC	SC	Ord	Ord
Truck, 2 1/2-ton, 6 × 6, van, K-60 G.M.C.	Ord	SC	SC	Ord	Ord
Truck, 2 1/2-ton, 6 × 6, van, K-61 G.M.C.	Ord	SC	SC	Ord	Ord
Trailer, 1/4-ton, 2-wheel, telephone cable splicer, K-38	Ord	Ord	SC	Ord	Ord
Trailer, 1/2-ton, 2-wheel, mobile communication, K-19	Ord	Ord	SC	Ord	Ord
Trailer, 1-ton payload, 2-wheel, house, K-29	SC	SC	SC	Ord	Ord
Trailer, 1-ton payload, 2-wheel, cargo, K-52	Ord	SC de to Ord	SC	Ord	Ord
Trailer, 1-ton payload, 2-wheel, cargo, K-63	Ord	SC de to Ord	SC	Ord	Ord
Trailer, 1-ton payload, 2-wheel, pigeon loft, PG-45	SC	SC	SC	Ord	Ord
Trailer, 1 1/2-ton payload, 2-wheel, photographic, K-45	SC	SC	SC	Ord	Ord
Trailer, 1 1/2-ton payload, 4-wheel, K-65	SC	SC	SC	Ord	Ord
Trailer, 2-ton payload, 2-wheel, telephone construction and pole hauling, K-36	SC de to Ord	SC de to Ord	SC	Ord	Ord
Truck, 4-5 ton, 4 × 4, tractor, K-32 Autocar	Ord	Ord	SC	Ord	Ord
Truck, 4-5 ton, 4 × 4, van, K-30 G.M.C.	Ord	Sc de to Ord	SC	Ord	Ord
Truck, 4-5 ton, 4 × 4, van, K-31 G.M.C.	Ord	SC de to Ord	SC	Ord	Ord
Truck, 5-6 ton, 4 × 4, van, K-30 Autocar	Ord	SC de to Ord	SC	Ord	Ord
Truck, 5-6 ton, 4 × 4, van, K-31 Autocar	Ord	SC de to Ord	SC	Ord	Ord
Truck, 5-6 ton, 4 × 4, van, K-62 Autocar	Ord	SC de to Ord	SC	Ord	Ord
Truck, 6-ton, 6 × 6, van, K-56 White	Ord	SC	SC	Ord	Ord
Trailer, 6-ton gross, 4-wheel, house type, K-35	SC	SC	SC	Ord	Ord
Trailer, 4-ton payload, 2-wheel, antenna mount, K-64	SC	SC	SC	Ord	Ord
Trailer, 4-ton payload, 2-wheel, antenna mount, K-22	SC	SC	SC	Ord	Ord
Trailer, 4-ton payload, 4-wheel, antenna mount, K-28	SC	SC	SC	Ord	Ord
Trailer, 4-ton payload, 4-wheel, K-39	SC	SC	SC	Ord	Ord
Trailer, 4-ton payload, 4-wheel, K-40	SC	SC	SC	Ord	Ord
Trailer, 4-ton payload, 4-wheel, K-41	SC	SC	SC	Ord	Ord
Trailer, 4-ton payload, 4-wheel, K-49	SC	SC	SC	Ord	Ord
Trailer, 4-ton payload, 4-wheel, K-58	SC	SC	SC	Ord	Ord
Trailer, 5-ton payload, 4-wheel, van, K-34	SC	SC	SC	Ord	Ord
Trailer, 5-ton payload, 4-wheel, K-76	SC	SC	SC	Ord	Ord
Trailer, 5-ton payload, 2-wheel, K-37, telephone constuction combination cable hauler	SC de to Ord	SC de to Ord	SC	Ord	Ord
Trailer, 10-ton gross, 4-wheel, antenna mount and operating cab, K-75	SC	SC	SC	Ord	Ord
Trailer, 5-ton payload, 4-wheel, K-77	SC	SC	SC	Ord	Ord
Semitrailer, 1 1/2-ton payload, van, K-55	SC de to Ord	SC de to Ord	SC	Ord	Ord
Semitrailer, 4-ton payload, 2-wheel, antenna mount, K-71	SC	SC	SC	Ord	Ord
Semitrailer, 6-ton gross, 2-wheel, K-67	SC	SC	SC	Ord	Ord
Semitrailer, 7-ton gross, K-72	SC de to Ord	SC de to Ord	SC	Ord	Ord
Semitrailer, 13-ton gross, K-78	SC	SC	SC	Ord	Ord

One of the first improvisations for transporting the wounded during manoeuvres in the United States at the beginning of 1942 (as is evidenced by the old-style helmet worn by the personnel). The Jeep is based on the first model, recognisable by its cubic fuel tank with straight fairings.

MEDICAL SERVICE VEHICLES

The Medical Corps of the US Army was only the user of medical motor vehicles and only had under its responsibility the GMC Truck 2½ Ton, Surgical because of the technical and specific nature of this material. All the other vehicles, in particular ambulance vehicles, were under the responsibility of the Ordnance.

Besides the field medical vehicles (four stretchers or six to eight men seated), whose capacity was in any case less than their European equivalents which were generally designed for six stretchers, the US Army used five other categories of vehicles, Metropolitan, high-capacity, field and front line ambulances, and specialised vehicles and trailers, as discussed below.

Ambulance vehicles known as Metropolitan were intended for rear hospitals. With an estate car body on special production chassis with a long wheelbase (Professional Chassis) LaSalle, Packard 4294-HDA or Cadillac (Henney, Superior equipment), they were a very comfortable vehicle, making it possible to transport a wounded person lying down. It should be noted that hearses existed with the same bodywork and on the same chassis, but of course with different internal equipment. These same vehicles were used by civilian hospitals.

High-capacity ambulance vehicles, produced through adaptation or conversion of standard buses, only permitted the transport of walking wounded because of their small doors, or specialised chassis. Twenty-five units of the Linn Type M 423 had been standardised in 1945. The Linn, thanks to its front-wheel drive, had been fitted with rear doors to permit it to take onboard wounded persons lying down (twelve stretchers).

Field ambulance vehicles permitted the transport of four wounded for the benefit of field units or hospitals. They were built on 1½ Ton Chevrolet or

Truck Surgical, 2½ Ton, the only motor vehicle directly supplied by the Medical Corps.

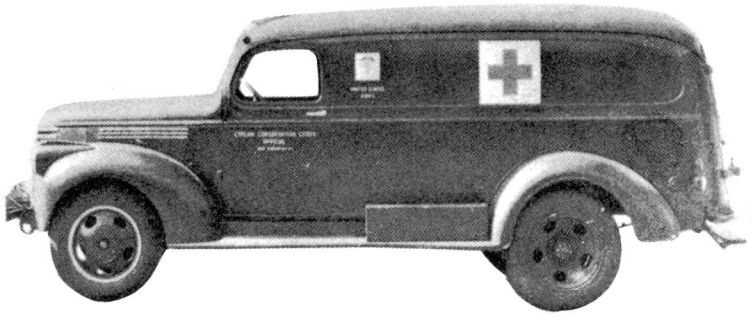

Field Ambulance, Chevrolet 4 x 2, 1½ Ton.

Dodge WC 27, ½ Ton.

Ford road chassis (sectional steel van), or on Dodge ½ Ton or ¾ Ton (WC 27/WC 54) off-road chassis with bodies by Wayne. As their body was of the sectional steel van model, they were quite bulky to transport. For this reason, it was decided to put in to production a model whose volume would be reduced and which, furthermore, could be fitted with a body requiring less steel for its manufacture.

By using wood, compressed oiled cardboard and tarpaulin fabric and other non-strategic materials, a dismantlable structure was created, the T214-WC 64 KD (Knocked Down) intended for former Command Car chassis without any use, reconditioned and lengthened, or Dodge M6s with 37 mm cannon. It was declared standard on March 24th, 1944. The WC 64 was equipped with extra sets of shock absorbers to improve comfort.

In view of the kind of material used to make its body, unsurprisingly, the WC 64 was not renowned for its solidarity. Therefore, after the war, still on the basis of reconstructed Dodge chassis, the Boyertown coachworks manufactured the S7 MA 51 medical vehicle with a body adapted from their production commercial transport van as is shown by the rather unaesthetic join under the windscreen and its sliding side doors.

Front Line Ambulances were just converted Jeeps with two to four stretchers carried across the bonnet or lengthwise on metal tubular structures, a modification that was not envisaged 'back home'.

Finally, the Medical services used specialised vehicles and trailers, such as the dental van on a GMC CCKW 353 or the Linn chassis which, besides its role as heavy medical vehicle, could be converted into an operating theatre or hospital logistic support vehicle.

In principal, only ambulance vehicles should have borne the regulation markings of the Geneva Convention, applied in a permanent fashion on the body (sides, rear, roof). In reality, this usage was very widespread and affected almost all vehicles used by the Medical Corps—flags on a staff, banners fixed on the tarpaulins, red crosses painted in a circle, etc.

Dodge ¾ Ton, WC 54 and 57 MA 51, photographed in Germany in 1960.

Right: *Dodge ¾ Ton, S7 MA 51 photographed in Indochina in 1954. Notice the sliding door and the way in which the front face joins the cowling (Boyertown production body for delivery vehicles envisaged for forward cab or semi-forward cab chassis).*

Dodge ¾ Ton, WC 64 KD.

The Medical service very frequently converted GMC or Dodge tactical cargo vehicles into vans, with makeshift wooden bodies, for it did not have sufficient specialised materials. This vehicle was seen in Italy in 1943.

Packard-Henney medical vehicle, on Professional Chassis 4294 HDA chassis, the acme of comfort at the time.

In the marshy terrain cut by rivers in the north of Europe, the Weasel replaced the Jeep as a front line medical vehicle. This adaptation had formed the object of a series of tests at Aberdeen in 1943. Here, one is seen during the crossing of the Rhine, in 1945.

CHEMICAL WARFARE SERVICE VEHICLES

A 500 Gallon (1,890-litre) chemical product tanker on a CCKW 352 chassis.

The Truck, Chemical Service, 6 x 6, 12½ Ton, model M1, was made with steel or wooden platform.

The Chemical Corps was responsible for studies and employment of chemical warfare products and operations for protecting and decontaminating personnel. For this reason, it had produced specialised handling vehicles, fumigation trailers and decontamination vehicles.

Chemicals could be handled and transported in bulk by, for instance, a 500-US Gallon (1,890-litre) tanker on GMC CCKW 353 chassis. Alternatively, they could be carried in containers or drums by a variety of vehicles, such as the Truck, Chemical Service, M1, platform with low spar sides, equipped with a gantry with cranes on a GMC CCKW 353 chassis.

M3 A1 decontamination apparatus on a GMC CCKW 353 chassis.

Telescopic jib crane lorry, Model M1, on a Diamond-T 4-Ton chassis.

Also used was the Truck Crane, Swinging Boom M1, on Diamond-T 6 x 6, 4 Ton, equipped with a cable type mechanical crane (capacity 2,500 kg to 5.8 metres). This crane was also used on Dodge-Canada 2 Ton D 60 road chassis for the handling of bombs by the Royal Canadian Air Force. The Corps also used the Saginaw three-wheel trailer with (Model M1) or without lifting gantry (M2), which is a derivative of the M5 bomb-carrying trailer. It was used almost exclusively in the depots.

Collective decontamination had been entrusted to a very powerful piece of equipment for the time, built either by John Bean, a renowned high pressure pump specialist, or by AB Farquhar. Each specialised company of the Chemical Warfare Service received twelve Apparatus Decontaminating, Power-Driven M3 A1 or M 4, on CCKW 353 chassis. The M3 A1 equipment of 400 gallons (1,500 litres) comprised a high pressure pump delivering 110 litres/minute at 28 bars pressure, and two manual high pressure nozzles. It was intended for dispersing by atomisation of disinfectants and deadening agents against the effects of chlorine combat gases and used, essentially for that purpose, chloride of lime or hypochlorite. Thirty-four vehicles of this first model were ordered in 1941 on a GMC CCKW X 353 chassis. *TM 3-220* includes a drawing showing the apparatus mounted on a Ford semi-forward cab chassis, converted to 6 x 6 by Marmon-Herrington, a vehicle corresponding to an unrealised pre-war project. The M4 was identical to the M3 A1, but with a tank capacity reduced to 1,200 litres, and was subsequently put into service in limited numbers. The M3 A1 was declared 'Standard' and was the only one retained after the war.

As gas was not employed as a weapon during the Second World War, these vehicles were used in other auxiliary roles incorporated in the technical manual of the material: field showers, since it could produce hot water under pressure; fire fighting; spraying of disinfectants (creosote) on rubble and spraying of anti-parasite products. The M3 A1, like the M4, was originally intended for treating large surfaces and buildings or supplying systems for disinfectant of personnel in series.

These vehicles were subject to breakdowns due to too strong concentrations of the mixture which obstructed the small diameter hoses and pipes and, furthermore, loading and preparation of the product were very long processes—for twenty minutes' of operation—the average time—it was necessary to reckon an hour for loading and the setting.

Table of Specific Vehicles of the US Army Chemical Corps

Extracted from *Technical Manual 9-2800*

TYPE	Purchase and Maintenance		Storage		
	Service Issuing Order		Complete Vehicle	Spares Maintenance	
	Chassis	Body		Chassis	Body
Chemical Warfare Service Truck 1½-3 Ton, 4 x 4 Bus Body (enclosed workshop and small manual pulverisation equipment)	Ord	Ord	CWS	Ord	Ord
Apparatus, Decontaminating, Power-driven, M3 A1 (2½ Ton, 6 x 6)	Ord	CWS	CWS	Ord	CWS
Truck, Chemical Service M1 (2½ Ton, 6 x 6)	Ord	Ord	CWS	Ord	Ord
Truck, Crane Swinging Boom, M-1 (4 Ton, 6 x 6 SWB)	Ord	CWS	CWS	Ord	Ord
Trailer, Chemical Handing, M2, 4 Ton Payload, 4 wheel	CWS	CWS	CWS	Ord	Ord
Trailer, Chemical Service M1 (4 Ton Payload, 4 wheel)	CWS	CWS	CWS	Ord	Ord
Tractor, Crane (wheeled)	CWS	CWS	CWS	Ord	Ord
Truck, 1½-3 Ton, 4 x 4 Bus Body GMC	Ord	Ord	CWS	Ord	Ord

A CCKW 353 with M3 A1 apparatus filling up with water (left).

Chemical product tanker on a CCKW 352 chassis (below).

A Dodge ½ Ton ambulance, a Dodge 1½ Ton, a great rarity in this use and in the Army Air Forces, and a fire fighting vehicle Class 325 on a Ford chassis wait at the end of the runway for the return of the planes from a mission. The inscriptions on the bumpers indicate vehicles belonging to the US Eighth Air Force. The airfield fire fighting companies depended operationally on the Air Service Command, itself divided into Air Service Divisions (5th ASD, 698th and 302nd vehicles TRK 698 and 302).

US ARMY AIR FORCES VEHICLES

Cushman Motor Works goods tricycle, Model 39, used by the Army Air Forces. The single-cylinder 244 cc engine developed 4 hp.

The aviation component of the American armed forces was, during the Second World War, always a branch of the ground forces, but was autonomous enough to benefit from its own hierarchy.

Titled US Army Air Corps until June 1941, and thereafter US Army Air Forces (USAAF), it would only become independent after the war in June 1947, when it became the US Air Force. The USAAF used its own tactical abbreviations, for example:

A.S.C.	Air Service Command
AF or ☆	Air Force
FG	Fighter Group
BG	Bomber Group
FS	Fighter Squadron
T	Transport Squadron
RCN	Reconnaissance Squadron
AB	Air Base

Air Force, Group and Squadron abbreviations were preceded by the formations number. The Air Base was preceded by one or two geographical identification letters or a name according to necessity.

Vehicles intended for aerodrome tasks were, for the most part, built on specific chassis for which the technical services were responsible for orders, equipping, storage and maintenance. For others functions, the USAAF used the vehicles supplied by the Ordnance or the Quartermaster Corps. Its fire fighting vehicles were supplied by the US Army Engineers. Three companies would be the privileged suppliers of the Army Air Forces: Reo, Federal and Biderman.

They manufactured, in its entirety, the Truck Tractor Fuel Servicing F1, 6 x 6, 7½ Ton, one of the biggest tractors built at the time, intended for towing 4,000-gallon (15,140 litres) refuelling semi-trailers.

The 6 x 6, 7½ Ton was also used for towing technical semi-trailers of the Army Air Forces who possessed, in this line, the largest and heaviest vehicle then made, the first order being allocated to

213

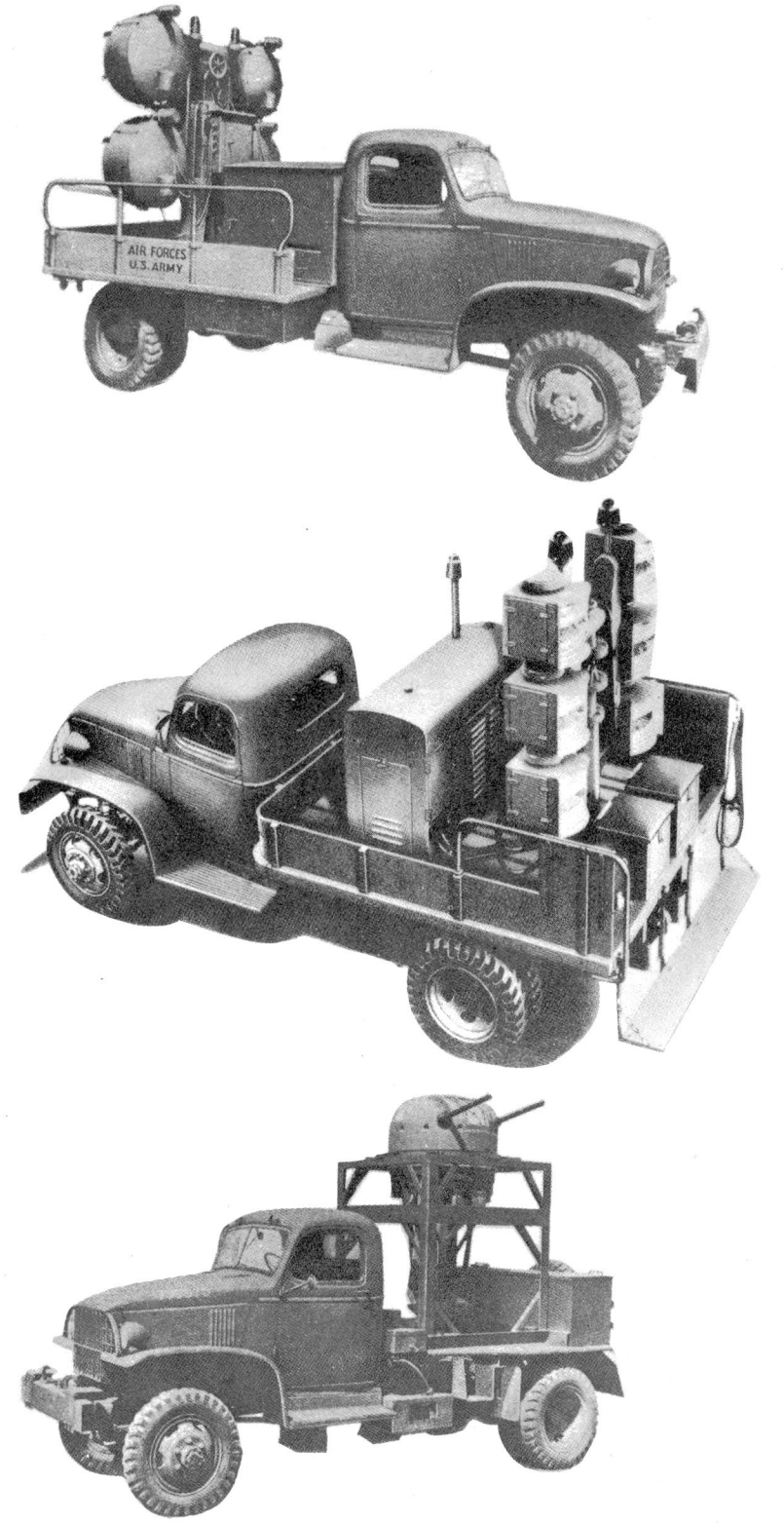

Chevrolet 1½ Ton, with Davey Compressor Company equipment for lighting runways, Type J5.

Fruehauf Trailer in 1940 for 237 semis of the 'Aerovan' model (soon to be a famous commercial name!)

This same chassis also served for the Truck, Tractor Wrecking C2, a recovery crane lorry which, according to the customs of the Army Air Forces, was equipped with a hitching saddle for the 12½ Ton C2 Wrecking 40-Foot or 25-Foot low platform semi-trailer fitted with a swan neck, manufactured by Trailer Co. of America. The combination was intended for the handling of aeroplanes, either dismantled during delivery or what remained of them after an accident, but also for transport of heavy vehicles.

Finally, Biderman also built a derivative of its tractor Model F1 with driver's cab in an off-centre position at the side to convert it into a crane carrier (cable type 10-ton trellis crane). Autocar also derived from its commercial range a series of forward-cab models with two driving axles which existed either as oil tankers or as tractors for semi-trailers in the 2½ ton class. The tractors for semi-trailers, all with 3.32 m wheelbase, were either 2½ Ton U 4044s (1940 model,

Chevrolet type Field Lighting J4 with American Gas Accumulator Company equipment. On August 5th, 1943, this equipment was rechristened AN 2505.

548 built) or U 4144Ts (1941 model, 274 produced) or U 5044s (1940 model, 97 manufactured). They could tow a Heil F2 tanker semi-trailer with 7,500 litres of petrol, to which it was possible to attach a second identical tanker converted into an ordinary trailer by means of a front undercarriage or Dolly Trailer Converter (extra front wheels fitted with a towing saddle fixing on to the pivot of the semi-trailer and enabling it to be converted into an ordinary trailer).

The cab chassis (wheelbase 3.25 m) of the Type U 2044 (1940 model, 233 built) or U 4144 (1941 model, 138 produced), all in the 2½ Ton class, received a 2,500 litre tank for oil (Oil Servicing Truck 660 gallons, L1) an essential of which the piston engines of the time were particularly greedy.

No Autocar appears in the 1947 edition of *TM 9-2800,* an edition published after the services of the

Chevrolet 1½ Ton Turret Trainer E5, equipped by Herman Body for ground training of air gunners.

Gunnery school for future machine-gunners of the US Army Air Forces. The turrets are without their perspex covers.

US Army had undertaken a great pruning among the stocks, workshops, fleets and units dispersed throughout the world. Only vehicles in good condition and of which the quantity held, both in parts and in complete vehicles, was sufficient were to be retained.

This equipment, very specialised, designed by Heil, was then replaced by a trailer with two twinned wheels 1½ Ton, Type L2 of 2,270 litres, which supplemented the services of the refuelling lorry F3 on a GMC chassis, a vehicle which was itself very versatile, since it could carry either oil or fuel (Truck, Fuel or Oil servicing 750 Gal, 2½ Ton—F3 2,840 litres). There also existed, in small numbers, a Truck Oil Servicing L1 on a GMC chassis absolutely identical to the F3 (2,840 litres) and an L2 (2,500 litres), both likewise built by Heil. These were, in fact the only bodies on GMC CCKW 353 designed for the Army Air Forces with the bomb carrier and the platform with Heil or Garwood scissor type elevator.

Chevrolet supplied its 4 x 4, 1½ Ton chassis as a basis for field lighting equipment for airfields. The Field Lighting Type J3 and J4 was equipped by American Gas Accumulator with six rectangular floodlights and an electricity generating unit behind the cab, while Davey Compressor's J5 carried four large circular floodlights and a generator powered by the vehicle's engine through the intermediary of the power take-off. The J4 was redesignated AN (Army/Navy) 2,505 on August 5th, 1943, and the J5 An 2,524 on December 27th, 1943. They were all classified 'Limited Standard' in 1947 except the AN 2,524 which would remain 'Standard'.

Another product, rather an original one, was the Turret Trainer E5, which succeeded a much more rudimentary material on a Dodge ½ Ton VC 3 (Turret Trainer T1). The aim of these vehicles was to train machine-gunners on the ground, therefore releasing aircraft for operations with the movements of the vehicle recreating, more or less, the unstable conditions in which they would have to man their weapons in the air. Between theory and practice there were a few miscalculations! Soon the large number of new training aeroplanes and obsolete bombers made it possible to do without this method of training. The vehicle was, however, still 'Standard' in 1947.

As for the Bomb Service Truck M1 (Ford 11 YS 1 Ton, Diamond-T 201 BS, GMC AC 251, equipped with a manual bomb handling gantry, all of 4 x 2 type), it was replaced by the Chevrolet M6 (G 7128). The M1 resembled and could easily be mistaken for the recovery vehicle of a field repair unit. Built on a short wheelbase (3.17 m) version of the standard 1½ Ton chassis, the body of the M6 was among the simplest: open cab (the only Chevrolet to receive one in the production version), platform with wheel passages showing and lifting gantry with manual crane (1,814 kg). Three seats were mounted on the platform. It could be twinned both in front and at the rear and towed a bomb-carrying trailer M1 (Bomb lift Truck M1) capable of positioning bombs of up to 2,000 lb thanks to its hydraulic elevator. A dismantlable version of the M6 transportable by air was also built. A total of 3,175 M6s was built. They were supplied by the Ordnance.

In view of the increase in weight of air projectiles, the US Army Forces had a more powerful bomb handling vehicle built for delivery to the units, either in the form of a kit which could be fitted on any GMC CCKW 353 with spar-sided platform or directly on the vehicle from the start. Designated Bomb Service Truck M27 or M27 B1, it consisted, for its 'handling' part, of a quadripod tubular superstructure, carrying

The Bomb Service M6 was the only Chevrolet with an open cab built in series. Production totalled 7,868. This model, NQ-G-7128, of the French air force is loading a Helldiver of the Aéronavale Indochina in 1954.

a rail on which a trolley and its crane powered by the truck's power take-off, travelled. The operator was installed on a seat above the cab of the GMC. In practice, only CCKWs with a winch were converted.

The M27 could also transport externally, hanging on the spars, light railway sections (one curve section, four straight sections, length 15 metres) and two four-wheel platforms forming the Dolly and Track Set 2 Ton.

This combination was intended to receive the bomb at the moment of its unloading from the truck and to transport it as far as the aeroplane, even on uneven or loose ground. The version M27 B1 was classified 'Standard' in 1953 and the M27 'Substitute Standard'.

One M27 was allocated to each squadron of fighter-bombers and two to each squadron of bombers. A total of 2,286 was produced by Heil with the co-operation of Holmes and Garwood.

The US Army Air Forces also used caterpillar tractors of which some were equipped with a cable Type 2 Ton or 6 Ton mechanical crane (International T6—Caterpillar D7) for aircraft maintenance operations in the field and notably for changes of engines or the towing of aircraft. For this last use, they ordered from Cleveland the Cletrac MG1 or 7 Ton High Speed Tractor M2. Standardised in February 1941, this elegant tractor was capable of travelling at more than 25 mph (40 km/hr) thanks to rubber

A 2½ Ton oil truck, on Autocar U 2044 chassis. This vehicle was ordered in May and November 1940, and a total of 233 was built (registration numbers W 80238 to 80287 and W 80568 to 80750). The tank built by Heil (Model L1) had a capacity of 660 gallons. An identical vehicle, U 4144, but equipped with a different engine, was built in numbers 138 (registrations W 80770 to 80907).

Tractor Model U 4044, intended for towing a 2,000 gallon aviation spirit semi-trailer, Type F2, built by Heil, equipped with two 160 gallons/minute pumps. A second tank of the same type could be hitched on to the semi-trailer thanks to a front undercarriage. A total of 548 was ordered in 1940, followed by 274 Models U4144 T in 1941.

Through replacement of the engine Type 358 by the Type 377 (these figures express the capacity in cubic inches), Autocar obtained the 4 x 4, 5 Ton, Model U 5044, also intended for towing fuel semi-trailers. A total of ninety-seven was ordered on September 24th, 1940.

A 750-gallon (2,843 litres) GMC petrol tanker F3.

caterpillars. It was also the only caterpillar tractor not to be equipped with metal caterpillar tracks.

Its very complete equipment enabled it not only to tow aeroplanes (traction capacity on the towbar: 4,600 kg), but also to start them with its 100 volt, 3 KWA generator. In addition, it was fitted with a 3,400 kg front winch and an air compressor, in theory to inflate the pneumatic shock absorbers, but of a more general use, of course, in reality.

Very low and very manoeuvrable (turning radius: 1.52 metres), it could move easily in crowded parking lots or slide under the wings of aeroplanes.

Derived from a commercial model, it was powered by a 6-cylinder side-mounted, petrol-driven Hercules WXLC 3 producing 150 hp at 3,000 rpm, the same as that of the Alligator. The gearbox had four forward gears and one reverse. Two passengers and a driver could be accommodated on the bench seat. It was fitted with a windscreen and a fabric hood, both of which could be folded down. Some received a hoist at the front for lifting principally engines.

Numerous other models were used for towing aeroplanes: Dodge, Jeep and quite commonly 4 x 4, 4-5 Tractors, which were anyway in very widespread service for all sorts of uses in the Army Air Forces.

In this use, the vehicles, like all those called upon to drive on the runways, were frequently painted yellow, while the Jeeps with the job of guiding aeroplanes on the huge airfields, notably in the Pacific, wore, on all or part of the body, yellow and black and more rarely red and white chequered paintwork, and a 'FOLLOW ME' placard.

Finally, although this vehicle was not originally ordered for this branch of the service, it was the US Army Air Forces that found the most rational use, as an aviation estate car for the transport of crews for the Dodge ¾ Ton Carryall, whose usefulness, beyond that was no longer very clearly evident to the equipment branches. Consequently, the Air Forces received most of them.

The US Army Air Forces themselves organised the setting up of radio telephone communications and the servicing of its radar installations on the using of *matériel* designed, acquired and set up by the Signal Corps. They principally used the following special vans, GMC. CCKW 353, K53, 57, 59, 61; Chevrolet 4 x 4, 1½ Ton, K51, K70; Autocar U 8144, K30, K31, K62; GMC AFKX 804, K30, K31; and White 666, K56.

In Britain the US Eighth Air Force, received large

Indian labourers load a Curtiss C-46 Commando with mortar shells destined for China. The GMC CCKW 353 chassis is equipped with a Heil elevator platform.

GMC CCKW 353 bomb transporter, Type M27.

6 x 6, 7½ Ton tractor, Model F1, Reo (Type 29x5). Like all vehicles of this series, this vehicle is fitted with Cleveland pneumatic shock absorbers in front.

Convoy of the US Army Air Forces, formed of Keystone AC 105 and Fruehauf Type A 3A workshop semi-trailers towed by 4 x 4, 4/5 Ton Tractors, and a 6 x 6, 7½ Ton, photographed on the Burma road, in 1944.

To refuel B-24 bombers, fuelling units composed of 4 x 4, 4/5 Ton tractors and 2,000-gallon (7,580 litres) Heil semi-trailers, Type F2, fill up at the terminal of a 220-mile (355-km) long pipeline. These tractors were very commonly employed in the US Army Air Forces. These were seen in Italy in October 1944.

Biderman F1 tractor.

Tractor 6 x 6, 7½ Ton, Model F1, Corbitt (Type 50 SD6). This vehicle, powered by a 165 hp Hercules HXC engine, is the least common of the tractors used by the US Army Air Forces for towing fuel tankers Model F1A. Some of these trucks were employed by the French air force.

quantities of British vehicles while waiting for its service vehicles, which were not classified as priority *matériel,* to be sent by sea.

Two very specialised tractors went into service for looking for crews of aeroplanes which had crashed in Alaska. The first model was a half-track derived from an Allis Chalmers agricultural tractor (Snow Tractor M7), which borrowed from the Jeep its engine, steering, clutch and differential. It was standardised in August 1943 and reclassified 'Limited Standard' in November 1944. It pulled a trailer on

C2 crane truck on a Federal 606 or Reo 29X5 chassis. Notice the bracing strut in position.

6 x 6, 7½ Ton recovery vehicle, Type C2, on Reo 29X5 chassis, participating in rescue operations following a railway accident in Great Britain.

C2 recovery vehicle on a Federal 605 chassis. This type of vehicle, designed on the basis of tractors for the refuelling semi-trailer F1, was intended for recovering and lifting crashed aeroplanes. It was equipped with a Gar Wood 10-ton crane and a hitching saddle enabling it to tow a C2 low semi-trailer adapted for transporting aeroplanes. On this series, the crane jib is curved.

Tractor type C2 towing a 12½ Ton semi-trailer, Type C2, built by Trailer Company of America.

The M7 was replaced by an entirely tracked vehicle, the Snow Tractor 36 from Iron Fireman Manufacturing, transporting two men in tandem in a sheet-metal clad cab. Its roof was painted flourescent red. It pulled an M1 or M14 sledge (Sled, Cargo, 1 Ton). It borrowed its mechanical elements from the Dodge ¾ Tonner. There were, for the same role, several trials of half-tracked Jeeps (cf. *The Jeep*).

4 x 4, 2½ Ton Truck Autocar U 2044 Heil L1 600 US Gallon Oil Tanker	
Length (metres)	4.89
Width (metres)	2.28
Height (metres)	2.64
Wheelbase (metres)	3.25
Weight Empty (kg)	3,978
All Up Weight (kg)	6,246
Ground Clearance (cm)	30
Climbing Gradient (%)	29
Angle of Approach (°)	50
Angle of Departure (°)	56
Speed (km/hr)	72
at Regulation rpm	2,600
Fuel Consumption on road (litres/100 kilometres)	35
Engine Make*	Hercules
Model**	JXD
Capacity (cc)	5,250
Cylinders	6, in-line
Fuel	petrol
Ignition	6-Volt battery
Tyres	9.00 x 20 rear twinned
Brakes	Air

Notes: The Model 4144 was powered by an Autocar 358 engine
The Hercules JXD also powered the Scout Car, the M8/M20 and the Studebaker 6 x 6, 2½ Ton

6 x 6, 7½ Ton Semi-Trailer Tractor		
	Reo 29X5	Federal 605/Bidermann
Length (metres)	7.32	7.31
Width (metres)	2.38	2.40
Height (metres)	2.60	2.61
Wheelbase (metres)	4.92	4.92
Weight Empty (kg)	8,160	8,350
All Up Weight (kg)	15,410	15,010
Ground Clearance (cm)	30	30
Fording (cm)	56	56
Climbing Gradient (%)	59	51
Angle of Approach (°)	54	54
Angle of Departure (°)	66	66
Speed (km/hr)	65	56
at Regulation rpm	2,100	1,750
Fuel Capacity (litres)	318	303
Fuel Consumption on road (litres/100 kilometres)	78.5	130
Engine Make	Hercules	Hercules
Model	HXD	HXC
Capacity (cc)	14,000	14,000
Cylinders	6, in-line	6, in-line
Fuel	petrol	petrol
Ignition	12-Volt	12-Volt
Tyres	10.00 x 22	10.00 x 22

Note: The Hercules HXD was common in 6 x 6, 6-Tonner bridge crane carrying version, and the Hercules HXC was also common with the same chassis, but not in cargo and artillery models.

skis M19 1 Ton, Snow Trailer, which could take two stretchers. The front wheels of the tractor and the trailer could take skis. Besides this role, the M19 trailer was also intended for transporting heaters for aero engines.

Autocar U 4044 2½ Ton Semi-Trailer Tractor	
Length (metres)	5.10
Width (metres)	2.36
Height (metres)	2.62
Wheelbase (metres)	3.32
Weight Empty (kg)	4,540
Ground Clearance (cm)	30
Climbing Gradient, Tractor Alone (%)	45
Angle of Approach (°)	50
Angle of Departure (°)	38
Speed (km/hr)	72
at Regulation rpm	2,600
Fuel Consumption on road (litres/100 kilometres)	59
Engine Make	Autocar
Model	358
Capacity (cc)	5,900
Cylinders	6, in-line
Fuel	petrol
Ignition	6-Volt battery
Tyres	9.00 x 20
Brakes	Air

Notes: The dimensions of the U 5044 5 Ton Tractor were identical. However, it was powered by a 6-cylinder Autocar 377 engine, and weighed 198 pounds (90kg) less when empty than the U 4044.

Recovery vehicle 6 x 6, 7½ Ton, Biderman C2. The crane, built by Silent Hoist Company, had a capacity of 10 tons.

Walter FGBS 4 x 4, 5 Ton snowplough, used to clear aerodrome runways. This example was photographed in 1942.

The prototype heavy recovery lorry Mack NO 4, designed for the Army Air Corps, was equipped with a towing saddle.

Cletrac MG-1 7 Ton High Speed Tractor	
Length (metres)	4.22
Width (metres)	1.78
Weight (kg)	6,486
Ground Pressure (kg/cm^3)	0.6
Ground Clearance (cm)	25
Fording (cm)	81.2
Climbing Gradient (%)	60
Angle of Approach (°)	45
Angle of Departure (°)	41
Speed (km/hr)	35
at Regulation rpm	3,280
Fuel Capacity (litres)	124
Engine Make	Hercules
Model	WXLC
Capacity (cc)	6,600
Cylinders	6, in-line
Fuel	petrol

Oshkosh W 700, 7½ Ton, with Klauer TGU 3 snow cutter. A total of seventy-five was ordered in the snowplough version and seventy-six in the tipper version, the latter for the ground forces. Extremely robust and resistant, these snowploughs, intended for clearing runways, remained in service for more than thirty years.

High Speed Tractor, 7 Ton, Model M2, built by Cletrac. This vehicle was intended for towing aeroplanes and facilitating start-up operations, for which it was equipped with a 110-volt 3,000-watt generator and an air compressor, both driven by the vehicle's engine. It was the only tractor equipped with flexible rubber caterpillar tracks.

The 3-inch Gun Motor Carriage T1 (M5). The design of this vehicle began in December 1940, based on the Tractor High Speed Cletrac. Its purpose was to transport a 3-inch anti-aircraft gun which was to be used as an anti-tank gun. Although its manufacture was at one time envisaged, serial production was never carried out.

Tractor Crane, 2 Ton, M5, built by International (Model T9) with Trackson CT9 crane.

International Harvester tractor TD14, with Hughes-Keenan equipment.

Caterpillar D7 with cable type crane for handling engines.

Biderman P1 crane lorry, equipped with a 20-ton Michigan TM 16 crane. The chassis was that of the F1 with offset cab, either of sheet metal or open topped.

Table of Specific Vehicles of the US Army Air Forces in September 1943 Extracted from Technical Manual 9-2800					
	Purchase and Maintenance		Storage		
Designation	Service Issuing Order		Complete Vehicle	Spares Maintenance	
	Chassis	Body		Chassis	Body
Army Air Forces					
Trailer, fuel servicing, type A-2-A-220-gallon (airborne)	AAF	AAF	AAF	AAF	AAF
Trailer, fuel servicing, 600-gallon, A-1 and A-3, 2-wheel	AAF	AAF	AAF	AAF	AAF
Trailer, 2-wheel, office	AAF	AAF	AAF	Ord.	Ord.
Trailer, laboratory, photo type A-1, 2 wheel	AAF	AAF	AAF	AAF	AAF
Trailer, laboratory, photo type A-2, 2- wheel	AAF	AAF	AAF	AAF	AAF
Truck, 1½-ton, 4×4, field lighting, J-3, J-4, J-5 Chevrolet	Ord	AAF	AAF	Ord	AAF
Truck, 1½-ton, 4×4, turret trainer, E-5 Chevrolet	Ord	AAF	AAF	Ord	AAF
Truck, 2½-ton, 4×4, oil servicing, type L-1 Federal	Ord	AAF	AAF	Ord	AAF
Truck, 2½-ton, 6×6, oil servicing, 600-gallon, L-2 G.M.C.	Ord	AAF	AAF	Ord	AAF
Truck, 2½-ton, 6×6, fuel servicing, or oil, 750-gallon, F-3 G.M.C.	Ord	AAF	AAF	Ord	AAF
Truck, 7½-ton, 6×6, fuel servicing (tractor), F-1	AAF	AAF	AAF	Ord	AAF
Truck, 7½-ton, 6×6, wrecking, C-2 (tractor)	AAF	AAF	AAF	Ord	AAF
Dolly trailer converter, fuel servicing, 2-wheel, type F-2 or F-1A	AAF	AAF	AAF	AAF	AAF
Dolly trailer converter, fuel servicing, 2-wheel, type F-2 or F-2A	AAF	AAF	AAF	AAF	AAF
Dolly trailer, technical supply, field shop and instrument shop	AAF	AAF	AAF	AAF	AAF
Dolly trailer, wrecking, C-2, 2-wheel	AAF	AAF	AAF	AAF	AAF
Semitrailer, 2-wheel, 10-ton gross, field shop repair, type A-3	AAF	AAF	AAF	AAF	AAF
Semitrailer, 2-wheel, fuel servicing, 2,000-gallon, F-2 or F-2A	AAF	AAF	AAF	AAF	AAF
Semitrailer, 2-wheel, 6-ton payload, instrument shop	AAF	AAF	AAF	AAF	AAF
Semitrailer, 2-wheel, 10-ton gross, photo laboratory, types N-1-2-3	AAF	AAF	AAF	AAF	AAF
Semitrailer, 2-wheel, 10-ton gross, technical supply	AAF	AAF	AAF	AAF	AAF
Semitrailer, 4-wheel, 15-ton payload, carry-all	AAF	AAF	AAF	AAF	AAF
Semitrailer, 4-wheel, fuel servicing, 4,000-gallon, F-1 or F-1A	AAF	AAF	AAF	AAF	AAF
Semitrailer, 4-wheel, 10-ton gross, oxygen generator	AAF	AAF	AAF	AAF	AAF
Semitraiter, 4-wheel, wrecking, 40-foot, type C-2	AAF	AAF	AAF	AAF	AAF
Semitrailer, 4-wheel, wrecking, 25-foot, type C-2	AAF	AAF	AAF	AAF	AAF
Tractor, medium (track-laying), high speed, M-2, prime mover	Ord	Ord	AAF	AAF	AAF
Tractor, crane, medium (track-laying), 6-ton, T-1, prime mover	Ord	Ord	AAF	AAF	AAF
Tractor, medium (track-laying), 2-ton crane, T-1, prime mover	Ord	Ord	AAF	AAF	AAF

The Jeep was not a vehicle specially designed for the US Navy, but was widely used in it and also in the Coast Guards and the Marines. This vehicle is equipped with the Fording Kit for travel in deep water (more than 18 inches [46 cm]).

US Navy, Marine Corps and Coast Guard Vehicles

One cannot talk of the equipment of the Navy and its two 'subsidiaries' without the name of International Harvester springing to mind, so much was this manufacturer associated with them all throughout the war. For the US Navy, International created three vehicles and almost exclusively devoted the production of a fourth to it.

First of all, the M-1-4, 4 x 4, ½ Ton, powered by a 6-cylinder International Green Diamond of 85 hp. It had either a steel pick-up body with, according to the custom of the Navy and Marines, two wooden transverse 'bench seats' resting on the spars, or a body from Boyertown with reducible height, used as a medical vehicle. The latter was particularly spartan, since the metal body had gaps between the spars in its upper part and was simply covered with a tarpaulin.

During the operations in the Pacific, one model of Jeep was specially converted by the Marines into a front-line ambulance vehicle (cf. *The Jeep*).

The load capacity of the M-1-4 was subsequently increased to 1 Ton, its silhouette pared down and its

A total of nine hundred International M-1-4 was built with folding Boyertown body, for use as a front-line ambulance vehicle.

GTB, to have been built (6,000 in total) either in the version with tarpaulin covered platform (GTB 4 x 4, 1½ Ton, Cargo—Low Silhouette, with twin tyres at the rear) or in the bomb transport/handling version (4 x 4, 1½ Ton, Bomb Service GTBS, tyres mounted singly at the rear).

Like Dodge, whose evolution the International series followed in its own manner, a version with three driving axles were extrapolated from the M-2-4,

M-3L-4 and M-3H-4 Chassis/Body Combinations	
M-3L-4	M-3H-4
Aviation Fire-Fighting Truck	Aviation Fire-Fighting Truck
Tipper	Searchlight Carrier
Aviation Refuelling Tanker 600 US Gallons Recovery Tanker	Chassis-Cab, without Body

A pre-production example of International's M-2-4, 4 x 4, 1 Ton Cargo whose spare wheels are curiously of a smaller diameter than those on the production vehicle.

engine power increased to 93 hp. It thus became the M-2-4, 4 x 4, 1 Ton Cargo. It could be equipped with T45 rocket launching equipment.

The larger tonnage was represented by the International M-3H-4 of which 3,742 were supplied and the M-3L-4 long-wheelbase (3.81 metres as against 3.30 metres) with 2,790 vehicles. It was put into service with a canvas-topped cab or with a metal-clad cab, which remains all in all rather exceptional, for the majority of the tactical vehicles of the Navy and Marines were open-topped and it was not traditional to retain the canvas roof! They were fitted with a high spar steel body or special equipment.

The Navy also received the greater part of the production of the only Low Silhouette lorry, the Ford

An M-2-4 firing a salvo of T 45 rockets on Okinawa in 1945.

International M-3-4, 4 x 4, 1½ Ton. The version M-3L had a wheelbase of 3.55 metres and the version M-3H-4 one of 3.83 metres. This chassis could be fitted with a cargo body, a tipper, a fuel tank, or alternatively be fitted out as a vehicle for fighting aircraft fires on the ground, or a recovery vehicle or a searchlight transporter.

International M-3-4 cargo vehicles and petrol tankers on Guam airfield in the Pacific. This vehicle also existed as a tipper, recovery vehicle and tanker. A total of 6,532 was built. The one in the foreground, photographed in August 1944, had a fabric roof.

4 x 4, 1 Ton. Christened M-3-6, it retained the improved version of the Green Diamond, received Hendrickson tandem rear driving wheels and a Thornton system of locking the differential and still included a front winch.

A particular feature of the series M1, M2 and M3 was the off-centre position of the radiator cap.

The 2½ Ton class only comprised a single vehicle, the International M-5-6, of which the greater part of the production went to the Navy and the Marines, but which, it may be said almost by exception, was also ordered by the US Army–3,000 M-5-6x4, fifty M-5-6 long chassis and 450 short chassis, both in 6 x 6 version, with a metal-clad cab.

International's 2½ Tonner supplied to the Marines still had a canvas roofed cab, and was either in the long wheelbase version (4.29 metres, Model M-5-6), or in the short wheelbase version (3.78 metres, Model M-5-6). Its tandem rear driving wheels were a Hendrickson unit which was fitted with a Thornton differential lock, a mechanical refinement with which only the sailors equipped themselves, the US Army

Ford 4 x 4, 1½ Ton, Bomb Service, Model GTB.

International Harvester M-5-6 tipper.

A prototype presented in 1940 by International for the future 2½ Ton tactical truck.

International's version M-3-6, 6 x 6, 1½ Ton presented itself in fact as a development of the M-2-4, 4 x 4, 1 Ton chassis, on which had been mounted a Hendrickson set of tandem rear wheels and a Thornton differential lock.

Minneapolis Moline 4 x 4, 1½ Ton aviation tractor. The vehicle is equipped at the rear with a compartment which can be filled with ballast to increase the grip and improve the traction capacity. The company still wanted it to be one of the first models of Jeep to have been built and called its vehicles this for quite a long time.

counting on power, underloading and good reduction ratios to get out of difficulties.

In 1933, International had signed an exclusive contract with Hendrickson for its method of converting a 4 x 2 chassis into 6 x 4 by a simple change of suspension. This suspension was composed of a central pivot mounted on spring leaves; on the axis of this pivot was mounted a connecting arm oscillating through its middle which ensures the cohesion and solidarity of the driving axle movements.

The engine of the M-5-6 was a Red Diamond. It was originally fitted with a high spar platform of sheet metal or wood, with the spare wheel carried at the side on the right in a corbelling. The short chassis version existed as a tipper, as a tractor for semi-trailer especially for aviation tankers on airfields, or as a bare chassis to have the body added.

Designed in the course of 1941, the M-5-6 carried out its trials in December of the same year at Virginia Beach and in the confines of the big base at Quantico. Following its trials, its cab was rearranged, losing, in particular, an ugly strip of sheet metal in front of the windscreen, with which the prototype of the M-1-4 ¼ Ton was also encumbered. Presented with an open cab, according to the design and well established custom of the Marines, the M-5-6 only was equipped with a metal-clad cab, whose elements came, by the way, from the K series, for the order placed by the US Army. In total, 33,588 units of the 2½ Ton International was supplied until September 24th, 1945, to the US Navy and the US Marines.

International M-5-6, long chassis, with high spar body, of the US Marines, on a Pacific island, towing a 1 Ton trailer specific to the Corps.

With International, FWD was one of the big suppliers of the US Marines and Coast Guards. The model HST-COE of the US Coast Guards was intended to transport a crew for laying and maintenance of the telephone lines. Similar vehicles were also built on FWD chassis, Types S and H. The Seabees used them in the Pacific as workshop vehicles.

It remained in service after the war since it was only withdrawn after the operations in Korea.

Numerous special bodies were used: recovery, fighting aircraft fires on the ground, etc.

Few were allocated to the allied powers. Some were, however, known to be in service in the French navy and the Dutch navy for the marines.

The letters and figures allocated by International to its tactical truck family had the following meaning: the letter 'M' stood for Military; the first figure indicated the useful load in pounds; the second figure gave the number of driving wheels; and the letter L, inserted after the first figure, characterised a short wheelbase, and the letter H a long wheelbase.

Of course, the whole range of K chassis was widely used by the three services, including, by the Marines, a KR 8 converted to 6 x 4 by Hendrickson in 1940 with a large-volume tarpaulin-covered metal body, intended for the transport of troops or the towing of anti-aircraft guns. The twinned rear driving wheels could be adapted to drive, in order to improve the traction on rough ground, flexible caterpillar tracks, according to an idea then very much in fashion in American military technical circles. These tracks, when they were not used, were fixed on the metal spars of the platform.

Some tractors for semi-trailer K8 or K11 remained in service on US Naval Air Service bases until the 1960s, whether they were acquired during the war or, some of them, after it.

The US Navy, and in particular its Bureau of Aeronautics (technical service of the air arm), was also a faithful customer of Autocar from whom it bought fuel tankers for the service of airfields (Autocar 9064,

An FWD, 5/6 Ton artillery tractor, Model SU COE Special. The engine was a 6-cylinder Waukesha SRKR. A version with an entirely metal-clad cab was also built for the British and Canadians.

An International M-5-6 with Couse Laboratories technical body, close in its design and employment to those on Ford chassis used by the aviation engineer battalions.

An Autocar, Model C 70, 4 x 2, 5 Ton, during the embarkation of a Marine unit for Korea. These vehicles had been acquired in 1942.

An FWD, 5/6 Ton, SU COE Special, with rock depositing tipper built by Heil.

6 x 4, 10 Ton; Autocar, 4 x 2, both with 6,000-litre tank) and road transport (C70) or aviation recovery (U90) trucks, of Sterling, a small manufacturer specialising in off-road heavy vehicles who was one of the last to remain faithful to chain transmission to the rear driving wheels (chassis DD 525 for recovery vehicle or fire engine, HC 5 330 recovery) and of FWD.

FWD developed a special version for the US Marines of its chassis SU-COE, which was intended for the British and Canadians. The sheet-metal clad cab, which was rounded and curved, was replaced by a steel, flat-faced, angular cab protected by a solid grille. The windscreen, reduced to its simplest form, consisted, in fact, of two windshields with a large space between them. No door, not even a fabric one, was provided. A canvas roof, the end of which did not join up with the windshields, could cover the two front seats. The engine was a 125 hp Waukesha SRKR. The tyres, generally mounted singly, were 14.00 x 20s, which, for the time, was particularly generous. It had either a metal platform or a shortened platform with a winch behind the cab (artillery tractor) or a Heil rock depositing tipper body.

One felt, only to look at it, that everything in the vehicle had been sacrificed to efficiency and that no concession had been made to items as foreign to the Marines as protection against the weather or comfort of personnel.

The US Coast Guard, a civil body with the job of protecting persons and goods along the coasts and on the great seaways in time of peace, came under the authority of the US Navy in time of war. Not only was a large number of its personnel employed in landing operations (landing craft crew, beachmaster, etc), but also a large number of its specific vehicles.

Thus it is that its FWD line fitter lorries (chassis H ST, 4 x 4) which were intended for the maintenance of its vast telephone and telegraph network were to a great extent allocated to the works battalions of the US Navy, the famous Seabees (from abbreviation CB: Construction Battalion), with whom they served as mobile workshops.

However, a large part of the motor vehicle *Matériel*

special to the Coast Guard, which was not in any case very 'rich' at the time, remained in the USA to ensure liaison between all the posts throughout the territory, the wearisome patrols along the coasts looking for the German or Japanese spy landing from a mysterious submarine, or guarding hundreds of kilometres of quays in the civilian harbours.

Besides the $\frac{1}{2}$, $\frac{3}{4}$ or 1 Ton Dodge, International or Ford vans, of which a large part was converted by Marmon-Herrington, and $2\frac{1}{2}$ Ton International or GMC road vehicles, the US Coast Guard received a large number of Jeeps, of which some were lengthened and provided with sand tyres of larger dimensions to permit the transport of ten men across the dunes. The jeep, lengthened by the efforts of the US Coast Guard workshops, was christened on the day of its presentation to the press 'Invader', which is at the very least curious for a vehicle intended precisely for tracking and repelling the latter. These 'innovations' show quite well that all was not rosy in the United States and that those services which were by definition non-combatant, very often had to 'go along with it' while waiting for better days. Admiral King, Chief of the US Navy, indicates besides in his report to the Navy Secretary for 1942 that "the coast is patrolled by detachments on foot or on horseback of the coastguards".

They were far from being completely motorised. As for the 'administrative' vehicles (buses, liaison cars, light and medium utility vehicles), the three services, besides the omnipresent International Harvester, turned to Ford or General Motors (Yellow Coach bus).

In spite of real effort, especially for units which were traditionally not very motorised, the US Navy and US Marines always experienced great difficulties in providing sufficient vehicles to the units dispersed in the immensity of the Pacific. In this theatre of operations its responsibilities were greater than anywhere else, which is certainly saying something.

Therefore, in spite of the traditional antagonism towards the Army and the individualism of the Marines, the latter received vehicles from the stocks of the Ordnance, notably DUKWs and Dodge $\frac{3}{4}$ Ton medical vehicles. The model properly meant for the Marines, International-Boyertown, had only been built in small series because of the rapid abandonment of the M-1-4 in favour of the M-2-4. In fair exchange, the US Army provided itself with the LVT amphibious caterpillar vehicles for which the Marines had carried out all the operational research work and remained the pioneers in their military use.

In the European theatre of operations, the Navy practically only used *matériel* of the US Army or of British origin, as its needs were very small there—indeed the US Marines did not fight in Europe. To introduce a new chain of logistic support for vehicles of no interest to other users who had priority and were in the majority on this front would have been defying common sense and economy of forces. On the other hand, in the Pacific, New Zealand received *matériel* from the US Navy, including International M-5-6 tractors with fuel supply semi-trailer.

The International Harvester KR 8, 6 x 4, was derived from the road chassis by fitting Hendrikson tandem rear driving axles whose wheels could drive flexible caterpillar tracks (mounted on this model) for the purpose of increasing the traction on uneven ground. This vehicle had been designed as an artillery tractor for anti-aircraft guns.

A Sterling DDS 235 of the US Navy, whose use was identical to that of the recovery crane trucks of the US Army Air Forces. Powered by a 6-cylinder Waukesha engine, this truck had a 10 ton Gar Wood lifting system with a field of action of 180°.

US Navy Sterling DD 525 Wreckers in the foreground and HC 530s (76 x 4, 15 Ton, chain drive to the driving rear wheels—Gar Wood US 7-T-28 equipment), stand next to M1 A1s.

The Mack FKSW was built from 1938 to 1941. This model, used as a tractor for semi-trailer by the US Navy, was in fact a vehicle designed for the civil market it was equipped with a Cummins Diesel engine. It is transporting a light cruiser's gun turret.

A Chevrolet pick-up is in the company of two tractors, an International K and an Autocar C70, and a Chevrolet petrol tanker of the US Navy, on the Lages base in the Azores. The aeroplanes are B-26s of the USAAF. All this matériel, except the ½ Ton pick-up, dates from the Second World War and was still in service in the 1950s.

VEHICLES SUPPLIED TO ALLIED NATIONS

Dodge TD 15, 4 x 2, ¾ Ton. This type of vehicle is typical of the first vehicles of civil manufacture used in small numbers by Great Britain or, like this one, by formations of civil volunteers engaged at the side of the British before the entry into the war of the USA. The name on the side is that of the lady who presented this ambulance to the corps of American volunteers serving in Britain.

Vehicles Supplied to Allied Nations		
Date	Form of Contract	Nations Involved
1938 to 3rd November 1939	Commercial contracts negotiated freely	Belgium, Britain, Egypt, Finland, France, netherlands, etc
4th November 1939 to 10th January 1941	'Cash & Carry' and/or commercial contracts negotiated freely	Britain and France, then Britain alone for 'Cash & Carry'. Egypt, China, Holland, etc, for commercial contracts
10th January 1941 to September 1945	Lend-Lease: contracts placed by US Army on Allied Nations' behalf. Commercial contracts negotiated freely without benefit of Lend-Lease until 1942 for some nations	Australia, Britain, Canada, CHina, Dutch, East Indies, USSR.

American industry produced vehicles for the benefit of the Allied countries at war under distinct and fairly complex administrative and legal forms, resulting from the slow evolution of the country which was going to lead it from isolationism to 'benevolent neutrality', then to direct involvement in the conflict. Furthermore, without counting the vehicles which were simply given by the United States, standard vehicles of the US Army, which remained its property, were handed over for the duration of the war to the Allied nations under Lend-Lease: Britain, China, Canada, Holland, Belgium, Italy (Cobelligerent Forces), Poland, USSR, Norway, France, Brazil, Mexico, etc. Finally, with the stoppage of production and export of civil models only intervening in 1942, it remained possible for the nations at war to buy certain models which were not retained by the US Army for its re-equipment from the manufacturers (Dutch Indies from Marmon-Herrington, China, etc) or to obtain supplies until that time in certain countries considered as sovereign and non-belligerent, directly from the

Ambulance, Indian Army Type. This vehicle was also built on Chevrolet, Ford, General Motors and International chassis, in Australia. Although designed for hot countries, this Dodge of the French First Army is engaged in Italy in winter operations but which its light body must have given little protection to the wounded and crew. It was originally allocated to the Indian divisions of the Eighth Army in the desert and it is because of the exchanges of vehicles carried out to preserve the operational potential of the combatant formations to the detriment of the units withdrawn from combat, that this type of truck found itself dispersed and engaged in regions for which it had not been designed.

Chevrolet 1543 x 2, 4 x 2, 3 Ton, Indian Pattern, in Mesopotamia.

dealers. That was the case, for example, for the French Army stationed in Syria or the British forces in the Middle East, which ordered vehicles in Egypt.

As for the subsidiaries of the Big American manufacturers (General Motors, Ford, Chrysler, International Harvester) in the British Empire (Australia, Canada, India, New Zealand, etc.), they ensured, in principle for their national armies alone, the assembly of chassis coming from the United States (P.K.D: Partly Knocked Down; C.K.D: Completely Knocked Down), or the manufacture under licence of commercial models—therefore in these two cases not standardised by the American armed forces—more or less fitted out or converted according to local needs and roles. But because of the reallocation of vehicles among units which moved from one theatre of operations to another, these vehicles were actually used by all the forces supported by the British (Polish, French, etc).

Australia had a privileged place, taking account of its geographical location and of the presence on its soil of large industrial units which enabled it to supply both its own army, whose needs increased every day, and the Commonwealth and notably the Indian Army (Indian Pattern). Not only American chassis, and notably K5s and 7s, were assembled on the spot, but also Canadian ones including numerous Chevrolet Maple Leaf vehicles. A reassembly activity on behalf of the US Army was also set up. Thus Holden, the local subsidiary of General Motors, received and assembled a number of FWD-HAR 1s, of which some

Ford FC 60 L, Canada, 1942 model, of the British Army in Tunisia drive past a field workshop of a French regiment equipped with Somua S 35 tanks. The singly mounted tyres are 150 x 16, an oversize mounting to improve the performance on sand tracks. The rear axle has two reduction ratios. The body is the British Army's classic metal platform with high spars, equipped on each side with a tubular support for a sub-machine-gun, permitting self-defence of the vehicle against air attacks. In accordance with the British custom, the headlights are removed, one of them being replaced by a simple black-out light. The US Army commonly used an identical vehicle in the $1\frac{1}{2}$ Ton class (Model G8 T), but with a 6-cylinder engine instead of the 100 hp V-8 of the FC 60 L.

Ford 098 T, Canada 1940 model, with high spar metal body of the British forces. Sun visors manufactured with the vehicle's own equipment have been installed.

Dodge, 4 x 2, Canada T 110 L4 of the British Royal Navy in Italy. The tyres are 10.50 x 16, oversized for the corresponding civil models. The US Army used a similar model (T 118), but in the 1½ Ton class. An L5 version with single-mounted rear wheels existed. The driving axle was an Eaton two-speed type.

Dodge D60 (T110) as it was despatched from Canada in the chassis without cab version with the body to be added.

Australian artillery tractors (Tractor, Artillery, Australian No 3) on Ford 1,500 kg V-8 chassis (1940 model in the foreground, 1939 model in the background), both converted to four-wheel drive by Marmon-Herrington. The artillery guns are first model 25-pounders and 18-pounders. These trucks were delivered as chassis-cab directly from the United States.

were allocated to Australia, and GMCs which came out of the workshops adapted to the local style, that is to say with a fixed windscreen, but the cab replaced by a fabric hood, an arrangement which, it seems, the Australians liked very much. Ford, for its part, turned out 35,510 vehicles, of which many were artillery tractors with Marmon-Herrington conversion to four-wheel drive and even six-wheel drive for special applications. Australia practised both P.K.D. and C.K.D.

It is interesting to note that the Canadian Chevrolets of the series CMP, with their famous pug nose, were nicknamed Blitz (Lightning) in Australia, a reminder of the Blitz of London, but also the commercial designation of Opel, the German subsidiary of General Motors!

Australia's neighbour, New Zealand, an essentially agricultural country, was from possessing such an industrial potential, and only Ford possessed workshops there. The archives of the manufacturer mention a figure of 15,199 vehicles, principally of Canadian origin, assembled in the islands (P.K.D.).

Chevrolet 4 x 2, 3 Ton, Model CC 60 L, assembled in Australia.

International Harvester 550-gallon (2,500 litre) refuelling tender, built in Australia and in service with the Royal Air Force, refuelling a squadron of Martin Baltimores on Malta in August 1943.

Australian International Harvester KS 5. This 3-Ton truck was also used by the US Army (fire fighting vehicle, bus) and the Royal Air Force. The metal cab with fabric hood is typical of Australian wartime manufactures.

Mack LM-SW 6 x 4, 10 Ton. This vehicle, equipped with a Holmes recovery system with double jib, was delivered to the Canadian Army. The rear driving axles have two-speed reduction.

Mack LM SW of the type supplied to the British Army with Gar Wood recovery equipment.

HAR 01 supplied to the Free French Forces.

FWD SU used as an artillery tractor for 5.5-inch guns by the British Army.

FWD HAR 03 tractor for semi-trailer.

Ford 2 GBT (1940 model), converted to 6 x 6 by Marmon-Herrington for the transport of searchlights and sound detectors of anti-aircraft batteries of the Dutch colonial army stationed in Java and Sumatra. In view of the fact that these vehicles should have been delivered in 1942 (chassis 2½ Ton, Type 198 T, 1941 model) but that at the time the islands were entirely occupied by the Japanese, they were in fact used on the major defence works in the USA and in Alaska. Notice the mudguards with cut-outs for off rod travel.

The Diamond-T version 975 which was built specially for Canada. Here it is equipped with a structure for the support of Bailey field bridges (Lorry, 4 Ton, 6 WH, Pontoon). All 975s had a metal-clad cab.

During the events in Bizerta, a group of civilians comes to fetch supplies of drinking water from a Diamond-T tanker of the French navy in 1961. This French conversion used Type 975 chassis.

In India, where Ford also had installations, things went further, since they went as far as assembling vehicles in railway workshops or simple fields promoted to the rank of assembly lines. There, too, the figures supplied by Ford give a total of 119,873 chassis (P.K.D.) of every type and every origin, including Australian.

South Africa produced fairly few utility vehicles, still Fords (35,510 were built), but specialised in the manufacture of armoured cars. Altogether 5,746 was built on the basis of Ford components and Marmon-Herrington driving axles and transfer boxes, either at the manufacturer's Port Elizabeth factory or by the firm of Dorman Long.

Canada, in this sphere, is an exception, since, besides vehicles of American origin produced under licence, the national industry designed and built in hundreds and thousands a range of integrated and standardised vehicles of its own conception (C.M.P: Canadian Military Pattern).

Altogether, Canada built 815,729, including 180,816 by Dodge, 381,530 for Ford etc for the whole Commonwealth. Some Dodges were used by the US Army (T 110). On the other hand, having concentrated the main part of its effort on an original range which only covered the medium tonnages, Canada had recourse to the US of America for its other vehicles and was notably a large user of Jeeps, for which modifications were agreed, of Diamond-Ts (Type 975 with extra long chassis, of which 1,100 was built, or with short chassis Type 969, of which 700 was built), of Macks (NR, LM, SW, NM), and of the Federal 20-ton tank transporter and tractor, and others.

Malaya, before being overrun by the Japanese, still had time enough to assemble 2,114 Fords (P.K.D.).

Ford Dagenham, in England, also reassembled imported chassis. It should be remembered that P.K.D. reassembly concerns complete vehicles simply dismantled to save volume and space during transport, and C.K.D. the local assembly from bodies and

A Diamond-T 975 containing a field workshop (metal body with high spars). The different machines for working wood and metal could be set up on the ground. This vehicle was known in the Canadian Army under the designation Truck 4 Ton Machinery RE 25 KW.

Mack NR 1, with single mounting at the rear and roof insulation for use in the desert by the Eighth Army. These vehicles were not only used as tank transporters, but also as transport vehicles, notably to supply the units of the Long Range Desert Group.

Tank transporter, 6 x 4, 13 Ton, Mack NR 4, supplied to Great Britain in 1941.

Station Wagon Heavy Utility 4 x 2, seven passengers, Ford-Canada C11 DF (year model 1941) photographed in a camp of the Canadian army in Britain on March 19th 1944. The body is wooden (Woodie type), a method of construction very widespread at that time for this type of vehicle. It existed also as a five-seater, with reinforced rear axle and suspensions and large-diameter tyres.

Car Light Sedan 4 x 2, four passengers, Chrysler, photographed in a Canadian park on March 28th, 1944. It was intended for the transport of authorities at division and army corps level.

Snowplough with Snogo equipment on Ford 4 x 4 chassis, converted by Marmon-Herrington, used by the Royal Air Force from 1942.

Under Reverse Lease-Lend the Americans received matériel *produced by Britain or the Commonwealth, such as this version, designed for them, of the Australian Scout Car under the name of Utility Car in 1943 and used in the Pacific.*

The British converted the Diamond-T 980. 6 x 4, into a tank transporter semi-trailer tractor in order to improve its ability to move over uneven ground, the M19 combination proving to be neither very manoeuvrable nor very stable. The tractor's wheels have been fitted with removable caterpillar tracks to improve the traction on loose ground. The 30-Ton semi-trailer was built by Shelvoke and Drewry.

Local French modification of the Diamond-T 6 x 6, as a tank transporter semi-trailer tractor seen in Indochina in 1951.

An international K5, a Ford and a GMC CCKW 353 chassis load up in a depot in India with supplies destined to be sent by air to China.

Harley-Davidson WLC photographed in a Canadian formation on March 19th, 1944, in England. Notice the black-out light specific to the WLC in the 'export' version.

mechanical components in pieces or partly assembled, which assumes larger capacities in personnel and machines but allows more flexibility in the final result.

The United States came out on top when the transport of wheeled service vehicles to distant zones would have overburdened the capacities of the merchant ships by making use of a good number of these 'native' vehicles, notably in Australia, of General Motors-Holdens and Internationals.

After the war, Holland was the principal user of Canadian vehicles in Europe. It is true that it was on its territory that Canada assembled the largest part of its armed forces in view of their return home and their demobilisation. The vehicles were abandoned in thousands at Drelen after a selection process had been carried out for the needs, at least in theory, of the Pacific war. No heavy vehicle was to be repatriated, as a result of an agreement with the Americans. This explains the large number of Diamond 975s (platform, workshop, Coles crane, pontoon transporter and fuel tanker and fire tender, the latter built in Holland), of FWDs and Mack LMSW 01s in the army of the Netherlands.

The Territorial Transport Corps, formed in Belgium in December 1944 to supply the basic necessities of the country, received trucks from the British and among these, a certain number of Studebaker US 6 x 4 U6 tractors for semi-trailers. (cf. *The GMC, A Universal Truck*).

Technicians of the US Army reassemble in a workshop in New Guinea vehicles bought in parts (P.K.D.) from the United States.

Dodge ¾ Ton delivered partly dismantled in sea transport packing case.

Dodge 8 cwt Model T212-DBA, built in the Canadian Chrysler factory, captured by the Afrika Korps and used for laying telephones lines.

Principle Vehicles Built in the USA for Allied Countries

Manufacturer	Type	Use	User Nation	Remarks
Harley-Davidson	WLC	Escort liaison	Canada Britain	Specially built for Canada-identical to the WLA
General Motors	Plymouth	Liaison car	Britain Canada	5 seats
White	760 920 & Ruxtall	Tank transporter	Britain	Platform with spars 10 Ton/18 Ton, 6 x 4—Loading ramp at rear of platform
Marmon-Herrington/Ford		Search-light carrier, special vehicles	Netherlands Australia Canada	6 x 6 chassis, reconnaissance vehicle, etc. Built and converted by Marmon-Herrington for the Dutch colonial army in Java and Sumatra. Some vehicles for recovery (Australia) and fighting aircraft fires (Canada)
	1½ Ton (year models 1939 and 1940)	Artillery tractor	Australia	Four-wheel drive version; Towing 25-pounder gun and its ammunition box
American LaFrance		Fire fighting vehicle Ladder-Motor pump	Australia Canada	Protection of American bases and war factories. Operated by municipal fire brigades. Includes five ladders. American LaFrance JO/JOX with forward cab for Australia, most modern produced in USA
Chrysler		Liaison car	Canada	5-seater
Mack	LMSW 01	Wrecker	Canada Britain	Equipment with opening jibs or single jib, 8 Tons' on one jib—16-Ton Garwood on two jibs
Mack	NR 1 to 5	Transport Tank transporter	Britain Canada	6 x 4 chassis, 13 Ton. Wooden platform with spars and tarpaulin, tank transporter platform. Ordered by the US Army on basis of NR 6. Used for supplying Long Range Desert Group, Cyrenaica
Mack	EXBX	Tank transporter	Britain	Wooden platform with two loading ramps, 6 x 6, 18 Ton. Converted later in Middle East to petrol tanker
Mack	EHU EHUT	Transport or semi-trailer tractor	Britain	Tarpaulined platform with forward cab 4 x 2, 5 Ton. 70 built
Mack	EH EHT	Transport or semi-trailer tractor	Britain	Tarpaulined platform. 510 built. 4 x 2,5 Ton. Used also by American Treasury Services (Treasury Dept)
Dodge	VH-48	Transport	Russia China	4 x 2, 3 Ton
	T234 170	Transport	China	Equivalent to Canadian T110. Less powerful engine. 15,000 built. Front redesigned. 2½/3 Ton
	VK-62	Transport	Britain	4 x 2, 3 Ton
	T203	Transport	Britain	54 x 4, 1½ Ton
	WK-60	Recovery	Britain	6 x 4, 3 Ton. Semi-forward cab. Steel platform. Recovery crane
Chevrolet	VA	Transport Bare chassis unequipped Reconnaissance vehicle for Long Range Desert Group	Britain Egypt	1½ Ton chassis. Bought on spot commercially or imported. Used principally in Middle East
	MS YS	Transport Transport	China China	
Diamond-T	975	Crane Mark VI	Canada	Coles electric crane of English origin. 3 Ton. Fixed trellis jib
Diamond-T		Crane Mark VII	Canada	American Bay City 4½ Ton mechanical crane. Curved trellis jib
Diamond-T		Folding boat transport (F.B.E.)	Canada	3 boats, system of British origin (Folding Boat Equipment)
Diamond-T		Transport of bridging elements, in particular Bailey. Units of field railway	Canada	Tarpaulined metal body with high spars. Used also for general transport (G.S.)
Diamond-T		Machinery 'H'	Canada	General usage workshop lorry. Metal platform with high spars and tarpaulin
Diamond-T		Machinery 'M'	Canada	Metal van. Car repair battery charging, painting of vehicles
Diamond-T		Machinery 'RE 25 KW'	Canada	Tows an electricity generating unit. Tarpaulined metal platform with high spars with handling crane. Engineering repair. Woodwork
Diamond-T		Pontoon	Canada	Body similar to F.B.E. Transport of float or Bailey element
Diamond-T	6 x 4 T980 and 981	Tank recovery	Britain Canada	Conversion to tractor for semi-trailer of tractor T 980 British Shelvoke and Drewry semi-trailer
Diamond-T	6 x 4 T980 and 981	Tank recovery	Britain	Ordered by Britain. Standardised subsequently by the USA. Tows a Rogers 40-Ton trailer

Caterpillar D-8 caterpillar tractor of the Canadian Army (Britain, March 1944).

Dodge Canada D15 15 cwt vehicle, supplied under Lend-lease and driven by French personnel, have just been loaded with the food landed on the Normandy beaches for supplying Paris. The chassis could also carry a 200-gallon water tank.

General motors 4 Door Sedan, Light Car of the Canadian Army in England in March 1944.

Principal Vehicles Assembled or Built for Allied Countries by the Foreign Subsidiaries of American Manufacturers

Manufacturer	Type	User	Nation	Remarks
Ford Canada	C11	Liaison vehicle	Canada Britain	5 or 7-seat estate car with wooden body
Ford Canada	DF/ADF C 21	ditto	ditto	7-seat estate car with wooden body, also as saloon
Ford Australia	As 01 Series	Light van	Australia India	
Ford Britain	01 Series	Liaison car	Britain	
Ford Britain	EO Series	Transport	Britain	Platform with tarpaulin
Ford Canada	FC 60	Transport recovery	Canada	4 x 2, 3 Ton. Holmes crane
Chevrolet Australia	1300 series	Pick-up	Australia	4 x 2, 750 kg
Chevrolet Canada	1300 series	Pick-up	India	
Chevrolet Australia	1500 Series	Transport, Tanker, ambulance	Australia	4 x 2, 1,500 kg—Version 15333 used by Long Range Desert Group
Chevrolet Canada	1500 Series	Transport	Australia Canada Royal Air Force	4 x 2, 3 Ton version. Platform with tarpaulin
	CC 60 L	Transport	Canada	4 x 2, 3 Ton. Platform with tarpaulin
Dodge Canada	T 130	Transport	Canada	3 Ton semi-forward cab. Platform with tarpaulin
	D 8	Pick-up	Canada Britain	500 kg version of US Army. Type Dodge T212. Less powerful engine
	D15	Transport, water tanker	Canada Britain	750 kg, 4 x 2. Civil metal-clad cab Produced in great quantity. Type T 222 for Dodge
Dodge Canada	D3	Weapons carrier	Canada	Version of the Dodge 750 kg 4 x 4
Dodge Canada	D 60	Transport, tipper, bare chassis to be equipped	Canada Britain	May receive an Eaton two-speed rear driving axle. Civil metal-clad body. Very widely used by all Allied forces, including USA. Type T110 for Dodge. Exists with short chassis (D 605), single-mounted wheels (L6) or twinned (L4).
FWD	SU-COE	Semi-trailer tractor Engineers Artillery tractor	Canada Britain	Tows 16 Ton semi-trailer for bulldozer. Artillery tractor for 5.5-inch guns. Special vehicles. Civil FWD. forward cab
	HAR 01	Off-road lorry.	Canada	Version with civil metal-clad cab of US Army's HAR 01.
	HAR 02	Semi-trailer tractor		1,200 produced as semi-trailer tractor. Also with spar-sided platform with tarpaulin or bare chassis for special equipment
General Motors Canada	Maple Leaf 1600	Artillery tractor. Transport. Chassis unequipped	Canada Australia	GM Canada designs 2½ Ton road chassis or 1½ Ton 4 x 4. Short and long wheelbase. Cab of the Canadian civil model and not American Chevrolet mechanical components. Maple Leaf, Canada's emblem
International Australia and Britain	K 7 and 8	Transport Semi-trailers Tractor Chassis un-equipped	Australia Britain	Part of K's assembled in Britain were for civil transporters with priority classification and Petrol Pool (transport of non-military petroleum products)
International Australia	K3	Pick-up. Ambulance	Australia India	4 x 2, 1 Ton
	K5/KS5 and K6	Transport Chassis un-equipped (bomb crane Aviation tanker, etc.)	Australia RAF	4 x 2, 3 Ton

Ford 12 cwt, 4 x 2, Model 01C, of the British Army destroyed in front of the Calais harbour station. Although of British manufacture, this van corresponds to Ford's American products.

THE POST-WAR PERIOD

The M26 was, for more than thirty years, the most widely used tractor in France for the transport of very large loads. This one has been fitted with sliding windows. Its front door has been eliminated. Such a combination could carry 100 tons of load. It belonged to Bourgey-Montreuil (1953).

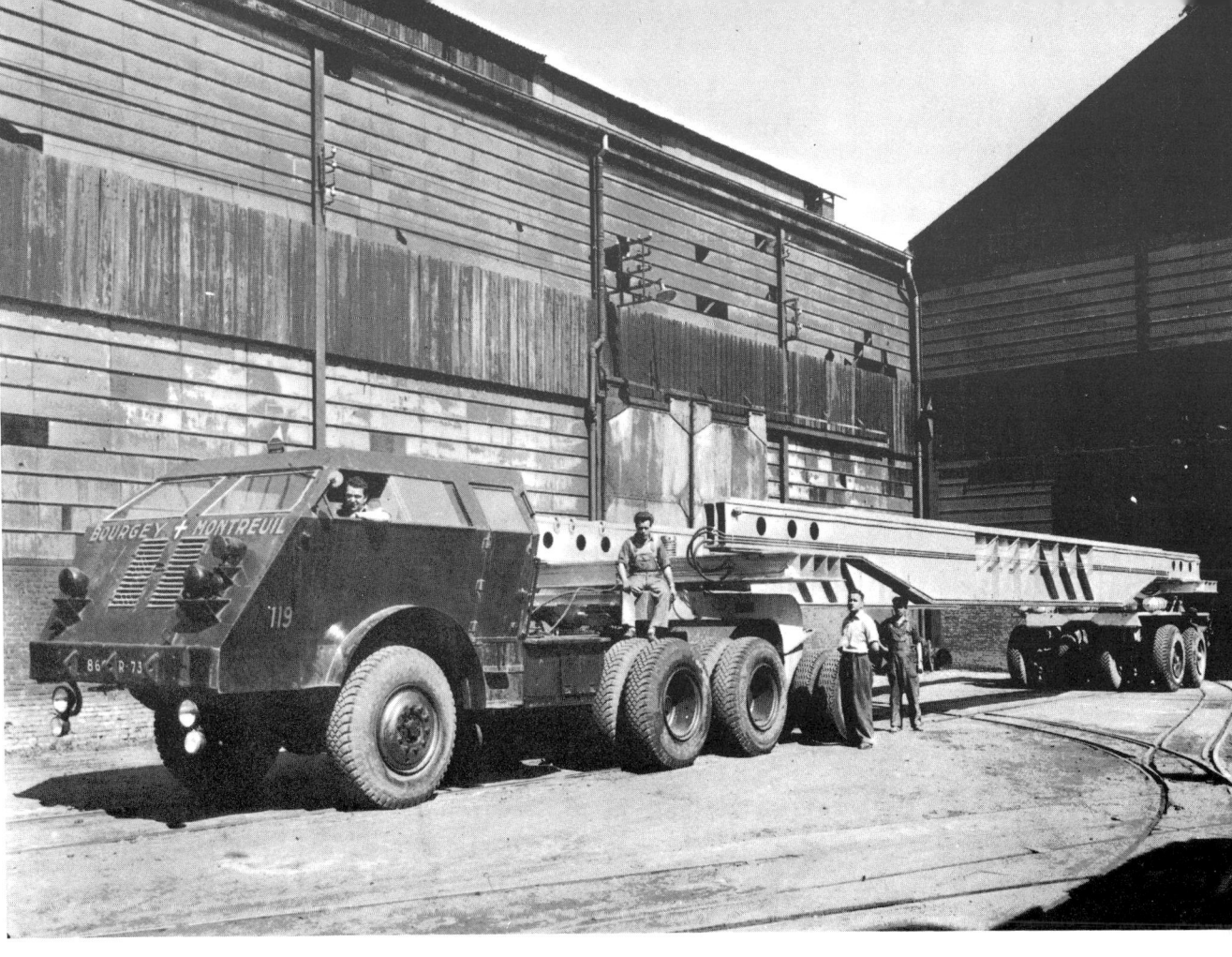

Left: During the operations against the Polisario, the Moroccan troops were on occasion supplied by sea and, notably, by this typical Duck belonging to a private contractor, whose crew have wedged open the bonnet with an old jerrycan to improve its ventilation.

Freed from their military obligations, hundreds of thousands of trucks and vehicles were acquired throughout the world by re-born firms. They helped the reconstruction and restarting of many national economies. However, regulations had been laid down in the United States to limit the sale of surplus vehicles in order not to aggravate the conditions of industrial resumption and to enable the automobile industry to expand as quickly as possible. However, it was difficult, not to say unthinkable for their country of origin to remain forbidden to them. So a few tens of thousands only, one could argue, managed to be employed there. The liquidation of war *matériel* was ensured by the War Assets Administration. Some commercial outlets were rather curious by any standards, such as the big New York stores Gimbels which in 1946 offered Chevrolets, Studebakers and International to their clientele via their enormous mail order catalogue.

Finally, large quantities of *matériel* were abandoned where they were, notably in the Pacific where 'war cemeteries' were to remain in existence in the islands for a long time, or even thrown into the sea, to reduce the total value of the surplus stocks.

The world and Europe in particular, would be driving American or more accurately 'surplus American', for, many years. Contrary to what the analysts of the end of the 40s predicted, the Detroit automobile empire did not succeed in its invasion of the World's vehicle market. Even with the help of the Marshal Plan and the quality which these surplus stocks advertised, it was unable to recover its pre-war commercial positions, at least in our countries.

Of the three million tons of *matériel* and vehicles assembled from 1945 in Europe, 46 per cent were acquired by France, 18 per cent by Italy, 12 per cent

The surplus vehicles were also used in the USA, like this Federal F1 with Standard Steel Works F1 A 4,000-gallon semi-trailer, in the process of refuelling a C-54 of the US Navy, then the largest American transport aeroplane at Burbank, California in 1947.

Esso-France used a fleet of Mack NRs in the immediate post-war period, notably based at its Nanterre depot.

respectively by Belgium and Britain. For South-East Asia, China made sure of 37 per cent of the stock of the zone, the Philippines 26 per cent and India 24 per cent.

The total value of American surplus stocks in the world amounted to 7 billion 584 million dollars: their sale only brought in one billion 495 million. Further, the United States had to agree to large loans to their Allies to enable them to finance their acquisitions.

To retrace in detail the history of the vehicles and their conversion would take a whole book, and even then it would still certainly be incomplete. All that could be done with or to a truck was done. From Pacifics operating with propane bottles for drilling work for a forced channel for a dam, Whites or Macks travelling at 26 tons AUW, to Jeeps converted into private cars or Federal tractors with their two driving axles put into service on the Paris Marseille run.

Schipol-Amsterdam airport operated this Allis-Chalmers tractor until 1980 as a fire tender. The equipment and the conversion had been carried out by Saval-Kronenbourg. It comprised two tanks (water and emulsifier) on trailers. The vehicle is here being used to cool down the asphalt runway which was melting under the burning sun of the scorching summer of 1976.

As after the First World War, some makes were created using as a basis the mechanical elements and chassis of surplus stocks, but provided with improvements to making them economical like European carburettors, cabs with an aesthetic form more in line with the fashion at the time and above all, giving better protection from the cold and the weather.

Thus it is that Labourier developed FWD technology under a licensing agreement. DAF became closely interested in the semi-trailers for tractors M 425/426, while Perez and Raimond created a new make on the basis of this same model with a Hispano diesel, then over the years, with Cummins, Henschel, etc. The list is long and also touches Austria, Italy, Holland, Belgium and Germany, where Deutz would become a specialist in 'remotorisation', China, Morocco and the Philippines, to mention only the most significant countries. A conversion of the GMC to 4 x 2 was even proposed by the Chantiers et Ateliers du Rhône to save tyres and fuel.

Well behaved as they were, the American trucks lent themselves to this game with good grace, as they knew that they were the best of their time. Their quality was such that thousands are still in use to-day and some have become irreplaceable; who has done better in recovery work than a Diamond-T or an M1; how many Pacifics are still on the road for the transport of very large loads; who has been able to replace the DUKW; who has not copied the Jeep and who does not dream of owning a Harley? And above all who can simply claim to have equalled the GMC?

Last but not least, they have lasted because they are simple and indestructible, even if some have become almost unrecognisable, like the 450 Tontons of M. Lohéac, 'Tonton' being none other than Antoine Lohéac himself, so nicknamed since the start of the company because of a little niece who followed him about in his workshops and called him this.

Janette Mallet recalled the story of Antoine Lohéac vehicles in an article in *Les Routiers,* No 578, which is the basis of this account.

In 1946, La Société Nationale des Ventes de Surplus (the National Surplus Sales Company), a body to which the French government had delegated full power in the matter of organisation and marketing of this immense collection of bric-a-brac left by the war on our soil, was then ruling as master. Indeed, it held in its stocks a multitude of vehicles, often almost new, which it only intended to release on the civil market on certain conditions, thus avoiding to a great extent a repetition of the anarchical situation which had prevailed in the 1920s, at the time of the liquidation of the surplus stocks of the First World War. Very strict rules prevented almost all those who were not registered car dealers from acquiring the *matériel.* The Company only granted a rebate, and only then a meagre 8 per cent to garage owners. Nothing was envisaged for other purchasers whatever

Wagon transporter unit hitched to a Diamond-T of SCETA, a subsidiary of the French railways specialising in road transport.

Opposite top: A very rare Truck-Crane-Swinging Boom M1 late of the Chemical Warfare Service employed as a crane lorry by a Savoy firm. The cab has been metal clad, the engine is a diesel, the rear platform has received spar side elements from a Diamond-T Wrecker and a seat has been installed for the crane operator.

Opposite middle: Another rare creature, this Federal 6 x 4 tank transporter tractor, Type 604, 20 Ton, is equipped with a recovery unit from a Wrecker 10 Ton M1. It is seen at Nemours in 1975.

Right: This M26, largely converted, was used as a recovery lorry in the Lille region. Notice, at the rear, the vehicle standard crane assembly which here is firmly fixed in place.

Above: Typical example of the mutations which surplus matériel *underwent, a Diamond-T with an equipment coming from a Wrecker M1 A1, 10 Ton.*

Below: This very fine White 6 x 4, which has even retained its tarpaulin carrying box on the cabin, had the job of supplying water to the exploratory drilling in the south of Algeria. The tanker had a capacity of 18,000 litres. The equipment was due to the Société Africaine des Transports Tropicaux (African Tropical Transport Company), presided over by Georges Estienne, son of the general who was father of the French fighting tank.

A Chevrolet drill of the Midland Electricity Board in England, during the first campaign of electricity line installation by helicopter (Hiller 360) in 1950. The Chevrolets (drill and telephone line maintenance versions), painted grey, were at the same time commonly used in the postal administration in France. One was still in service in 1982 with the central laboratory of the Pont et Chaussées (Roads and Bridges Authority).

the size of the offers they made.

The brothers Bouglione, at le Havre, requested Antione Lohéac to tender on their behalf for forty tractors, convinced, wrongly, that they would benefit from a rebate which they could not obtain. He would thus become aware of this anomaly and submit the problem to the director of surplus stocks in person. Fruitful negotiations, since he would obtain a rebate of 10 per cent for the purchase of twenty-five vehicles and of 20 per cent beyond that number. Thanks to a loan, he was able to acquire a batch of sixty-five tractors in one go. His choice fell on an American vehicle with semi-forward cab which had proved itself during the war: International Harvester's M425/426.

Antoine Lohéac acted at that time with the idea of setting up a big garage and selling his material, but he discovered that buyers were rare. It needed more than that to discourage him. He then decided to use his trucks for his own advantage and to enter into the world of transport. While others did one trip in the day with their old chain-driven Berliets or Dewalds, he did three with his American tractors that nobody wanted. A good means of lowering prices. From the eight francs a ton charged by his competitors, he went down to five francs, and obviously the customers were numerous. Subsequently, the refineries came and established themselves around Rouen. A lot of fuel and asphalt to be transported.

From the beginning Antoine Lohéac had two preoccupations, first, to improve constantly the quality of his vehicles and, secondly, to lighten them as much as possible, for, he said, one is always paid only for the goods transported. He would fix an objective for himself to reach a dead weight lower than 6 tons. His conversions would always be made according to three basic principles, reliability, profitability and safety. His first objective was to reduce the fuel consumption and at the start he would replace the original engine which literally 'drank' petrol, by MAN diesels bought from the State Property Department, recovered from German half-tracks. He would try out the Somua 130 hp engine identical to that of the Paris buses for about thirty vehicles; he would then fit the Berliet 150 hp unit of the GLR8, then the Magic 190 hp engine which lent itself marvellously to the 35-ton AUW limit then instituted in France, and some DAF 210 hp types. He would finally select the DAF 260 hp and the Scania 6-cylinder 300 hp unit when it went up to 38 tons. At present these two engines each equip half the Lohéac fleet.

The body of this Dodge T 110 shows a little local colour! On the door and the mudguards are the emblems of Nationalist China.

A Federal 4 x 4 tractor of the first series, recognisable by the 'metal flag' on the bonnet which replaces the manufacturer's plate, equipped with a Poclain hydraulic crane.

PRP, or Perez and Raimond, before taking over Willeme, had converted numerous American vehicles, such as this recovery vehicle, still in service at Nogent-le-Rotrou. Although this Federal tractor chassis bears the Henschell emblem on its radiator grille, it is fitted with a 200 hp General Motors diesel. At this stage of conversion there remain, quite obviously, very few elements of the original vehicle, generally the chassis and the driving axles.

An M426 of Prost transport, with tandem hitching of F2 tankers. This method of hitching, frequently used by the US Army Air Forces on its airfields, was authorised for a short period in France, prohibited, then authorised again in the 1960s. As for the tractor, fitted with a metal-clad cab, it was much used by transporters in France, Belgium and Holland. DAF even built semi-trailers for it in the immediate post-war period.

Above right A conversion by Jamet brothers, specialist in American vehicles, this Federal tractor has become a 6 x 6 which, in company with others like it, undertook a long self-sustained journey as far as Africa to be delivered to its future users in the 1950s.

The American driving axles were too weak and were replaced by the Berliet FPDM21 which, in addition to its strength, offered the advantage of being easily adapted to the vehicle, it being sufficient to change the drive shafts. Today all the Lohéac 38-tonners are fitted with an Eaton single-reduction rear driving axle, and the front axles and chassis longerons are original after over forty years of service. The gearboxes are Fuller type Roadranger RT 9509 with nine speeds without split.

A matter of great principle with Lohéac, he never skimps on quality including that of the accessories which are made "in house".

Reducing the weight of the cabin made the greatest contribution to lightening the vehicles. In fact, it is the cabins that give the 'Tontons' their great individuality. At the start, the Internationals' steel cabs with canvas roof were replaced by entirely enclosed, aluminium cabs. Progressively, from 1968 onwards, aluminium gave place to polyester, an idea which came to him after a visit to the Chantiers de Normandie (Normandy Workshop). First the wings, then the battery box, the roof and the bonnet, then finally the designing of a mould and production in the Lohéac workshops of a complete, moulded, synthetic resin and fibreglass cab. They ensured, that it kept a family resemblance to the American original.

It was fixed, fireproofed, in a semi-forward position, as a driving position behind the engine ensures more safety for the driver. Its nose hinged forwards, thus permitting easy access to the radiator and most of the accessories. It only weighted 350 kg. Fitting only a single seat in the cab for Lohéac was an extra means of saving weight, and no spare wheels, and another 250 kg gained.

There was a double advantage for this cab: maximum lightening but also a minimum maintenance

One of the concrete mixers built specially with White 666 components for a building programme initiated by M. Lohéac for accommodation for his drivers.

Above left: One Dodge WC 41, of which only 343 were produced, found a new career in a Saint Moritz garage, immaculate as every Swiss citizen should be (1980).

Above: The first model built by M. Lohéac on the M425/426 tractor used Berliet engine and driving axle, light metal body.

because it did not suffer the ill effects of corrosion. When they went from 35 to 38 tons, the nose was shortened because it was necessary to add an extra ton on to the front axle because of the weight distribution imposed by the new AUW, and an obligation to advance the attachment saddle by 30 cm as well as the cab.

The fruit of these improvements was a chassis-cab with attachment saddle, driver and fill of fuel which only reached 5,659 kg. As a comparison, the original International tractor with canvas-roofed cab and petrol engine lighter than a Diesel weighed 5,179 kg and had an authorised AUW of 15 tons. The same Lohéac model with 850 kg more attained an AUW of 38 tons. An enviable result!

All the 'Tontons' are not tractors, some, fairly rare, are carriers.

A Dodge T 234, 3 Ton, of which fifteen thousand were built for China, converted after the war into town buses with passenger trailer. The new design of the simplified military radiator grille, adopted by Dodge on this truck, would be taken up again for the Power Wagon.

FWDF HAR 01, with Bros Brothers snow cutter, of the Royal Air Force, in service at Kastrup airport, Copenhagen.

A rare example, this M425/426 whose plate indicates that it was built by Kenworth, belonging to M. Trouillet and powered by gas in 1948!

BIBLIOGRAPHY

All data figures and tables of specific equipment are extracted from different editions of *Technical Manual 9-2800* of the US Army

The production figures come from the manufacturers' reference tables of chassis numbers or from their archives, and from the series of the US Army serial registration numbers mentioned in the contracts. In general, manufacturers' archives have yielded source material.

The essential information on Crabs and Alligators in Indochina has been extracted from a series of articles 'We don't only have guns', in *Képi Blanc*, the monthly journal of the *Légion Etrangére*.

MAGAZINES

Frères d'Armes N° 13 February-March 1965: 'French use of LVTs'
4 x 4 Magazine
Jours de France 'Les Dossiers de Notre Temps' GUILIANO, Salvatore & CUNY, Marie-Thérèse & BELLEMARE, Pierre
Képi Blanc 'Nous avons pas que des fusils' Series of articles ['We don't only have guns']
Les Routiers N° 578
Militaria Magazine Articles particularly by BONIFACE, J. M.,
Relics of the Road 'Impressive International' RICE, Gini Truck Tracks Inc., 1975
Relics of the Road 'Keen Kenworth Trucks' RICE, Gini Truck Tracks Inc., 1973.
VMI International [French-language military vehicles enthusiasts' magazine] Particularly, N°S 8 ('Corps of Territorial Transport'), 6, 7, 10 and 11
Wheel and Tracks [Magazine of the history of Allied vehicles] ed. VANDERVEEN, Bart H.

BOOKS

ANDRADE & FERNANDEZ *Veiculos Militares Brasileros (Brazilian Military Vehicles)* Aquarius, 1983
Army Motors
BURNESS, T. A. D. *American Truck Spotters Guide 1920-1970* Motorbooks International, 1978
CHAMBERLAIN, Peter, and ELLIS, Chris *British and American Tanks of World War II*
CRABB, Richard *Birth of a Giant* Chilton Book, 1969
CRISMON, Fred W. *US Military Wheeled Vehicles* Crestline
Dodge Military Vehicles Brooklands publishing
GUNNELL, John *The Complete Four-Wheel Drive Manual* TAB Books
HOGG, Ian V. *British and American Artillery of World War II*
KAROLEVITZ, Robert A. *This Was Trucking* Bonanza Books, 1966
LEWIS, F. *The Public Image of Henry Ford* Wayne University, 1976
SCHMIDT, E. J. Hoff, and TANTUM IV, W. H. *US Military Vehicles of World War II*
SLOAN, Alfred P. *My Years With General Motors* Doubleday Company, 1964
Mobilized Chrysler Corporation, 1949
Motor Trucks of America Motor Vehicle Manufacturers Association of the United States Inc. University of Michigan, 1979
POPTA, Van & SCHULTZEN, C. M. *Nederlandse Militaire Voertuigen (Dutch Military Vehicles)* 1978
VANDERVEEN, Bart H. *Observers Army Vehicles Directory to 1940.*
VANDERVEEN, Bart H *Observer's Fighting vehicles Directory, World War II*
WILKINS, Mira and HILL, Ernest *American Business Abroad* Wayne University
WOODS, Jeff *Weasel* Iso Publications, 1977

OFFICIAL

Corps of Engineers, Troop and Equipment, The Office of the Chief of Military History, 1958
FM 5 - 20 B, Camouflage of Vehicles
Handbook of Motor Vehicles used by the United States Armed Forces Timken-Detroit Axle Company, 1944
King, Admiral 'Report to Secretary of the US Navy', March 27th, 1944
Ordnance Department Procurement and Supply, The Office of the Chief of Military History, 1960
Tables of organisation and Equipment of the US Army (TO&E), April 1943
Technical Manual 9-2800 September 1943, October 1947, September 1957, Motor Vehicles Ordnance Corps, US Army
US Army Engineers. Notice on the Mechanical Equipment of the 1952

Acknowledgements and Photographic Credits

To Bart H. Vanderveen, the faithful friend whose vast knowledge has often been drawn upon for contribution and who remains the first among us.

To Aimé Van Ingelgom; Alfred Krenn; Philippe Page of the AFP; Josette Chardan of Sigma; the officers and photographic section of the CMIDOM; Harley-Davidson Company; Mr Poisson of American Motors; Mr Dailloux for his fine photographs; Poclain; Daniel Tard; Mack; Renault Véhicules Industriel, *Camion-Magazine* for documents extracted from the 'Mysterious Lorry'; André Horb; president of La Rosalie et l'Association; M. Lohéac for his memoirs; *4 x 4 Magazine*; the magazine *Les Routiers* which allowed us to use some of its texts and notably those of our colleague Janette Mallet; René Boucher who gave us the rare Technical Manuals which we did not have; Bill Murray; Le Musée des Blindés (Museum of Armoured Vehicles), Saumur and all its team with, as leader, its director Colonel Aubry; l'Établissement Cinematographic et Photographic des Armees; Sirpa; Expéditions Polaires Françaises; Jean-Paul Leroy, our 'very special' envoy to '*Nouvelle-France*' and our friend Professor Albert Legault, advisor to the Ministry of Defence of Canada; Ford-France; Hubert Pavie and Christine Rahard of RVI, to whom we gave so much trouble with our requests for 'exotic' documents; Sven Bengtson; Edward J. Sawtell of the Ford Motor Company; W. C. Colin Chisholm of Mack; White-Volvo; Volvo-France; Christopher Foss; Alain Pelletier; Borgé and Viasnoff; Antique Trading Supply; the French specialist of the Harley-Davidson, Fred W. Crismon; and IVECO.

Photographic Credits

AFP; Austrian Embassy; Swiss Embassy; American Motors; Public Archives of Canada; Sven Bengtson; *Camion Magazine*; Chrysler; CMIDOM; Crismon; Dailloux; ECPA; EPA; Ian Allan; ESSO; Expéditions Polaires Françaises; Ford; Christopher Foss; FWD; GMC; Harley Davidson; Herminghaus; André Horb; Idées et Éditions; National Geographical Institute; IVECO; IWM; Kieffer, *L'Enthousiaste*; Mack; Bill Murray; Pelletier; Poclain; SYGMA; Tararine; US Army; USIS-IPS; Bart H. Vanderveen; Van Ingelgom; White-Volvo.